John Gibb
from
A. N. Salmond

In memory of
his friend
J. D. F. S.
20th April 1905 —

THE

SIBYLLINE ORACLES

TRANSLATED

FROM THE GREEK INTO ENGLISH BLANK VERSE

BY

MILTON S. TERRY

Professor in Garrett Biblical Institute

NEW YORK: HUNT & EATON
CINCINNATI: CRANSTON & STOWE
1890

PREFACE.

THE Sibylline Oracles are a collection of pseudepigraphal poems, venerable for their antiquity, and valuable for their exhibition of the spirit and thought of the early Christian centuries. In assuming to be the utterances of the most ancient Sibyls they are obviously spurious, but, like the Book of Enoch, the Assumption of Moses, and the Ascension of Isaiah, these Jewish-Christian poems possess a permanent value for the theologian and the student of history. They represent a notable phase of ancient religious life and sentiment, and their very imperfections as literary productions reveal to the critical reader tendencies in human civilization and intellectual activity which he can nowhere else so clearly trace.

These Sibylline books are quoted by Josephus, Justin Martyr, Athenagoras, Clement of Alexandria, Lactantius, and other Christian fathers, and are treated by some of them as if they were as authoritative as the Holy Scriptures. The relation, accordingly, of these and similar books to current discussions in the department of biblical criticism and canonics is of a very noteworthy character. They have also acquired no little importance in the modern study of apocalyptics. Lücke and Stuart give them much space and attention in their learned works on the Revelation of John, and a considerable literature has grown up around them, as will be seen in the following Introduction.

It seems very desirable that these oracles should be made accessible to English readers. The old version of Floyer has long been out of print, contains only the first eight books, and is given to discussions which have become obsolete by the progress of scientific criticism. The present work is an attempt to put these famous Sibyllines into as readable English as is consistent with accuracy of translation. The form of heroic blank verse has been chosen as on the whole best representing to English readers the spirit of the Greek hexameters. It would not have been difficult in numerous passages to have made better poetry and better sense than can be found in the Greek original, but such a liberty would violate the obligations and proprieties of a work that assumes to be a faithful translation.

It must be remembered that the Greek text of these books has come down to us in a very corrupt state, mutilated in a number of places, and notable for its imperfect meters. Many of the geographical and historical allusions are obscure and uncertain, and the several books contain numerous repetitions. For the convenience of the critical reader the corresponding lines of the Greek text are indicated at the foot of each page of the translation, and in the notes references are furnished to the places in the writings of the Christian fathers and other ancient authors where the Sibyl is quoted, or where similar sentiments occur. It is hoped that our Introduction and foot-notes will also supply the information which readers in general will desire; but it should be observed that there are many passages which all the learning and ingenuity of scholars have hitherto failed to make clear.

I desire, in conclusion, to acknowledge my indebtedness to Professor Joseph R. Taylor, of the North-western University, for his very helpful co-operation in the preparation both of the translation and the notes; also to Professor Charles Horswell for assistance in the translation of the third book. My thanks are also due to Professors Baird and Bradley for valuable suggestions.   M. S. T.

EVANSTON, *September*, 1890.

TO

MY BELOVED COLLEAGUES

IN THE

FACULTY

OF

GARRETT BIBLICAL INSTITUTE,

M. RAYMOND, D.D., LL.D.,   C. W. BENNETT, D.D., LL.D.,
H. B. RIDGAWAY, D.D., LL.D., C. F. BRADLEY, D.D.,

THIS VOLUME

IS

Affectionately Inscribed.

INTRODUCTION.

THE Sibyls occupy a conspicuous place in the traditions and history of ancient Greece and Rome. Their fame was spread abroad long before the beginning of the Christian era. Heraclitus of Ephesus, some five centuries B. C., compared himself to the Sibyl " who, speaking with inspired mouth, without a smile, without ornament, and without perfume, penetrates through centuries by the power of the gods." Various oracles, purporting to have been uttered by the Sibyls, are found in the writings of Pausanias, Plutarch, Livy, and other ancient authors of less celebrity. From all which it appears that they were female prophets, believed to be gifted with a knowledge of the future, and inspired to make known the fate of individuals, cities, and kingdoms.

The most ancient and famous of the Sibyls was the one who dwelt in the cave at Cumæ, near Neapolis, on the coast of Italy. To her solemn and sacred place Æneas journeyed when he would learn the destinies of the future, and she opened to him the secrets of the lower world, and served as his guide therein, as Virgil has so finely described in the sixth book of the *Æneid.* The ancient story about this Cumæan Sibyl is that Apollo became enamored of her, and offered her whatever she might ask of him. She asked that she might be permitted to live as many years as she held grains of sand in her hand. The god at once granted her request, but she refused to reciprocate his love. He thereupon decreed that her long life should be to her a burden rather than a blessing, for she should be without freshness and beauty. She is said to have been seven hundred years old when Æneas came to Italy, but she was doomed to live nearly as many more before the number of her years would equal that of the sands she had held, and her ultimate destiny was to wither quite away, and become only a voice. She also bore the names of Herophile, Deiphobe, Demophile, Phenomine, Demo, and Amalthea.

One of the oldest specimens of a heathen oracle is that of Delphi, as preserved in Herodotus (vi, 86). Glaucus, son of Epicydes, is said to have received from the Milesians a large sum of money, and given a pledge to restore it when properly demanded. When, however, the demand was made by the Milesians, Glaucus professed to be ignorant of any such obligation. While the matter was pending he went to Delphi and consulted the Pythian oracle, and received the following response :

> Glaucus of Epicydes, greater gain
> Immediate is it by oath to overcome,
> And take the money as by force; swear then,
> Since death awaits the man that keeps his oath.
> But Orcus has a nameless son, nor hands
> Nor feet are his, but swift he moves along,
> Till, having seized a whole race he destroys,
> And all the house. But the race of the man
> Who keeps his oath is better afterward.

In this response we observe what was so characteristic of the heathen oracles, an element of uncertainty, an enigmatical obscurity. While the answer contains a wholesome word of counsel, it also palters with us in a kind of double sense. Many other examples might be collected from the writings of the ancients. Some of these writers speak as if there were but one Ṣibyl, others mention several. Pausanias, in his *Description of Greece* (book x, chap. xii), mentions " the first Herophile" as the most ancient of all the Sibyls, a daughter of Zeus and Lamia ; and a second Herophile, who was, however, earlier than the Trojan War, and foretold the ruin Helen was destined to bring upon Asia and Europe. He also mentions a woman of the name of Demo, who delivered oracles, and a Hebrew prophetess called Sabbe. He adds to these the names of two women, Phænnis and Peleæ, who prophesied under divine inspiration, but were not called Sibyls. But the fullest account of the Sibyls which we possess is found in the writings of Lactantius, one of the Latin fathers who flourished about the close of the third century of our era, and who refers to Varro as his authority. As this passage seems to have been the principal source of information for later writers, we can do no better service for our readers than to produce it here:

"Marcus Varro, than whom no one more learned ever lived, neither among the Greeks nor even among the Latins, in books on sacred subjects which he wrote to Caius Cæsar, the chief pontiff, when he was speaking of the fifteen men,[*] says that the Sibylline books were not the work of one Sibyl, but were called by one name, Sibylline, since all female prophets were called Sibyls by the ancients, either from the name of the one at Delphi, or from their announcing the counsels of the Gods. For in the Æolic manner of speaking they call the gods *sious* ($\sigma\iota\sigma\acute{\nu}\varsigma$), not *theous* ($\vartheta\varepsilon\sigma\acute{\nu}\varsigma$), and counsel is not *boule* ($\beta\sigma\nu\lambda\acute{\eta}$), but *bule* ($\beta\nu\lambda\acute{\eta}$); and so Sibyl is pronounced as *siobule* ($\sigma\iota\sigma\beta\nu\lambda\acute{\eta}$). But the Sibyls were ten in number, and all these he enumerated under authors who had written of each one. And first there was the Persian of whom Nicanor made mention, who wrote the history of Alexander of Macedon; the second was the Lybian, whom Euripides mentions in the prologue of the *Lamia;* the third was the Delphian, of whom Chrysippus speaks in that book which he composed on divination; the fourth was the Cimmerian in Italy, whom Nævius in his books of the Punic War and Piso in

---

[*] The Quindecemviri, a college, or board of fifteen priests, to whom the care of the Sibylline books was intrusted at Rome.

1*

his annals names; the fifth was the Erythræan, whom Apollodorus of Erythræa affirms to have been his own countrywoman, and that she prophesied to the Greeks who were moving against Ilium both that Troy would be destroyed and that Homer would write falsehoods; the sixth was the Samian, of whom Eratosthenes writes that he had found something written in the ancient annals of the Samians; the seventh was the Cumæan, by name Amalthea, who is by others called Demophile or Herophile. She brought nine books to King Tarquinius Priscus, and asked three hundred philippics for them, but the king spurned the greatness of the price and laughed at the insanity of the woman. She thereupon in sight of the king burned three of them, and for the rest asked the same price; but Tarquinius all the more thought the woman was insane. But when again, having destroyed three more, she persisted in the same price, the king was moved, and bought what was left for three hundred pieces of gold.* Afterward their number was increased, the capitol being rebuilt, for they were collected out of all the cities both of Italy and Greece, and especially of Erythræa, and brought to Rome in the name of whatever Sibyl they chanced to be. The eighth was the Hellespontine, born in the Trojan country, in the village of Marpessus, near the town of Gergitha. Heraclides of Pontus writes that she lived in the times of Solon and Cyrus. The ninth was the Phrygian, who prophesied at Ancyra; the tenth was the Tiburtine, by name Albunea, who is worshiped at Tibur as a goddess, near the banks of the river Anio, in which stream her image is said to have been found, holding a book in hand. Her oracular responses the Senate transferred into the capitol."

So far Lactantius appears to quote substantially from

---

* Dionysius Halicarnasseus also records this story of Tarquin and the Sibyl, and adds that, having delivered over the books, she disappeared from among men.—*Antiq. Rom.*, iv, 62.

Varro, and then he adds, as if contributing further information, the following: " Of all these Sibyls the songs are both made public and held in use except those of the Cumæan, whose books are kept secret by the Romans; neither do they hold it lawful for them to be inspected by any one except the fifteen men. And there are single books of each which, because they are inscribed by the name of a Sibyl, are believed to be the work of one; and there are also confused ones, nor is it possible to discern and assign to each its own except that of the Erythræan, who both inserted her own true name in her song and foretold that she would go by the name of the Erythræan, although she was born in Babylon. . . . All these Sibyls proclaim one God, but especially the Erythræan, who is held among the others to be more distinguished and noble, since indeed Fenestella, a most careful writer, speaking of the fifteen men, says that upon the restoration of the capitol the consul Caius Curio proposed to the Senate to send embassadors to Erythræ, who should search for the songs of the Sibyl and bring them to Rome. And so Publius Gabinius, Marcus Otacilius, and Lucius Valerius were sent, and they brought to Rome about a thousand verses written down by private persons. We have shown above that Varro said the same thing." *

Lactantius and many other Christian writers of the first four centuries seem to have accepted this tradition as genuine fact, and they cite numerous passages from the Sibyllines current in their time as if they were as authoritative as the Hebrew prophets. Few scholars of the present day, however, regard this tradition as entitled to much credit. It undoubtedly rests upon some foundation of fact, and there is no good reason to question that some such collection of oracles existed in the ancient time. Such books would naturally have been kept at the capitol and confided to the priestly

* Lactantius, *Div. Inst.*, book I, chap. vi. Migne's *Latin Patrology*, vol. vi, 140–147.

authorities. There is no room to doubt that in times of
public peril they were consulted with a superstitious reverence, and not a few instances of the kind are mentioned by
the old historians. But the capitol was destroyed by fire in
the time of Sylla (B. C. 84), and again in the time of Vespasian (A. D. 69), and whatever Sibylline books were kept
therein then doubtless perished in the flames. The subsequent collections, made as Lactantius reports, were doubtless
fragmentary, and there is no certainty that any of them are
now extant. But, on the other hand, it is not improbable
that various temples and cities of the empire possessed some
sacred books, and among them oracles purporting to be Sibylline were gathered up and brought to Rome.

The Greek books of Sibylline Oracles, which exist at the
present time, and of which this volume furnishes the first
complete English translation, are obviously not identical with
those of heathen antiquity referred to by the old classic
authors. They belong to that large body of pseudepigraphal
literature which originated near the beginning of the Christian era (about B. C. 150–A. D. 300), which consists of such
works as the Book of Enoch, the Testaments of the Twelve
Patriarchs, the Book of Jubilees, the Assumption of Moses,
the Psalms of Solomon, the Ascension of Isaiah, and the
Second Book of Esdras. The production of this class of
literature was most notable at Alexandria in the time of the
Ptolemies. The influence of Greek civilization and culture
upon the large Jewish population of the Egyptian metropolis,
and the marked favors shown this people in that country,
turned them far from the strict usages of their Palestinean
brethren. No fact could more strikingly show the results of
this foreign influence than the building of the temple and
altar at Leontopolis, as described by Josephus (*Ant.* xiii, 3).
If the son of the high-priest Onias saw propriety in convert-
ing a heathen temple to the worship of Almighty God, and
building it after the pattern of the one in Jerusalem, we need

not wonder that the religious and literary taste of the Alexandrian Jews found gratification in harmonizing Hebrew traditions and Greek philosophy. The ingenuity that found in Isa. xix, 19, a warrant for the building of such a temple and altar might easily discover among the responses of heathen oracles much that was capable of appearing to great advantage in a Jewish dress. In this way, no doubt, arose the Jewish Sibyl, assuming to be a daughter of Noah, and skilled in all prophetic knowledge. And this passion for reproducing famous oracles spread beyond the land of Egypt, and gathered breadth and volume with its years of growth. Not only were the historical and philosophical productions of the Greeks made use of, but the speculations of the Persians, the mysteries of Egyptian priests, and the poetical myths and legends of all nations contributed to the medley which Hellenistic Jews were fond of turning to a pious purpose. And just as the allegorical method of interpreting Scripture was handed over as a sort of inheritance to the early Christian Church, so the passion for producing pseudonymous books took easy possession of many Christian writers of the first centuries. Hence the large number of apocryphal Gospels and Acts and Apocalypses.

Our Sibylline books are found to contain Greek, Jewish, and Christian elements. The oldest portions appear to be the work of an Alexandrian Jew, who probably made use of various fragments of the old Greek and Roman Sibyllines which were current in his day.* This work was probably enlarged by later writers and then taken up by Christian enthusiasts, who turned it to account in their assaults upon heathenism. The result is that, after various revisions and alterations and additions, we have twelve books, which

---

* From this work Josephus quoted the passage which now appears in our book iii, 116–123 (Greek text 99–104). His language in connection with the quotation is: "The Sibyl also makes mention of this tower and of the confusion of the language, when she says thus."—*Ant.* i, iv, 3.

exhibit little coherency. They contain numerous repetitions, and many passages exist only in a mutilated form. "Even at this day," writes a learned critic, " we might safely undertake to compress into three books all that is distinctive, not to say valuable, and could very well afford to imitate the example of Tarquin, and give the same price for the smaller collection which was asked for the whole. By this procedure we should lose nothing but abridgments, modifications, or repetitions." *

Very noticeable is the manner in which many of the early Christian fathers refer to these spurious oracles. Justin Martyr cites verses of the Sibyl and treats them with as much regard as if they were a portion of the Hebrew Scriptures. He urges upon the Greeks that their own ancient Sibyl taught the same great truths as the prophets. † Clement of Alexandria pursues the same method, often quoting passages that served his purpose, and in one place (*ad Græcos*, vi) he repeats several lines now found in the Proem of our books, and attributes them to a "prophetess of the Hebrews." Theophilus of Antioch quotes the words of the Sibyl as if they were holy scriptures, and he has preserved in his writings our only copy of the ancient Proem. Tertullian says (*ad Nationes*, chap. xii) that the Sibyl was earlier than all literature and the prophetess of truth, from whom the priests of the demons borrowed their titles. Eusebius, Augustine, Jerome, and other fathers still later occasionally refer to the writings of the Sibyl as an inspired authority. But of all the fathers Lactantius makes most frequent appeal to the Sibyls, and his writings abound with citations of verses from their books. To him they seemed an invaluable weapon with which to confute the superstition and idolatry

---

* *Methodist Quarterly Review* of October, 1854, p. 502.

† Athenagoras in his *Legatio pro Christianis* quotes a passage from the oldest portion of the third book in the same way as Josephus does the passage mentioned in a foregoing foot-note.

of the heathen world. He evidently regarded the Sibylline books from which he quoted as substantially identical with those of which Varro wrote.

Some of the fathers, however, as Irenæus and Cyprian, make no use of the Sibylline Oracles. Whether they were ignorant of them, or suspected their genuineness, or found no occasion to cite them, we need not attempt to say. According to Origen (*ad Celsus,* lxi) Celsus derided the Christians for their belief in the Sibyl, and the learned Alexandrian father undertook no defense of the Sibylline prophecies. But those early years of Christianity were not an age of scientific literary criticism, and whatever certain scholars here and there might think or say, pseudepigraphal books obtained a wide circulation, and in many places met with general credence. About the close of the fourth century the emperor Honorius is said to have issued an order for the destruction of these books and of the heathen temples in which they were deposited. But, whatever the result of this order, many copies probably escaped the flames, and were subsequently multiplied and scattered abroad. Like many other writings, they were lost from sight during the Middle Ages, but were recovered and published at the revival of Greek learning about the beginning of the sixteenth century. Eleven different manuscripts have been discovered, but they exhibit great diversity of matter and arrangement. Whole sections are wanting in some copies which are supplied in others. The language and versification betray the work of different authors and revisers. Some passages are hopelessly mutilated in all the manuscripts. The earlier published copies contained only the first eight books. Angelo Mai found and published a manuscript of the fourteenth book in 1817, and afterward two Vatican Codices, both containing books xi–xiv, and so nearly alike as to show that one must have been copied from the other. The character and condition of the manuscripts are such as to make it impossible to construct an edition of the Greek text which will be fully satisfactory. We may, however, sympathize with the critic referred to above, who suggests "that all that is to be learnt from the Sibylline Oracles may be most readily gathered from them in their sluttish and mutilated state as exhibited in the manuscripts. Their rugged wretchedness is more suggestive than they would be in a more purified form. They are the tattered remnants of an ignorant, bigoted, superstitious, and often fraudulent phase of declining civilization ; and the Sibyls, who profess to be co-etaneous with the birth of antiquity, and contemporary with Noah, deserve to be lapidated according to the sentence and prayer put forth by one of them on her own behalf."＊

The first printed edition of the Greek text was brought out by Xystus Betuleius at Basel in 1545. A metrical Latin version of this by Sebastian Castalio appeared in 1546, and another edition of the Greek text, emended by the same scholar, in 1555. In 1599 Johannis Opsopœus published at Paris an edition of the Greek text, accompanied with the Latin version of Castalio, and with brief prolegomena and notes. But all these editions were superseded by that of Servatius Gallæus, published at Amsterdam in 1687–89, in two quarto volumes. One volume contains the Greek text, with the Latin version and extensive annotations ; the other consists of dissertations on the Sibyls and their oracles.† This text and translation was republished at Venice in 1765, in the first volume of Gallandius's *Collection of the Fathers,*

＊ See the close of book vii.

† An English translation from the texts of Opsopœus and Gallæus was published in London, 1713, by Sir John Floyer. This, of course, contains only the first eight books. In a preface of twenty pages the translator maintains the genuineness of the oracles, cites numerous testimonies from the Christian fathers, and finds the papacy and the Turks predicted therein. The book is out of print, and its dissertations attempting to answer the objections of Opsopœus and Vossius (pp. 249–262) are obsolete and worthless.

and accompanied with numerous notes, largely taken from the work of Gallæus. The next important contribution to the Sibyllines was the discovery in the Ambrosian library at Milan of the fourteenth book, which was published by Angelo Mai in 1817. The same distinguished prelate subsequently found in the Vatican library at Rome four books numbered xi–xiv, and published them in that city in 1828. The first to edit and publish the entire collection of twelve books (books i–viii and xi–xiv) was J. H. Friedlieb, whose single volume, issued at Leipsic in 1852, contains the entire Greek text, with a remarkably close metrical version in German, a valuable introduction, and a collection of various readings. But the latest and most complete edition of the whole work is that of C. Alexandre, whose first volume appeared at Paris in 1841, and contained the Greek text and Latin version of the first eight books, and extensive critical and exegetical notes. Two subsequent volumes (Paris, 1853 and 1856) supplied the remaining books, seven *Excursus*, and a bibliography of the Sibyllines. A new edition, condensing the former into briefer space, and presenting all in a single volume, appeared at Paris in 1869, and is entitled to the honor of *editio optima.**

The critical study of these books makes it evident that

---

* There was published in 1878 at Breslau a very scholarly and valuable dissertation on the fourth book of the Sibylline Oracles, by D. Badt, in which we have, besides critical and exegetical discussions, a revised Greek text of the fourth book. Other special essays are by C. L. Struve, *Fragmenta Librorum Sibyllinorum quae apud Lactantium reperiunter*. Regiomonti, 1817. F. Bleek, Die Entstehung und Zusammensetzung der uns erhaltenen Bücher Sibyllinischer Orakel, in Schleiermacher's, De Wette's & Lücke's *Theol. Zeitschrift* for 1819 and 1820 (vol. i, pp. 120–146; vol. ii, pp. 172–239). R. Volkmann, *De Oraculis Sibyllinis Dissertatio* (Leipsic, 1853), and *Sectiones Sibyllinæ* (Phritz, 1861). Hilgenfeld, Die Jüdische Sibylle, in his *Jüdische Apokalyptik*, pp. 53–90 (Jena, 1857). H. Ewald, Abhandlung über Entstehung, Inhalt, und Werth der Sibyllischen Bücher. Göttingen, 1858.

they are the work of a variety of authors, the oldest of whom
were Alexandrian Jewish, but the greater number of whom
were Christian, belonging to different times and places. They
all assume to speak in the name of the ancient Sibyl, and
employ for their purpose a studied imitation of the language
and hexameters of Homer. " The collection as we now have
it," says Schürer, " is a chaotic wilderness, to sift and arrange
which will ever baffle the most acute criticism. For, unfor-
tunately, it is not the case that each book forms of itself
an original whole, but that even the single books are some
of them arbitrary aggregates of fragments. The curse of
pseudonymous authorship seems to have prevailed very
specially over these oracles. Every reader and writer al-
lowed himself to complete what existed after his own
pleasure, and to arrange the scattered papers now in one, now
in an opposite manner. Evidently much was at first cir-
culated in detached portions, and the collection of these
afterward made by some admirer was a very accidental one.
Hence duplicates of many portions are found in different
places. And the manuscripts which have come down to us
exhibit great discrepancies in the arrangement." * The oldest portion is believed to be our present book iii, beginning
with line 114 (Greek text 97), and including most of the following lines as far as 960 (Greek, 807). To this was
formerly attached the Proem preserved to us in Theophilus.
This portion was probably the work of an Alexandrian Jew
of the second century B. C. Next in the order of time is
probably the fourth book. The reference to the burning of
the temple (line 159), and the eruption of Vesuvius (lines
165–170), which occurred A. D. 79, make it probable that it
was written not far from A. D. 80.

It is not the purpose of the present work to enter upon a
detailed criticism of the various elements of the Sibylline

* *The Jewish People in the Time of Jesus Christ,* vol. iii, p. 276. English
Translation, Edinburgh, 1886.

books as they now exist. Such an essay would necessarily involve much that would be unsuitable for English readers, and needlessly enlarge this volume. A summary of contents is furnished at the beginning of each book, and the foot-notes are believed to be sufficient to help the common reader to an understanding of the various parts. Where no certainty exists as to the meaning the fact is indicated, and sometimes the views of different scholars are briefly stated. The printed texts of Alexandre and Friedlieb have been constantly before us in making the translation, and various readings and conjectural emendations are occasionally mentioned. But these have been sparingly introduced, since they could be of little value to the English reader. The citations made by the Christian fathers are duly noted, and as they have all been verified by means of Migne's complete collection of the Greek and Latin fathers, the place of citation is designated, not only by the common reference of book and chapter, but also by the volume and column in which the passage appears in Migne's edition. This latter designation is always put in brackets, the letter G denoting the Greek, and L the Latin patrology ; and the numbers which follow these letters refer respectively to the volume and column. The numbers inclosed in parentheses at the foot of each page of the translation indicate the corresponding lines of the Greek text as represented on that page.

As the compiler of our present collection of Sibylline Oracles is believed to be the author of the *Anonymous Preface*, the readers of this volume are herewith provided with a translation of that document, which, according to Alexandre, belongs to the sixth century of the Christian era.

THE ANONYMOUS PREFACE.

IF the diligent perusal of the writings of the Greeks affords
much profit to them who are proficient therein, inasmuch as
it enables those who toil for such things to acquire much
learning, far more fitting is it for those who are happily disposed to devote themselves assiduously to the sacred writings, inasmuch as they disclose the things of God and those
which profit the soul, yielding thence the twofold advantage
of availing to benefit both themselves and also those that
read.　It seems good to me, therefore, having read again
and thoroughly studied them, to collect into one systematic
and harmonious order the so-called Sibylline Oracles, found
in a scattered and confused condition, so that, being readily
seen at a glance by the readers, they would afford them the
profit arising therefrom, disclosing not a few necessary and
useful things, and representing the work in a more valuable,
and at the same time more varied, form.　For they also speak
very clearly concerning Father, Son, and Holy Spirit, the divine and life-originating Trinity, and concerning the incarnate dispensation of our Lord and God and Saviour Jesus
Christ, born, they say, of a virgin, without generation, and of
the healing of those by him made perfect ; in like manner,
of his life-giving passion and resurrection from the dead the
third day, and of the judgment to come, and recompense of
what we have all done in this life.　Furthermore, they
clearly treat of things which are made known in the Mosaic
writings and the books of the prophets, concerning the creation of the world, the formation of man, and expulsion from
paradise, and renewal again.　Concerning things that have
happened, or also in like manner of things to come, they
variously prophesy ; and, in a word, are able to profit not a
little those who read.

Now the Sibyls, according to many writers, have in various places and times been ten in number. But Sibyl is a Romaic term, meaning a prophetess—that is, a soothsayer; hence the female soothsayers have been designated by one name. First, then, there was the Chaldean—that is, the Persian—called by the proper name Sambethe; being of the race of the most blessed Noah, who is said to have prophesied of the affairs of Alexander of Macedon, whom Nicanor mentions, who wrote the life of Alexander. The second was the Libyan, of whom Euripides makes mention in the prologue of the Lamia. The third was the Delphian, having been born among the Delphians, concerning whom Chrysippus speaks in his book on Divination. The fourth was the Italian, who was in Cimmeria in Italy, and whose son Evander founded in Rome the temple which is called Lupercal. The fifth was the Erythræan, who also prophesied of the Trojan War, and concerning whom Apollodorus, the Erythræan, made strong affirmation. The sixth was the Samian, called by the proper name Phyto, concerning whom Eratosthenes wrote. The seventh was the Cumæan, called Amalthea, also Herophile, and with some Taraxandra. But Virgil calls the Cumæan Deiphobe, a daughter of Glaucus. The eighth was the Hellespontine, born in the country of Marmessus, near the small town of Girgitha, which was once within the boundaries of Troas, in the times of Solon and Cyrus, as Heraclides of Pontus wrote. The ninth was the Phrygian; the tenth the Tiburtine, named Albunea.

They say, moreover, that the Cumæan brought nine books of her oracles to Tarquinius Priscus, who at that time ruled the public affairs of the Romans, and asked three hundred philippics for them; but being treated with scorn and not questioned as to what they were, she consigned three of them to the fire. Again in another audience with the king she brought the six books, and demanded still the same amount. But not being treated as worthy of a word, again she burned three more. Then, for the third time, bringing the three that remained, she came asking the same price, and declaring that, if he would not take them, she would burn them also. Then, they say, the king read them, and, being filled with wonder, gave for them a hundred philippics, and took care of them, and made a demand for the rest. But she declared that neither had she the like of those that were burned, nor could any such be known except by divine inspiration; but that at one time certain persons had taken out of various cities and places things that were deemed necessary and useful to themselves, and that from them a collection ought to be made. And this was as quickly as possible done. For that which was given from God, however faithfully laid up in the innermost place, did not escape notice. And they deposited the books of all the Sibyls in the capitol of the older Rome; those of the Cumæan being kept concealed and not given out to many, since she had more particularly and distinctly announced the things that were to come to pass in Italy; but the others were made known to all. But those of the Erythræan before mentioned have this name which was given her from that place; but the rest were not inscribed as to what sort or whose they were, but remained undetermined.

Firmianus, therefore, a philosopher not unadmired, being also priest of the aforementioned capitol, having turned his attention to our eternal light, the Christ, in his own works compared the things spoken by the Sibyls concerning the ineffable glory, and mightily refuted the irrational errors of the Greeks. His able exposition is in the Ausonian tongue, but the Sibylline verses were published in the Greek language. But that this may not appear incredible I will produce the testimony of the man previously mentioned, which runs in this manner: [Since therefore the Sibyllines which are found with us are not only, as being easily procured, held in contempt by those who are morbidly fond of Greek

matters (for things that are rare seem precious), but also as
all the verses do not preserve the accuracy of the meter, they
have small credit. But this was the fault, not of the
prophetess, but of the rapid writers, who kept not pace with
the rush of words, and were unskillful. For with the inspiration the remembrance of that which was spoken ceased.
To which also Plato had reference when he said that they
speak correctly of many and great matters, knowing nothing
of the things they say.] We therefore will set forth from
those things which were preserved in Rome by the elders as
much as possible. Moreover, concerning the God who is
without beginning they declare these things:

> One God, who reigns alone, supreme, unborn.
> But God is one alone, high over all;
> He made the heaven, and sun, and stars, and moon,
> And the fruit-bearing land, and swelling sea.
> He is sole God, Creator uncontrolled,
> Who himself fixed the figure of the form,
> And mixed the light of mortals, and the nature
> And generation of all things that live.

Whatever he said, whether it be the things which are
brought together and made into one flesh, or whether it be
of the four elements which are opposites of one another,
also the world under heaven, and man himself, he created it.

PROEM.

FIRST FRAGMENT.

Ye mortal men and fleshly, who are nought,
How soon are ye puffed up, nor see life's end!
Ye tremble not, and have no fear of God,
Your Overseer, the Most High One, who knows,
5 The All-Observer, witness of all things,
All-nourishing Creator, who in all
Implanted his sweet Spirit, and made him

This Proem, consisting of two sections, is found only in the writings of Theophilus, a bishop of Antioch, who lived in the latter half of the second century. It forms no part of the Sibylline Oracles as they exist in the manuscripts and printed editions, but seems to have formed the beginning of an older collection which is no longer extant except in fragments, many of which, perhaps, have been worked into our present third book. See the Introduction, page 18. Theophilus near the close of his second book addressed to his friend Autolychus, ii, cap. 36 [Migne, G., 6, 1109], cites the first of these fragments (vers. 1–41) with the following introductory words: "Now the Sibyl, who among the Greeks and other nations was a prophetess, in the beginning of her prophecy upbraids the race of men, saying."

Line 1. Cited by Clement of Alexandria, *Strom.*, iii, 3 [Migne, G., 8, 1117], who also in the same connection quotes a similar passage from Empedocles. Comp. Homer, *Od.*, xviii, 130: "Earth nourishes nothing feebler than man."

Line 4. *Overseer.*—Same word (ἐπίσκοπος) referred to Christ in 1 Pet. ii, 25. Comp. also Clem. Rom., 1 *Cor.*, 58 [G., 1, 328].

Line 7. *Made him the guide.*—Made the Spirit guide. These two lines are quoted by Lactantius, iv, 6 [L., 6, 462], who, however, inserts the word *God.* He observes: "The Erythræan Sibyl in the beginning of her song, which she commenced by the help of the Most High God, proclaims the Son of God as leader and commander of all in these verses:

"All-nourishing Creator, who in all
Sweet breath implanted, and made God the guide of all."
(1–5)＝Corresponding lines of Greek text.

The guide of mortal men.　One God there is
Who reigns alone, supremely great, unborn,
10　Almighty and invisible, himself
Alone beholding all things, but unseen
Is he himself by any mortal flesh.
　For who is able with the eyes of flesh
To see the heavenly, true, immortal God,
15　Whose dwelling is the sky?　Not in the beams
Of the bright sun can men endure to stand,
Mortal-born men, mere veins and flesh in bones.
Honor him, then, sole ruler of the world,
Who only through eternal ages bides,
20　The self-existent, unbegotten One,
Ruling all things through all, and to all men
Imparting judgment in a common light.
Of evil counsels ye shall surely have
The merited reward, because ye failed
25　To glorify the true, eternal God,
And offer him the holy hecatombs,
But unto demons made your sacrifice—
Even those in Hades.　And ye walk about
In pride and madness, leave the path of right,
30　And go away among the thorns and briers.
Why do ye wander?　Pause, O foolish ones,

Lines 8–10. *One God.*—Quoted by Justin Martyr, *ad Gr.*, 16 [G., 6, 272].
Comp. Theodoret, *Hist. Eccl.*, i, 3 [G., 82, 904]; Basil, *adv. Eunom.*, iii [G.,
29, 668]; Greg. Naz., *Orat.*, xxvi, 19 [G., 35, 1,252]; Lact., i, 6 [L., 6, 140];
Orphica, ed. Hermann, *Frag.* i, 10; ii, 11.

Lines 13–16. Cited by Clem. Alex., *Strom.*, v, 14 [G., 9, 165], and Eusebius, *Præp.*, xiii, 13 [G., 21, 1,121].　Comp. Cyril, *Contr. Jul.*, i, 32 [G., 76,
lxxvi, 549]; Philemon in Just. Mar., *de Monarch*, 2 [G., 6, 316]; Xenophon,
Memor., iv, 3, 13; Cicero, *de Nat. Deorum*, i, 12.

Lines 18, 19. Cited by Lact., *de fals. Relig.*, vi [L., 6, 147].

Line 22.　*Common light.*—An allusion to the universal moral sense of men.
Comp. book i, 409; iii, 588; John i, 9.

(7–25.)

2

Who rove in darkness, and black night obscure,
And leave night's darkness, and receive the light.
Lo, he is clear to all, he cannot err.

35 Come, chase not gloom and darkness evermore.
Behold, the sun's sweet light shines wondrous fair.
Know how to treasure wisdom in your hearts.
There is one God who sends rain, earthquakes, winds,
Lightnings and famines, plagues and mournful cares,

40 And snows and ice.   But why should I speak all?
He governs heaven, rules earth, and self-exists.

      *   *   *   *

Lines 34-41. Cited by Clem. Alex., *Cohort.*, viii [G., 8, 97].   Line 34 is also cited in *Strom.*, v, 14 [G., 9, 173].

* * *—Friedlieb appends to this first fragment the following lines, found in Lactantius, ii, 12 [L., 6, 319], and also in the Anonymous Preface:

> He only is God, who not being ruled
> Is the Creator; he has stamped the form
> Of mortals, and the nature of all things
> Compounded, giving each its kind of life.

Between the two parts of the Proem Alexandre inserts the following from Theophilus, *ad Autol.*, ii, 3 [G., 6, 1049]:

> But if the gods have offspring, and remain
> Immortal also, greater far than men
> Are the begotten gods, and not a place
> Were there for mortals, nor could ever be.

There is no authority for the insertion of either of these fragments at this place, although it may be admitted, as Alexandre claims, that this last cited passage suits the context and forms part of a syllogism when read with what follows in the text of the second part of the Proem.

Both of these fragments were evidently a part of the Sibylline Oracles as they once existed in a more ancient form; but they became displaced by various revisions and transcriptions.   Two other fragments are also cited by Lactantius as prophetic utterances of the Sibyl, the first in *Div. Inst.*, vii, 19 [L., 6, 797]:

> When he comes,
> Fire shall be darkness in the midnight black.

This may possibly be a modification or corruption of the passage in book iv, line 66. The other passage is in *Div. Inst.*, vii, 24 [L., 6, 808], and consists of but a single line:

> Hear me, O men, a King eternal reigns.
> (26-35.)

SECOND FRAGMENT.

But if all that is born must also perish,
It cannot be from thighs of man and wife
God has been formed.   But God is one alone,
Highest of all.   He has made heaven, and sun,
5 And stars, and moon, and the fruit-bearing earth,
And ocean's swelling streams, and lofty hills,
And the perennial fountains.   And he brought
The countless millions of the waters forth ;
And nourished life in all the creeping things
10 That move on earth, and clear-toned twittering birds
Of various colors, and of whizzing wings,
That cleave the air.   And in the mountain glades
Disposed he the wild races of the beasts,
And to us mortals made subordinate
15 All cattle ; the God-formed one made chief
Of all things ; and subordinate to man
He put all variegated forms of life,
And things that are incomprehensible.
For all these things what mortal flesh can know ?
20 He only knows who himself made these things
From the beginning, incorruptible
Creator, everlasting One, who dwells
In the pure ether.   He rewards the good
With an abundant bounty, but fierce wrath
25 He rouses for the wicked and unjust,

SECOND FRAGMENT.

Theophilus adds the second Sibylline fragment (verses 42–102) immediately after the first with only the connecting words : "Also in regard
to those (gods) which are said to have been born, she thus speaks."
  Line 2. *It cannot be.*—Cited by Lact., i, 8 [L., 6, 154].
  Lines 3–6. Cited by Lact., i, 6 [L., 6, 147].
  Lines 21–25. Cited by Lact., *de Ira Dei,* xxii [L., 7, 143].
(1–19.)

And war, and pestilence, and tearful woes.
O men, why vainly puffed up do ye bring
Yourselves to ruin?   Blush to deify
Polecats and monstrous beasts.   And is it not
30 A madness and a frenzy of the mind
If gods steal plates, and plunder earthen pots?
And when they might inhabit in their power
The golden heaven, see them moth-eaten there,
And thickly woven under spiders' webs !
35 Ye worship serpents, dogs, cats—O ye fools,
And reverence birds, and creeping things of earth,
Stone images and statues made with hands,
And stone heaps by the roads.   These ye revere,
And also many foolish things besides,
40 Which it would even be a shame to tell.
These are the baneful gods of thoughtless men,
And from their mouth pours deadly poison down.
But of him is life and perennial light
Imperishable, and he sheds a joy
45 Sweeter than honey on the sons of men.
For him alone should any bend the neck
And tread the eternal paths of piety.
Leaving all those, the full cup of revenge,
Pure, strong, pressed down and unadulterated,
50 Drain off with madly eager soul, all ye.
But ye will not arouse you from your sleep
And come to sober reason, and know God,
The mighty King, who oversees all things.
Therefore on you the flame of burning fire
55 Is coming; ye through ages every day

Line 26. *Tearful woes.*—Comp. Clem. Alex., *Strom.*, v, 14 [G., 9, 188];
Just. Martyr, *de Monarch.* [G., 6, 316]; *Cohort*, xv [G., 6, 272]; Euseb.,
Præp., xiii, 12 [G., 21, 1100].
  Lines 48, 49. Comp. Psa. lxxv, 8; Isa. li, 17; Juvenal, 25, 15.

Shall be by gleaming torches set on fire,
For false and worthless idols put to shame.
But they who fear God and eternal truth,
Life shall inherit, and forever dwell
60 Amid the verdant fields of Paradise,
Feasting on sweet bread from the starry heaven.

Lines 58–61. Cited by Lact., ii, 13 [L, 6, 324]. In these last verses we may note allusions to such passages of Scripture as Matt. xix, 29; Luke xxiii, 43; 2 Cor. xii, 4; Rev. ii, 17; Psa. lxxviii, 24; cv, 40; John vi, 31.
(44–49.)

BOOK I.

CONTENTS OF BOOK I

Announcement, 1–4. Creation of the earth and man, 5–46. First sin and penalty, 47–78. Condition of the first race, 79–104. The second race of men, 105–123. Third and fourth races, 124–140. The race of giants, 141–146. Call and preaching of Noah, 147–232. Entrance into the ark, and the flood, 233–270. Abatement of the waters, 271–308. Exit from the ark, 309–332. The sixth race, 333–361. The Titans, 362–380. Prophecy of Christ, 381–450. Dispersion of the Hebrews, 451–466.

THE SIBYLLINE ORACLES.

BOOK I.

BEGINNING with the earliest race of men,
Even to the latest, I will prophesy
Of all things past, and present, and to come
In the world through the wickedness of men.

5   And first, God bids me utter how the world
Came into being. And do thou declare,
O crafty mortal—prudently declare,
Lest ever thou disparage my commands—
How the celestial King, who made the world

10 And all things, said: Let it be, and it was.
For he the earth established, casting it
Round about Tartarus; and he gave forth

Although first in order, this book is doubtless one of the latest of the collection. It is obviously of Christian origin, and belongs probably to the third century A. D.

Line 3. *Past, present, and to come.*—The Sibyl's pompous purpose is in painful contrast with the intrinsic value of her prophecy. This is quite characteristic of the pseudepigraphal prophecies generally.

Line 5. *God bids me.*—She claims to be the passive and helpless organ of a higher power. Comp. book ii, 1–6; iii, 1–10.

Line 12. Tartarus, the prison of the Titans, here conceived as encompassed by the earth and forming its interior. Hesiod (*Theog.*, 720, *ff*) represents it as surrounded by a brazen fence and situated far beneath the earth as earth is beneath the heaven; it would require nine days and nights, he says, for an anvil to fall from heaven to earth, and as many more for it to fall from earth to Tartarus. Comp. Homer, *Il.*, viii, 13–16. Virg., vi, 577–581. It will be seen in line 123 and elsewhere that Gehenna is regarded as a part of Tartarus or identical with it, and Hades (line 97) comprehends the abode of all the dead.   (1–10.)

2*

The soft sweet light, and raised the heaven on high,
And spread abroad the ocean's blue expanse,
15 And crowned the pole with hosts of brilliant stars,
And decked the earth with plants, and mixed the sea
With rivers, and the air with vapors fused,
And watery clouds.   And then another race
He put forth, fishes in the seas, and gave
20 Birds to the blowing winds, and to the woods
The shaggy beasts, and crawling dragons vile,
And all things whatsoever now are seen.
These made he by his word, and all was done
Quickly and well.   For he as self-produced
25 Existed sole, and looked from heaven down;
And the world was complete.   And then again,
He fashioned afterward a living work,
Man, after his own image, newly formed,
Beautiful, godlike, whom in Paradise
30 Ambrosial he assigned a dwelling-place,
Where elegant labors might become his care.
  But in that verdant field of Paradise
He was alone; discourse he longed to hold,
And much desired another form to see
35 Like to himself.   Then opened God his side
And from it took a bone, and made fair Eve,
His wedded spouse, and in that Paradise
Brought her to dwell with him.   On her he gazed,
And a great admiration held his soul,
40 Being suddenly rejoiced to look upon
A pattern so exact.   And with wise words
He answered, words that flowed spontaneously;
For God cares for all things.   And neither lust
Obscured their minds, nor from a sense of shame

Line 29. *Paradise.*—Here referring to the Garden of Eden as described
in Gen. ii, 8.

(11–35.)

45 Were they clothed, but remote from evil hearts,
   Even like beasts they walked with limbs exposed.
     Then to them also God commandments gave,
   And showed them that they must not touch the tree.
   But the vile serpent led them off by guile
50 To meet the doom of death, and to receive
   Knowledge of good and evil.   But the wife
   First became traitress to him; she gave him,
   And foolishly persuaded him to sin;
   And he, persuaded by the woman's words,
55 Forgetful of the immortal Maker grew,
   And treated plain commandments with despite.
   Therefore instead of good received he evil,
   According to his deed.   And then, the leaves
   Of the sweet fig-tree sewing, they prepared
60 Garments for one another, and concealed
   The sexual parts, because they were ashamed.
   But on them the Immortal set his wrath,
   And forth he cast them from the immortal field.
   For it was now appointed unto men
65 To dwell upon the soil, since he kept not
   The word of God, the Immortal, Mighty, High.
   Then went they forth upon the fertile globe,
   Moistened with tears and sobs, and God himself,
   The Immortal, spoke these memorable words:
70   "Increase and multiply, and work on earth
   With skillful hand, that by your toilsome sweat
   Ye may receive sufficiency of food."
     Thus spoke he; but the author of deceit
   Prone on the dusty earth he made to crawl,
75 And harshly banished; and dire enmity
   He sent between them; this to save his head

Lines 49–51.   Cited by Lact., *Div. Inst.*, ii, 13. [L., 6, 325.]
(36–62.)

Is watchful; man his heel; for death is near,
Neighbor of men and poisonous vipers sly.
  And then the race was multiplied, as bade
80 Himself the almighty Ruler, and increased
One nation with another far and wide.
Houses of various sorts they reared aloft,
And cities and their walls they builded well
And wisely.   And a long-continuing day
85 Was given them for the life they loved so much.
For they died not by grievous ills consumed,
But as o'ercome by sleep.   Happy the men
Of great soul whom the immortal Saviour loved,
The King most high.   But also they transgressed,
90 And gave themselves to folly; for bold-faced
They mocked their fathers, and their mothers shamed;
Acquaintances they knew not, and they met
Brothers with treason.   Then became they vile,
And armed with helmets red with human gore
95 They also made wars; and upon them fell
The last calamity from heaven sent forth,
And took life's fears away, and Hades then
Received them.   Hades it was called where first
Adam arrived when he had tasted death
100 And earth had covered him on all sides round.
Therefore all earthborn men are said to go
Into the halls of Hades.   But all these
Having arrived in Hades have received
Honor, for they to the first race belonged.

Line 84. *Long-continuing day.*—Reference to the remarkable longevity
of the patriarchs as given in the genealogy of Gen. v.
  Line 98. *Hades.*—The conception of Hades here set forth, as the great
receptacle of the souls of men after death, is in essential harmony with both
the Jewish and the Christian doctrines.   The derivation of the name from
Adam is noticeable as a purely arbitrary conjecture.   Comp. book iii, 30,
note; comp. Plato's explanation of the word in *Cratylus.*
                              (63–86.)

105　But when these he had taken, then again
　　　Of the surviving and most righteous men
　　　Another race he formed, much varied, which displayed
　　　Works pleasing, good, and fair, and high respect,
　　　And thorough wisdom. They brought forward arts
110　Of all kinds, meeting difficulties with skill.
　　　And one devised to till the land with plows,
　　　Another worked in wood; one sailed the deep,
　　　Another made a study of the stars;
　　　Another practiced augury with birds;
115　Sorcery and magic arts were others' care;
　　　Others intently practiced other arts,
　　　Watchful inventors, worthy of the name
　　　Because within they held a sleepless mind.
　　　Immense in body, and to look upon
120　Compact and huge were they, but they went down
　　　Under Tartarean chambers terrible,
　　　Held in strong chains to expiate their crimes
　　　In the Gehenna of burning, quenchless fire.
　　　　And after these again appeared a race,
125　Mighty-souled, third race of perfidious men.
　　　Fearful and many were the evil deeds
　　　They wrought among themselves. And these by war
　　　And carnage and calamity were slain
　　　Continually, having a haughty heart.
130　And from these afterward another race
　　　Proceeded, late completed, fit for war,

Line 114. *Augury.*—Augurs were Roman priests who predicted the future from the flight and song of birds. See Cicero, *de Divinatione* i, 17; Livy, i, 36.

Line 125. *Third race.*—The successive races here mentioned appear to be in imitation of Hesiod's ages or races of mankind. Hesiod applies to them the epithets of golden, silver, brass, and iron. See *Works and Days*, 108–190, and comp. Aratus, *Phænom.*, 100–134; Ovid, *Met.*, i, 89–150; Juvenal, *Sat.*, xiii, 27–30.

Murderous and rash; of the fourth race were they.
Much blood they shed, nor feared they God or man,
For fierce, excessive passion urged them on,
135 And impious wickedness.   And they by wars,
Carnage, and strife were hurled to Erebus,
Wretched and impious men.   Them that survived
The heavenly God himself in wrath removed
Out of his world, and in vast Tartarus
140 Cast down, beneath the bottom of the earth.
    Again thereafter yet another race
Much worse than men he made, for whom no good
Will ever the immortal God prepare,
Since they wrought many evils.   For they were
145 Wanton and violent beyond compare,
Giants perverse, uttering foul blasphemies.
    Single among all men, most just and true,
Was Noah, faithful, and to all good works
Attentive.   And to him the Lord himself
150 From heaven spoke these things: "Noah, be thou bold,
And preach repentance to the people all,
That they may all be saved.   But they will not
Regard it, having souls devoid of shame,
And all the impious race will I destroy
155 With mighty floods of waters.   But straightway
I bid thee from the non-imbibing root
An indestructible house of wood to build.
I will put understanding in thy heart,
And skill in art, and measurement, and space,

Line 136. *Erebus.*—The name of a deity of the lower world came to be used as a designation of the lower world itself.   In Homer Erebus is conceived as the region between earth and Hades.   See *Iliad,* viii, 368.   Tartarus was still lower down.   Comp. note on line 12.

Line 146. *Giants.*—The mighty *nephilim* mentioned in Gen. vi, 4, whose wicked violence brought on the flood.

(111–134.)

160 And in all things will I have anxious care
That thou be saved and all that with thee dwell.
Now I am he who is (and in thy heart
Meditate it); I clothe me with the sky
And cast the sea around me; and to me
165 Earth is a footstool. Round my form I pour
The air, and all around me dance the stars.
Nine letters have I, and four syllables.
Mark me: The first three have two letters each,
The other has the rest, and five are mutes.
170 Of the whole sum the hundreds are twice eight,
And thrice three tens, with seven. Know who I am
And be not unacquainted with my love."
  Thus he spoke, and a mighty trembling seized

Line 167. *Nine letters.*—The connection shows that the name intended must be some title or designation of the Creator, but no word has been discovered that fully meets the conditions of the puzzle. The nearest solution is found in the word ἀνέκφωνος. This word has nine letters, four syllables, and five mutes, or consonants. The first three syllables have two letters each, and the sum of all the letters taken at their numerical value is 1,696. But the number stated in the text is twice 800, plus three times thirty (— 90) and seven — 1,697. 'Ανέκφωνος must also be supposed to be a shortened form for ἀνεκφώνητος, used in ecclesiastical Greek writers to denote the *unutterable* name, Jehovah. Another name proposed is Θεὸς Σωτήρ, but an obvious objection is that we have here two words, not, as the text suggests, one word of four syllables. Besides, these letters amount to only 1,692. There is perhaps an error in the text. If for the words *with seven* (line 171) we read *with two*, the numerical difficulty of the last-named solution would be met; or if we read *with six*, then the word ἀνέκφωνος solves the problem. Comp. the similar puzzle in lines 383–387 of this same book, and the well-known enigma of the number of the beast in Rev. xiii, 18. A like example is also found in Capella (book ii, 193), who thus addresses the sun: "Hail, thou veritable face and paternal countenance of God, eight and six hundred in number, whose first letter forms a sacred name, a surname, and a sign;" which Kopp explains by the letters φρη (— 608), representative of the Egyptian name of the sun. Comp. also the designations of the Roman emperors in book v, 16, and following.

(135–147.)

Him who heard such things, and then in his mind,
175 Having prepared each matter, he implored
The people and began with words like these:
"O men, filled with all unbelief and fallen
In madness great, ye will not hide from God
Whate'er ye do, for all things he beholds,
180 Immortal Saviour, all-surveying. He
Bade me exhort you that ye perish not.
Be sober, cease ye from your wicked deeds,
Nor fiercely fight, nor hold a murderous heart,
Nor moisten many a land with human gore.
185 Adore, O mortals, the supremely great
And fearless heavenly Maker, the great God,
Imperishable, whose dwelling is the sky;
And him let all entreat, for he is good;
Entreat him for the life of all the world,
190 Of cities and four-footed beasts and birds,
That unto all he may be merciful.
For when the whole vast world of men shall be
By waters ruined, ye'll wail a dreadful song.
And suddenly to you the ambient air
195 Will be unsettled, and the wrath of God
Will come from heaven upon you; and be sure
On men the immortal Saviour it will send,
Unless God ye appease, and now repent,
And unto one another be no more
200 So petulant and wicked and unjust,
But with a holy life be fortified."
But when they heard him each turned up his nose;

Line 175. *Implored the people.*—The O. T. narrative of the flood records
nothing of Noah's preaching, but in 2 Peter ii he is called a "preacher of
righteousness" (comp. 1 Pet. iii, 20), and Josephus (*Ant.*, i, iii, 1) confirms
this tradition of the Jews. Comp. also Theophilus, *ad Autol.*, iii, 19 [G., 6,
1.145].

(148–171.)

They called him mad, a man with frensy fired.

And then again did Noah sound this strain:

205 " O cowardly, vile-hearted, wavering men,

Forsaking reverence and loving shame,

Rapacious tyrants, violent transgressors,

Liars, filled with all unbelief, untrue,

Workers of evil, sly adulterers,

210 Flippant, and pouring slanders forth, the wrath

Of God ye do not fear, and ye are kept

To the fifth generation to atone.

Ye nowise weep, ye monsters, but ye laugh.

Sardonic smiles will ye laugh, let me say,

215 When God's approaching fearful flood shall come;

When a pure race on earth the wave renews,

Springing perennial from the dry, dead roots;

In one night root and branch becomes unknown,

And cities with their people from the deep

220 The Earth-shaker scatters and their walls destroys.

And then the whole world of unnumbered men

Shall die.   But how will I weep, how lament

In wooden house !   How mingle tears with waves !

For if the waters at God's word shall come,

225 Earth shall swim, hills swim, even air shall swim;

Water shall be all over, and all things

Shall be destroyed by waters.   And the winds

Shall stand still, and a second age shall dawn.

O Phrygian, from the lofty water first

Line 214. *Sardonic smiles.*—Expression supposed to have originated from a Sardinian plant so bitter as to cause the face of the eater to writhe in pain, though he might attempt to laugh.

Line 220. *Earth-shaker.*—In the Greek poets an epithet of Poseidon (Neptune), the god of the sea, here evidently applied to the God of Noah.

Line 229. *Phrygian . . . first.*—Comp. the statement of Herodotus (ii, 2), that the Phrygians were the most ancient of mankind.

(172–196.)

230 To go forth, thou another race of men
    Shalt nourish up, as from another new
    Beginning, and shalt be a nurse for all."
      But when he to that lawless generation
    Had vainly spoken thus, then the Most High
235 Revealed himself, and called again, and said:
    " The time has come, O Noah, to make known
    Each thing, whatever daily I to thee
    Have promised and decreed; to execute
    In all the world, because of human guilt,
240 All things, whatever myriad wrongs were done
    By former generations.   But do thou
    Make haste and enter with thy sons, and wife,
    And their wives.   Call as many as I bid,
    The tribes of beasts and creeping things and birds,
245 And in the breasts of such as I ordain
    To keep alive will I then straight impart
    The prompt and willing mind to enter in."
      Thus he spoke; and he went and cried aloud.
    And then his spouse and sons and their young wives
250 Entered the house of wood.   And then straightway
    Went every other thing, even as God willed.
    But when the key was fitted to the lid,
    Adjusted crosswise in its polished place,
    Then was the will of the celestial God
255 Accomplished.   Then he drove the gloomy clouds
    Together, and concealed the sun's bright disk,
    And moon and stars and circle of the heavens,
    Obscuring all things; and loud thunders rolled,
    Terror of mortals, and the lightnings flashed;
260 And all the winds together were aroused,
    And all the streams of waters were unloosed,
    And from heaven opened mighty cataracts,
    And earth's recesses and the tireless deep

            (197–223.)

Disclosed their myriad waters, and the wide
265 Illimitable earth was covered o'er.
But that divine house floated with the storm,
And, tossed by many a furious wave and swept
By blast of winds along, rose fearfully.
But still the keel cut through the mass of foam,
270 While the loud-murmuring waters dashed around.
But when the whole world God had drowned with
rains,
In Noah's mind 'twas given to understand
The purpose of the Immortal ; and he went
Sufficiently in Nereus. But straightway
275 The lid he lifted from the polished wall,
Where crosswise it was joined with skillful stays,
And, looking out upon the mighty mass
Of boundless waters, Noah's eyes surveyed
Death all around. Fear seized him, and his heart
280 Quaked mightily. And then the wind was stayed
A little, for it had toiled many days
To wet the whole world ; then it broke apart,
Disclosing, as if pale and stained with blood,
The great and fiery surface of the sky
285 Hard toil-worn. Noah difficultly held
His courage. And procuring then a dove,
He sent her forth alone to learn if the earth
Appeared yet solid ; but with wearied wing
She flew around all things and returned again,
290 For the great water was not yet assuaged,
For greatly was it filling every place.

Line 269. *Keel cut.*—Comp. Homer, *Iliad,* i, 481.

Line 274. *Nereus.*—A sea-god dwelling in the bottom of the ocean, called
in Homer (*Iliad,* i, 556) the "old man of the sea." His daughters were
nymphs of the sea and called Nereides. The Sibyl here declares that Noah
went sufficiently far into the domain of this aged monarch of the deep.

(224–246.)

But having rested other days, he sent
The dove again, to learn if yet had ceased
The many waters ; and she flew afar
295 And went upon the earth, and having paused
To rest a little on the humid ground,
Again to Noah back she came, and bore
An olive-branch, the sign of tidings great.
Then was he full of boldness and great joy,
300 For earth he hoped to look upon again.
And thereupon another bird, black-winged,
He straight sent forth ; and, trusting in his wings,
He promptly flew, and coming to the earth,
Remained there.   Then knew Noah that the land
305 Was very near.   But when the ark had tossed
Here and there on the furious waves, controlled
By skill divine, it swam o'er the sea's surge,
And was made fast upon the narrow shore.
There is upon the Phrygian main-land dark
310 A steep, tall mountain, Ararat by name,
Because thereon all were to be restored ;
And in it there is great and strong desire.
There the great river Marsyas draws his streams.
There the ark rested on the lofty height,
315 The waters ceasing.   Then again from heaven
Uttered the holy voice of the great God
This word: "O rescued Noah, faithful, just,
Come boldly forth with thy sons and thy wife
And their three young wives, and fill all the earth,
320 Increasing, multiplying, rendering justice

Line 310. *Ararat.*—Comp. the legends of this mountain and the remains
of the ark in Josephus, *Ant.*, i, iii, 6.
Line 313. *River Marsyas.*—Two rivers of antiquity bear this name, one
a branch of the Mæander in Asia Minor, the other a branch of the Orontes
in Syria. Neither of those seems to meet the conditions of our text.
(247-272.)

One to another, on from age to age,
Until to judgment all the race of men
Comes, for a judgment shall be unto all."
Thus spoke the heavenly voice, and Noah rushed
325 As from his couch forth boldly on the earth,
And his sons with him, his wife, and their wives,
And creeping things, and birds, and quadrupeds;
And all else from the wooden house went forth
Into one place. And then, most just of men,
330 Went Noah forth, the eighth, having fulfilled
Upon the waters twice one hundred days
And one; such was the will of the great God.
Then a new age of life again appeared,
First golden, which was now the sixth and best
335 Since man was first formed; heavenly it was called,
Because in all things it had care toward God.
O prime race of the generation sixth!
O mighty joy which I shall then obtain
When I escape dire ruin, having been
340 Much tossed with mine espoused, and brothers-in-law,
And husband's father and with husband's mother,
And having suffered with the wives like me.
Now I will sing: a many-colored flower
Shall on the fig-tree bloom, and in mid-time
345 The royal power and scepter it shall show.

Line 331. *Twice one hundred days.*—From Gen. vii, 11, compared with Gen. viii, 13, 14, it appears that Noah must have been over a year in the ark.

Line 334. *Sixth.*—"The Erythræan Sibyl says that she lived in the sixth age after the flood," says Eusebius, *Orat. ad Sanct.*, xviii [G., 20, 1285]. Here we note that she assumes to be a daughter-in-law of Noah. Comp. close of book iii.

Line 343. *Many-colored flower.*—Here employed as an image of the fertility of the royal race of whom she is about to sing.

(273–293.)

For three kings, great-souled and most just of men,
Shall show the lots and reign full many a year,
Awarding justice unto men, to whom
Labor and amiable deeds are dear.
350 And earth productive shall show many fruits
Spontaneous, and yield much corn for the race.
And then the nursing fathers, far apart
From cold dire plagues, shall not be growing old
All their days ; they will die as cast in sleep,
355 And pass down to the Acheronian shores,
In Hades' habitations, and down there
Shall they have honor. For they were a race
Of blessed ones, fortunate heroes, whom
The God of Sabaoth gave a noble mind ;
360 And they shall ever in his counsels share.
And blessed shall they be, even though they come
To Hades.   Then again rose fierce and strong
Another second race of earthborn men,
The Titans.   Like in form were each and all,
365 In aspect, size, and nature ; and their speech
Was one, like that which from the earliest race
God formerly implanted in their minds.
But these with haughty heart against the Highest
Took counsel, hastening to destruction on,
370 And waging war against the starry heaven.

Line 346.   *Three kings.*—The three sons of Noah would seem to have
been identified in the Sibyl's thought with Kronos, Titan, and Japetus of
the Greek mythology. Comp. book iii, 130.

     Line 355.   *Acheronian.*—Acheron was a river of the lower world. Virg.,
Æn., vi, 295.

     Line 364.   *Titans.*—Mythical sons of heaven and earth who figure much
in Greek legend and poetry. See book iii, 130–185. Lactantius records
a number of the legends and observes: "The truth of this history is taught
by the Erythræan Sibyl, who says almost the same things, varying only in
a few unimportant details." *Div. Inst.*, i, xiv [L., 6, 190].

(293–314.)

And then would the great ocean's flood have poured
Its maddened waters on them, but the great
Sabaoth checked and held it, though incensed,
For he had promised not to bring again
375 A deluge on malevolent mankind.
But when the many waters' boundless flood,
Wave rolling here and there on wave, he made
From wrath to cease, the great high-thundering God
In other depths of ocean, less profound,
380 Marked off the land by harbors and rough shores.

   *   *   *   *

And then the Child of the great God to men
Shall come incarnate, being fashioned like
To mortals on the earth. And he shall bear
Four vowels, and the consonants in him
385 Two times are told ; and the whole sum I name :
For eight ones, and as many tens to these,
And yet eight hundred will the name reveal
To men who are given up to unbelief.
Now do thou in thy heart consider Christ,
390 The Child of the immortal God most high ;
He shall fulfill God's law, and not destroy ;
His image he shall bear, and teach all things.
To him shall priests come bearing gold and myrrh
And frankincense ; for all things will he do.
395 But when a voice shall come through desert land

Line 381. *The Child.*—Jesus, whose name in Greek letters is indicated by the enigma which immediately follows. The sudden introduction of this reference to Jesus Christ makes it probable that a passage once immediately preceding it has fallen out of the text.

Line 384. *Four vowels.*—The name Jesus in Greek, Ἰησοῦς, contains four vowels and the consonant s twice told, and the numerical value of all the letters is 888. Comp. line 167, and note.

Line 395. *A voice.*—Comp. Isa. xl, 3 ; Matt. iii, 3.

Preaching to men, and all, with a loud cry,
Make straight the ways, and cast forth wickedness
Out of the heart, and let men's bodies all
By water be illumined, that, being born
400 From above, they may never more at all
Turn from the righteous (now, won by the dance,
His head will one of barbarous mind cut off,
And give for a reward), then shall a sign
Suddenly be to men, when, guarded well,
405 From Egypt's land shall come a beautiful stone,
At which the Hebrews shall be scandalized,
But nations shall be gathered, led by him,
For God who rules on high shall be made known
Through him, and a way in a common light.
410 For life eternal he'll show men elect,
But for the lawless lasting fire prepare.
And then the sick will he heal, and all men
Worthy of blame, who will show faith in him.
Then shall the blind see, and the lame shall walk,
415 The deaf shall hearken, and the dumb shall speak,
Demons be cast out, and the dead be raised,
Billows he'll walk, and in the desert place,

Line 399. *Illumined.*—An expression relating to Christian baptism quite common with the early fathers, many of whom understood the word φωτισθέντες in Heb. vi, 4, as referring to baptism. Justin Martyr, 1 *Apol.*, lxi [G., 6, 421], says: "This washing is called *illumination*, inasmuch as those who learn these things have their understanding illuminated." Cyril of Jerusalem wrote eighteen books of religious instruction, which are entitled *Catechesis of the Illuminated* [G., 33, 369–1060]. See also *Apost. Const.*, viii, 8. For other references see Suicer, Thesaurus, under φώτισμα.

Line 401. *Dance.*—See Matt. xiv, 6–10.

Line 404. *Guarded.*—By God and angels, as told in Matt. ii.

Line 405. *From Egypt's land.*—See Matt. ii, 13–15, 21. *Stone.*—Comp. Matt. xxi, 42, 44, and 1 Pet. ii, 4–8; Zech. iii, 9.

Line 409. *Common light.*—Comp. John i, 4–9.

(337–356.)

From five loaves and a fish of the deep sea,
Will sate five thousand, and what then remains
420 Will fill twelve baskets for the virgin pure.
    And then will Israel, drunken, not perceive,
Nor shall they hear, weighed down by sickly ears.
But when the burning wrath of the Most High
Upon the Hebrews comes, and from them faith
425 Be taken away, because the heavenly Child
Of God they injured, then will Israel give
With foul lips buffetings and scorn to him.
For food gall, and for drink strong vinegar
Impiously they give, with evil madness stricken
430 In breast and heart ; not seeing with their eyes,
More blind than moles, more terrible than beasts
That crawl envenomed, fettered by deep sleep.
But when he stretches out his blameless hands
And metes out all things, and a crown of thorns
435 Bears, and they pierce his side with spears—
For which dark night prodigious in midday
Three hours shall come—then shall the temple
Of Solomon disclose great signs to men,
And then shall he in Hades' mansion walk,
440 And resurrection to the dead proclaim.
But in three days he'll come to light again
And show his form to men, and teach all things,
And in the clouds ascending will depart
Into a heavenly mansion, having left
445 Unto the world the gospel covenant.
    And in his name shall a new sprout bloom forth
Among the nations, guided by great law.

Lines 414–420. Comp. book viii, 256–259 and 339–346, which is quoted in *Div. Inst.*, Lact., iv, 15 [L., 6, 493].   Instead of the reading *for the pure virgin* in line 420, book viii, 346, has *for the hope of the people.*   The whole concluding part of this book should be compared with book viii, 356–403.

(357–384.)

3
•

But also after these things have transpired,
Apostles shall be guides; and afterward
450 Of prophets a cessation there shall be.
      But when the Hebrews their ill harvest reap,
Much gold and silver will the Roman king
Plunder from them.   And other princes then
Continually will be, as kings expire,
455 And they will oppress mortals.   Great will be
The fall of those men when they shall commence
Unrighteous insolence.   But when the temple
Of Solomon on ground divine shall fall,
Hurled down by barbarous men, in brazen mail,
460 The Hebrews shall be driven from the land,
Wandering afar, and plundered, and much tares
In the wheat will they mingle, and will stand
An evil faction among all mankind.
And all their cities, outraged, will lament
465 Each other, since an evil work they wrought,
Receiving the great God's wrath in their hearts.
                   (385–400.)

BOOK II.

CONTENTS OF BOOK II.

Introduction, 1–6. A time of plagues and wickedness, 7–15. The tenth race, 16–28. A time of peace, 29–37. Great sign and contest, 38–63. A chapter of proverbs, 64–188. The contest, 189–194. Woes of the last generation, 195–221. Events of the last day, 222–260. Resurrection and judgment, 261–307. Punishment of the wicked, 308–372. Blessedness of the righteous, 373–392. Some saved from the fire, 393–402. The Sibyl's wail, 403–412.

BOOK II.

Now when my song of wisdom God restrained,
Much I implored, and in my breast again
He put the charming voice of words divine.
Trembling at every form I follow these,
5 For what I speak I do not comprehend,
But God commands each thing to be declared.
   But when on earth shocks, and strong thunderbolts,
Thunder and lightning, and mildew of earth,
Madness of wolves, and slaughter of mankind,
10 And ruin both of men and bellowing bulls,
Four-footed cattle, and laborious mules,
And goats and sheep, even then the barren field
Shall become much abandoned from neglect,
And fruits shall fail, and license shall abound
15 Among most men, and temple robbery.
And then of men the tenth race will appear,
When the earth-shaking Thunderer will break
The zeal of idols, and will shake the people
Of seven-hilled Rome, and all their treasured wealth
20 Will perish, burned by Vulcan's fiery flame.
   And then shall bloody signs from heaven descend.—
      *   *   *   *

Line 2. *I implored.*—Comp. beginning of book iii. This book is a continuation of the preceding, and probably belongs to the same author and date.

Line 5. *I do not comprehend.*—Comp. Plato, *Apol.*, where Socrates observes that "not by wisdom do poets write poetry, but by a sort of genius and inspiration; they are like diviners who also say many fine things, but do not understand the meaning of them."

Line 20. *Vulcan.*—The Greek Hephæstus, the god of fire.

Line 21. After this line something seems to have been lost from the text.
(1–20.)

But the whole world of men, enraged, will kill
Each other, and in tumult God will send
Famines and plagues and thunderbolts on men
25 Who without righteousness condemn the just.
And of men will the whole world be deserted,
So that, if any one beholds a trace
Of man on earth, he will be wonderstruck.
But then will the great God who dwells in heaven
30 Devout men's Saviour in all things become
And then shall peace profound and union be,
And the fruit-bearing earth shall yield again
Abundant fruits, nor shall it longer be
Divided, nor with toilsome service tilled.
35 But every port and harbor shall be free
To all men, even as they were before.
And brazen impudence shall be destroyed.
　　Then a great sign will God thereafter show.
A star will shine forth like a lustrous crown,
40 Bright, all-resplendent, from the radiant sky,
Days not a few; for then will he from heaven
Display the victor's garland unto men
Who struggle for the prize ; and then will be
That mighty contest of triumphal march
45 Into the heavenly city, and all earth
Having the fame of immortality
Shall be all men's possession, and all people
In the immortal contests will contend
For glorious victory.　Nor shamefully

Line 44. *Triumphal march.*—Allusion to the iselastic (εἰσελαστικός) contests the victors in which were conducted into their own city through a broken part of the wall. See Pliny, book x, Epis. 119 and 120, in which these games are mentioned.　Alexandre conjectures that this whole passage (lines 38–63) concerning contests and crowns was first written in a time of persecution to inspire to fidelity; but after persecution had ceased it was accommodated to the more common struggles of the Christian life.

(21-43.)

50 Can any then with silver buy a crown,
   For to them will the holy Christ assign
   The righteous things, and crown the ones approved,
   And give his martyrs the immortal pledge,
   And such as waged the contest unto death.
55 And he will give the incorruptible prize
   Of contests unto virgins who strove well;
   And to all men the right things will he grant,
   And to strange nations that live righteously,
   And know one God. And such as love the bonds
60 Of marriage, and adulterous acts despise,
   Will he give rich gifts and eternal hope.
   For every soul of man is God's own gift,
   And men should not stain it with any woes.
   [Become not rich unjustly, but be pure .
65 In all thy life. Assist those near to thee,
   And stand aloof from strangers. Speak no lies,
   But guard all true things. Reverence not thou
   Vain idols, but the everlasting God
   Hold first in honor, and thy parents next.
70 Dispense all righteous things, but do not come
   Into unrighteous judgment. Cast not off

Line 64. The passage beginning here and ending with line 188, and consisting mainly of proverbs, has every appearance of an interpolation. It breaks the connection of thought, and the figure of the iselastic contest, which is continued in lines 189–194. The passage is for the most part taken from a poem of 217 lines in hexameter verse, entitled ποίημα νουθετι-κόν (*admonitory poem*), and attributed to Phocylides, a gnomic poet of Miletus (born about B. C. 560). Very few, however, will seriously accept these lines as a genuine production of a contemporary of Theognis. They are without much doubt the composition of a Christian writer, and possibly, but not probably, by the author of the second book of the Sibylline Oracles. The variations between the two texts are considerable, the Sibyllines adding many lines not found in Phocylides, and Phocylides having a few not found in the Sibyllines.

(44–61.)

The poor unjustly, nor judge outwardly.
'{ If thou judge wickedly, God will judge thee.
False witness fly, and righteous things make known.
75 Keep thy virginity, and in all things
Guard love. Unrighteous measure do not give;
But beautiful is measure full to all.
Strike not the scales outside, but draw them equal.
Swear not in ignorance, nor willingly;
80 God hates false oaths, whatever one may swear.
Never receive in hand a gift that came
From unjust works. Seeds steal thou not; accursed
Through countless generations will he be,
Whoever takes it, for he scatters life.
85 Yield not to vile lusts, slander not, nor kill,
Give to the toilworn laborer reward;
The poor afflict not. Hold thy tongue with care,
And secret things fast in thy heart restrain.
To orphans, widows, and the needy give.
90 Will not to act unjustly, nor allow
Unrighteous things. Give to the poor at once,
And say not, Come to-morrow. Of thy grain
Give to the toilsome with a ready hand.
Know, he that gives alms lendeth unto God.
95 Mercy from death frees when the judgment comes;
Not sacrifice, but mercy God desires
Rather than sacrifice. Clothe therefore thou
The naked; with the hungry share thy bread.
Him without shelter in thy house receive,
100 And lead the blind. On shipwrecked mariners
Have thou compassion, for the sailor's art

Line 81. Comp. Exod. xxiii, 8 ; Prov. xvii, 23.
Line 94. Comp. Prov. xix, 17.
Line 96. Comp. Hos. vi, 6; Matt. ix, 13.
Line 97. Comp. Tobit iv, 16.
(62–85.)

Is perilous. To the fallen give a hand.
And save the man that stands all unassisted.
Suffering is common; life is as a wheel;
105 Riches uncertain. If thou hast wealth, reach
Thy hand unto the poor, and of the things
Which God gave thee bestow thou on the needy.
Common is all the life of mortal men,
But it comes out unequal. When thou seest
110 A poor man, never banter him with words,
Nor rudely accost a man that should be blamed.
The life in death is tested; if one did
The unlawful or just, it shall be discerned
When he comes into judgment. Injure not
115 The mind with wine, nor drink excessively.
Eat not blood, and from idol offerings keep.
Gird not the sword around thee 'gainst a friend,
But for defense; would that thou use it not
Unjustly or justly; for if thou put to death
120 An enemy thou hast defiled thy hand.
Keep from thy neighbor's field, and cross it not.
Each boundary is just, and troubles come
By trespass. Wealth is profitable
Unto the upright, but to the unjust an evil.
125 Harm not the growing produce of the field.
Let foreigners be equally esteemed
Among the citizens; for all should break
A painful hospitality, as guests
Of one another; but let no one be
130 A stranger with you, since of one blood all
Ye mortals are, and for mankind no realm
Affords a permanent abiding place.
Wish not nor pray to be rich, but pray this:

3*

To live of few things, and possess no thing
135 Unjustly. Mother of all wickedness
Is love of gain. Yearn not for gold or silver,
But be assured that in them there will be
A deadly two-edged instrument of iron.
Gold and silver are ever a snare to men.
140 O gold ! source of all evils, bane of life,
Full of vexation, would that thou wert not
To mortals such a longed-for misery.
For through thee come wars, plunders, homicides,
Children with parents in a bitter strife,
145 And brethren hating those of their own blood.
Plot no deceits, and do not arm thy soul
Against a friend. Conceal not in thy heart
Another thing from what thou speakest forth,
Nor change with place even as a polypus
150 Grown to a rock. But be thou frank with all,
And those things which are of the heart declare.
Whoever willfully commits a wrong,
An evil man is he; but he that sins
Under constraint, his end I do not tell;
155 But let the will of every man be right.
Boast not of wisdom, nor of power, nor wealth;
God only is wise and mighty, and abounds
In riches. Do not wear thy heart away
With evils that are past, for what is done
160 Can never be undone. Send not thy hand
Forth in a hasty deed, but curb wild wrath.
For often as one strikes he may commit
Unwittingly a murder. Let there be
A common suffering, neither great nor strong.
165 Excess of good has not been wont to yield

Lines 133–134. Comp. Theognis, 1151, 1152.
Line 135. Comp. 1 Tim. vi, 10.
(110–132.)

Profit to mortals, but much luxury
Brings on excessive lusts.   Great wealth puffs up,
And waxes into wanton insolence.
Desire, obtaining mastery, effects
170 Destructive madness.   Anger is a lust,
And when it passes further, it is wrath.
The zeal of good men is a noble thing,
But of the vile is vile.   Destructive is
The boldness of the wicked ; glory crowns
175 That of the good.   The love of virtue holds
Deserved esteem, but Cyprian loves add shame.
Agreeable is the amiable man
Among his fellows.   Moderately he eats,
Drinks, and discourses ; moderation is
180 Of all things best; excess brings many a pain.
Nor envious nor distrustful be, nor be
A railer, nor a man of evil thoughts,
Nor yet a false deceiver.   Exercise
Prudence, and keep thyself from shameful works.
185 Follow not malice, but by righteousness
Blot out revenge ; for useful is persuasion,
But strife engenders strife.   Do not believe
Too quickly, ere thou truly see the end.]
This is the contest, this is the reward,
190 This is the prize, this is the gate of life,
And entrance into immortality,
Which God in heaven to righteous men appointed
As victory's reward.   They that obtain
The crown shall enter gloriously by this.
195   But when this sign appears through all the
      world,

Line 176. *Cyprian.*—Belonging to the isle of Cyprus, where the lewd
worship of Venus was notorious.
(133–155.)

Children are born gray-haired, then human woes,
Famines and plagues and wars, and change of seasons
And many tearful sorrows will abound.
Alas ! How many children in the lands
200 Will mourn, and sadly for their parents weep,
And, wrapped in shrouds, bury the flesh in earth,
The mother of the peoples, mingling them
With blood and dust.   O miserable men
Of the last generation, evil-doers,
205 Cruel and foolish; nor perceiving this,
That when the tribes of women cease to bear,
The harvest-time of mortal men is come.
And ruin threatens when impostors come
Instead of prophets speaking on the earth.
210 And Beliar will come, and many signs
Will work for men.   And then of holy men
Elect and faithful there will be confusion,
And a plundering of them and of the Hebrews.
And there will come fierce wrath, when from the East
215 Shall come a people of twelve tribes, and seek
A people, whom the Assyrian branch destroyed,
Tribe-kinsmen of the Hebrews ; and with them
Shall nations perish.   Afterward again
Will they rule over the surviving men,
220 Elect and faithful Hebrews, and subject
Them as before, since their power will not fail.
The Most High, all-surveying, who abides

Line 196. *Gray-haired.*—Comp. a similar passage in Hesiod, *Works and Days*, 184. Children will become prematurely old by reason of the woes destined to visit the race in the last generation.

Line 210. *Beliar.*—Same as Belial, named here for antichrist, whose coming in the last time is depicted in harmony with Paul's doctrine in 2 Thess. ii, 8–10.

Lines 214–221. A passage inexplicably obscure in its historical allusions, but apparently connected with the notion of the ten tribes of the Assyrian exile, who, according to 2 Esdras xiii, 40–50, are concealed in the Far East, and to be restored in the last time.

(156–177.)

In the pure heaven, will scatter sleep on men,
Covering their eyelids round.   O blessed servants,
225 Whom when the Master comes he finds awake.
Awaken all, and watch with sleepless eyes ;
For he will come at morning, or at eve,
Or in midday; but he will surely come,
And it will be as I say ; it will be
230 To those at ease, that from the radiant heaven
The stars to all at midday will appear,
With the two luminaries ; and the time
Is pressing on.   And then will light on earth
The Tishbite, drawing from the heaven above
235 His heavenly chariot, and three signs will show
To all the world, of life to be destroyed.
Alas !   How many women in that day
Will be found with a burden in the womb;
How many infant children at the breast ;
240 How many will be dwelling on the waves.
Alas!   How many that day will behold.
For a dark mist will wrap the boundless world,
East, west, and south, and north; and from the heavens
Will flow a mighty stream of burning fire,
245 And every place consume—earth, ocean, sky,
And sea, and pools, and rivers, and harsh Hades,
And heaven's axis.   And the lights of heaven
Will rush together, and take on a form
All-desolate.   For all the stars will fall
250 Into the sea, and all the souls of men
Gnash their teeth, burning in the stream below,

Line 224. Comp. Matt. xxiv, 46.
Line 227. Comp. Mark xiii, 35; Homer, *Iliad*, xxi, 111.
Line 232. Comp. Matt. xxiv, 29.
Line 234. *Tishbite* . . . *chariot.*—Comp. 2 Kings ii, 11; Mal. iv, 5.
Line 237. Comp. Matt. xxiv, 19.
(178–203.)

That burns with brimstone and the force of fire.
And then the elements of all the world
Shall be forsaken—air, earth, sea, light, heaven,
255 And days and nights. No longer through the air
  Will fly the insatiate birds, nor swimming beasts
Pass through the sea, nor vessels sail the waves,
Nor cattle plow the field, nor sound of trees
Under the winds ; but all things then will melt
260 Together, and will come out purified.

    Then will the angels of the immortal God
Come, Michael, Gabriel, Raphael, Uriel,
Who know whatever evil things men do,
And from the dark and murky gloom below
265 Up to the judgment will lead forth all souls,
To the tribunal of the immortàl God.
For One alone imperishable is,
Himself the Almighty; he shall judge mankind,
And then to nether realms, souls, spirit, and voice,
270 The heavenly God will give, and also bones
Fitted to joints, and made divinely fair.
And flesh and sinews in all parts will join,
And veins and skin; and afterward the hair
Will spring forth as aforetime. So one day
275 Shall earthly bodies moved with breath be raised.

    And then will Uriel, mighty angel, break
The bolts of harsh and lasting adamant,
Which, monstrous, hold the awful gates of hell,
And hurling them aside, to judgment bring
280 All the sad forms exceeding sorrowful,
Chiefly the phantom forms of Titans old,

Line 262. These four angels are mentioned in the Book of Enoch (chaps. ix and x), and are frequently referred to in the later Jewish angelology.

Line 281. *Titans.*—Comp. book i, 364, and iii, 130–185,

(204–232.)

And giants, whom the deluge swept away;
And such as perished in the billowy seas,
And all that furnished banquet for the beasts,
285 And creeping things, and winged fowls—all these
Uriel will summon to the judgment-seat;
And also those whom flesh-devouring fire
Destroyed in flame, even these shall rise and stand
Assembled at the judgment-seat of God.
290   And when the dead are raised, and fates resolved,
And the high fulminating Lord of hosts
Is seated on his heavenly throne, and sets
The mighty pillar, then amid the clouds
In the glory of Christ, with blameless angels thronged,
295 The Incorruptible himself will come
Unto him who is incorruptible,
And on the right hand of the great tribunal
Sit, judging lives of just and unjust men.
Moses will come, great friend of the Most High,
300 And Abraham, himself also great, will come,
Isaac and Jacob, Joseph, Daniel,
Elijah, Habakkuk, and Jonah, all,
And those whom persecuting Hebrews slew.
But all those Hebrews after Jeremiah,
305 At the tribunal judged, he will destroy;
That they may worthy recompense receive,
And pay for what in mortal life they did.
And then all through the burning stream shall pass
Of fire unquenchable; but all the righteous
310 Shall be saved.   But the ungodly to all ages
Shall be undone, who erst wrought wickedness,
And knowingly committed murders vile;

Line 293. *Pillar.*—Comp. vers. 344, 355, and book vii, 35.
Line 294. Comp. Matt. xvi, 27.
Lines 308–310. The following passage from Lactantius, vii, 21 [L., 6, 802],
(233–257.)

Liars and thieves and ruiners of home,
Crafty and terrible; and parasites,
315 And marriage-breakers, pouring slanders forth;
The fearful, insolent idolators;
Those who, forsaking the immortal God,
Become blasphemers; robbers of the just,
Destroyers both of faith and holy men;
320 Presbyters, priests, and ministers revered,
Who practiced with a double face their guile,
And shamelessly perverted others' rights;
Impostors, credulous, but more destructive
Than wolves and leopards, vilest of the vile;
325 Also the arrogant, and usurers,
Who pile up compound interest at home,
And wrong the widow and the fatherless;
And such as give to widows and to orphans
The product of unrighteous deeds, and such
330 As, giving out of hardships, cause reproach;
All who forsake their parents in old age,
Not reverencing or requiting them,
But disobedient, contradicting sires
With harsh words; those who take assurances
335 And then deny; and servants who have turned
Against their masters; also the impure,
Who by lasciviousness defile the flesh
And loose the maiden's girdle secretly;
And such as having burdens in the womb

---

is worthy of comparison here: "When He shall have judged the righteous
he will also try them with fire. Then they whose sins shall exceed either
in weight or number shall be scorched by the fire and burnt; but they
whom full justice and maturity of virtue has imbued will not perceive that
fire, for they have something of God in themselves which repels the violence
of the flame."

Line 331. Comp. a similar passage in Hesiod, *Works and Days*, 183, *ff.*
(258–282.)

340 Produce abortion, and their offspring cast
    Unlawfully away; and sorcerers
    And sorceresses—all these will the wrath
    Of the immortal God cause to approach
    The pillar, where around a circle flows
345 The river inexhaustible of fire.
    Then will the angels of the immortal God,
    Who ever liveth, direly punish them
    With flaming scourges and with fiery flames,
    Bound from above with ever-during bonds.
350 Then in Gehenna, in the midnight gloom,
    Will they be to Tartarean monsters cast,
    Many and fierce, where darkness is supreme.
       But when all punishments have been entailed
    On all whose hearts were evil, then straightway
355 From the great river will a fiery wheel
    Circle them round, pressed down with wicked
       works;
    And then in many a way most piteously
    Will fathers, mothers, nursing children wail;
    Nor will there be satiety of tears,
360 Nor will the piteous cry of those who mourn
    Be heard elsewhither, but worn down afar
    Amid the darkening shades of Tartarus
    They cry aloud, and pay the penalty
    Threefold for all the wicked works they did,
365 Burning in fire; and they shall gnash their teeth,
    All consumed by devouring thirst and force,
    And wish to die, but death shall flee from them,
    For nevermore will death nor night give rest.
    Much will they vainly pray to God most high,
370 But he will turn his face away from them.

Line 358. Comp. Virg., *Geor.*, iv, 475, *ff*, and *Æn.*, vi, 306, *ff.*
(283-311.)

[For seven ages a day of penitence
Gave he to men by a pure virgin's hand.]
　But others, with whom right and good works weighed,
Most upright in their piety and thoughts,
375 The angels, bearing through the burning stream,
Shall lead to light and life exempt from care.
There is the immortal way of the great God,
And fountains three, of honey, wine, and milk.
The land, alike for all, divided not
380 By wall or fence, shall bear abundant fruit
Indigenous ; the means and modes of life
Common will be, and riches without lot.
For there no longer will be poor nor rich,
Tyrant nor slave, nor great, nor small, nor kings,
385 Nor chieftains, but all share a common life.
No more will any say the night has come,
Or morrow comes, or yesterday has been.
They have no trouble about many days.
Spring, summer, autumn, winter will not be
390 [Marriage nor death, nor will they buy and sell,
Nor will there be sunset or sunrise more],
For he will make it one long, lasting day.
　Then to the pious will the almighty God
Grant yet another thing, when they shall pray
395 For men to be saved from devouring fire
And lasting torments ; and this he will do.
For having plucked the steadfast from the flame
That rests not, and removing them elsewhere,

Lines 371, 372.　Comp. book viii, 445–447.
Line 375.　　This, together with lines 398–400, has been thought to teach
the doctrine of purgatory.　See note below.
Line 378.　Comp. Virg., *Eclogue* iv.
Lines 383, 384.　Comp. viii, 139, 140.
Lines 386–392.　Comp. book viii, 537–542.
　　　　　　(312–335.)

He for his people's sake will send them on
400 Unto another and eternal life,
In fields Elysian, where are the great waves
Of the deep-bosomed Acheronian lake.
Ah, wretched I ! what shall I in that day ?
For, ill-disposed and anxious for all things,
405 I sinned and had no care for marriage-bonds,
Nor reason.   But within my sumptuous halls
I shut the needy out, and knowingly
Aforetime did unlawful things perform.
Thou, Saviour, rescue me, the shameless one,
410 From my tormenters, me who did the shame.
I pray thee, let me rest a while from song,
Holy Giver of manna, King of the great realm.

Lines 393–402.   *Then to the pious.*—This passage, which savors of a final restoration from future punishment, has been thought to be contrary to orthodox teaching ; and we find appended to some manuscripts the following lines, headed, "Contradiction of the 'To the pious will the Almighty,'" and professedly a disproof of the doctrine of Origen on this subject :

> " False manifestly, for the penal fire
> Shall never cease from those who are condemned ;
> For even should I pray to have it thus,
> I'm marked by greatest scars of trespasses,
> Which call for still a greater clemency.
> But be ashamed of Origen's vain talk,
> Who says that punishments will have an end."

Line 401.   *Fields Elysian.*—In Homer (*Od.*, iv, 563) these are represented as situated on the western border of the earth by the ocean stream, and thither heroes beloved by the gods passed without dying.   Hesiod (*Works and Days*, 169) calls them "the isles of the blessed, beside deep-eddying ocean."   But later, and with the Roman poets, Elysium was in the lower world, the blessed part of Hades, and is here conceived as bordering on the Acheronian lake.

Line 405.   Comp. the conclusion of book vii.

(336–348.)

BOOK III.

CONTENTS OF BOOK III.

Introduction, 1–10.   Unity and power of God extolled, 11–34.   Oracle
against idolatry and sin, 35–54.   Coming and judgment of the great King,
55–74.   Coming of Beliar, 75–88.   Reign of the woman and end of the
world, 89–108.   All things subject to Christ, 109–113.   The tower of Babel,
114–126.   Kronos, Titan, and Japetus, 127–151.   Kronos, Rhea, and the
Titans, 152–183.   End of the Titans and rise of many kingdoms, 184–189.
The Sybil's message, 190–195.   Rule of the house of Solomon, 196–200.
Rule of the Hellenes, 201–209.   The Western Kingdom, 210–225.   The Sibyl's burden, 226–231.   Woes on the Titans and on many nations, 232–248.
The righteous race, 249–269.   The exodus and giving of the law, 270–307.
Desolation and exile, 308–336.   Restoration from exile, 337–345.   The Sibyl
ceases and begins again, 346–354.   Woe on Babylon, 355–368.   Woe on
Egypt, 369–374.   Woe on Gog and Magog, 375–379.   Woe on Libya, 380–
391.   Great signs and woes on many cities, 392–409.   Retributive judgment
on Rome, 410–427.   Doom of Samos, Delos, Rome, and Smyrna, 428–431.
Peace of Asia and Europe, 432–446.   The Macedonian woe, 447–455.   The
unnamed rulers, 456–470.   The sign for Phrygia, 471–486.   The fate of
Ilion, 487–493.   Songs of the blind old man, 494–510.   Woes of Lycia,
Chalcedon, Cyzicus, Byzantium, and Rhodes, 511–530.   Woes of Lydia, Samos, Cyprus, and Trallis, 531–548.   Italy's tribal wars, 549–556.   Woes of
Laodicea, Campania, Corsica, and Sardinia, 557–572.   Woes of Mysia, Carthage, Galatia, Tenedos, Sicyon, and Corinth, 573–579.   The Sibyl ceases
and begins again, 580–583.   Woes of Phenicia, Crete, Thrace, Gog, Magog,
Maurians, Ethiopians, and provinces of Asia Minor, 584–620.   Oracles
against Greece, 621–684.   The holy race, 685–724.   Egypt subdued, 725–
733.   Time of blessedness, 734–742.   Exhortation to worship God, 743–753.
Time of judgment, 754–775.   The God-sent king, 776–784.   Removal of
envy and strife, 785–795.   Fearful time of judgment, 796–828.   The Sybil's
testimony, 829–833.   A Jewish millennium, 834–869.   Exhortation to the
Greeks, 870–884.   Day of prosperity and peace, 885–905.   Exhortation to
serve God, 906–911.   The Messianic day, 912–944.   Signs of the end,
945–959.   The Sibyl's account of herself, 960–986.

BOOK III.

Thou blessed One, loud Thunderer of the heavens,
Who holdest in their place the cherubim,
I pray thee give me now a little rest,
Since I have uttered what is all so true.
5 For weary has my heart within me grown.
Why should my heart be quivering now again,
And my soul, lashed as with a whip, be forced
To utter forth its oracle to all?
Yet once more I will speak aloud all things
10 Which God impels me to proclaim to men.
   O men, in godlike form and image made,
Why do ye vainly wander, and not walk
The straight path, keeping ever in your mind
The immortal Maker?   One God rules alone,
15 Unutterable, dwelling in the sky,
Self-constituted, and invisible,

This book contains a great variety of matter, and doubtless embodies the most ancient Sibylline verses now extant.   See Introduction.   Some of the manuscripts preface this book with the line,

" Again, in her third tome, these things she says."

In some editions the first seventy-four (Greek text, sixty-two) lines are appended to the preceding book.

Line 2. *Cherubim.*—Allusion to such passages as 1 Sam. iv, 4; 2 Sam. vi, 2; Psa. xviii, 10; lxxx, 1; xcix, 1, where the Most High is conceived as dwelling or riding upon the cherubim.

Line 3. *I pray.*—Here, as at the beginning of the first and second books, we note the Sibyl's claim to be controlled by God.   In many things she assumes to be an unwilling prophetess.

Line 11. *O men.*—Here and in the following lines we have much that reminds us of the language of the Proem.

Line 16. Comp. Rev. i, 4, 8.

(1–12.)

Though he himself alone beholds all things.
No sculptor's hand formed him, nor by man's art
Appears his image in gold or ivory;
20 But he proclaims his own eternity
As one who is, and was, and yet shall be.
For who is he, frail mortal, that with eyes
Can look on God?   Or who could bear to hear
The name alone of the great God of heaven
25 Who rules the world?   He by a word all things
Created, heaven, and sea, and tireless sun,
And the full moon, and stars that shed forth light,
The mighty mother Tethys, fountains, streams,
Imperishable fire, and days and nights.
30 This is the God who made four-lettered Adam,
The first one formed, whose name fills east and west
And south and north.   The same is he who fixed
The type and form of man, and made the beasts,
And creeping things, and such as spread the wing.
35 Ye do not reverence or worship God,
But vainly go astray and bow the knee
To serpents, and to cats make sacrifice,
And other idols, statues made of stone,
And sit before the doors of godless shrines.

Line 28. *Mother Tethys.*—Wife of Oceanus, mother of the rivers and the nymphs, three thousand in number. See Hesiod, *Theog.*, 335, *ff.*   Comp. Homer, *Iliad*, xiv, 201, 302.

Line 30. *Four-lettered Adam.*—The ingenuity which sees in the four letters of this name the Greek initials of the words for east, west, north, and south surpasses even that noted in book i, 98, where Hades is traced in the word Adam. But Augustine adopts this, and says: "According to the Greek tongue, Adam himself signifies the whole world. For there are four letters, A, D, A, M, and in Greek speech these are the initial letters of the four quarters of the earth." *Enarratio in Psalmum*, xcv, 15 [L., 37, 1236]. See also *Tractatus in Joannis*, ix, 14, and x, 12 [L., 35, 1465, 1473].

(12–32.)

40 Ye guard against the God who keeps all things,
And in the wickedness of stones delight,
Forgetful of the immortal Saviour's judgment,
Who made the heaven and earth. Woe to a race
That has delight in blood, deceitful, vile,
45 Ungodly, double-tongued, malicious men,
Unchaste, idolatrous, designing fraud,
An evil madness raving in their breasts.
They plunder, and maintain a shameless soul ;
For no rich man will with another share.
50 But a dire evil shall to all men come,
Faith they will nowhere hold, and many wives
And widows will in secret others love
Because of gain, and they will not observe
Life's sacred bond if only they get men.
55 But when Rome also over Egypt rules,
Having one end in view, then shall appear
The mighty kingdom of the immortal king
Set over men. A holy king shall come
Wielding the scepter over every land
60 Unto all ages of advancing time.
And then will the stern wrath of Latian men
Rome thrice expose to pitiable fate.
And all mankind shall perish in their homes,
When from the heavens a fiery cataract flows.
65 Ah me, unhappy ! When shall that day come,
And judgment of the immortal God's great king ?
Now surely, O ye cities, ye are built
And all adorned with temples and race-grounds,
Markets, and images of precious stone,
70 All that ye may come to a bitter day.
For it will come whenever there shall pass

Line 56. *One end in view.*—The subjugation of all to her power.
Line 58. *Holy king.*—Comp. book viii, 211.

(38–60.)

4

The smell of sulphur among all mankind.
But these things severally I will tell
In as many cities as men carry vice.

75 From the great Cæsars Beliar shall come
Hereafter, and shall stand on mountain height,
And stay the sea, and the great fiery sun,
And shining moon, and make the dead stand up,
And perform many miracles with men.

80 But nothing to perfection will he bring,
But many mortals he will lead astray,
Elect and faithful Hebrews; also men
Without law, such as never heard God's word.
But when the threatenings of the mighty God

85 Shall draw near, and upon the earth shall come
The flaming power as in a billowy wave,
It shall burn Beliar too, and faithless men,
All, even as many as put their trust in him.

And then the world shall by a woman's hands
90 Be governed and persuaded in all things.
And when o'er all the world a widow reigns,

Line 75. *Beliar.*—Comp. book ii, 210, note. The miracle-working antichrist is first depicted in Dan. vii, 25; viii, 23–25; xi, 36, from which Paul drew the imagery of his description in 2 Thess. ii, 8–10. This Beliar is to come *from the Cæsars* (not from the *Samaritans*—that is, Sebastenes, as Ewald, p. 89, after an old Jewish superstition imagined), and hence the widespread notion that Nero was the person, and that he had fled beyond the Euphrates and would again return. Comp. book iv, 150–157, 175–177; v, 38–47; viii, 88, 193–201. Some have supposed that Rev. xvii, 10, 11, refers to this legend of Nero, but the notion is more likely to have sprung from a misapprehension of that passage.

Lines 77, 78. *Sun* . . . *moon.*—Comp. Hesiod, *Theog.*, 18 and 371.

Line 91. *Widow.*—This widow woman to rule all the world in the last time seems to be derived from the apocalyptic image in Rev. xvii, 3; comp. xviii, 7, and refer to Rome itself as the mistress of nations. Comp. also book viii, 249–251. Ewald's idea, that Julia Domna, widow of Septimius Severus, is intended, seems to have nothing to support it.

(61–77.)

And flings the gold and silver in the sea,
And brass and iron of perishable man
Flings in the flood, then all earth's elements
95 Shall widow-like be waste and desolate.
And God who dwells on high will roll the heaven
Together, even as a scroll is rolled.
And on the noble land and on the sea
The entire multiform arch of heaven shall fall.
100 A cataract of glowing fire shall flow
Unceasing, and burn land and sea and sky;
Creation itself will he melt into one,
And take out that which tends to purity.
The luminous laughing spheres shall be no more,
105 Nor night, nor dawn, nor many days of care,
Nor spring-time, summer, winter, autumn more.
And then shall come God's judgment, in the midst
Of a great age when all these things shall be.

* * * *

O navigable waters, and all lands
110 Wherever the sun rises and goes down,
All things shall be subjected unto him
Who comes a second time into the world;
For from the first he recognized his power.

* * * *

But when the threatenings of the mighty God
115 Had been fulfilled, which once he threatened those
Who made a tower in the Assyrian land
(And they were all one language, and resolved
To mount aloft into the starry heaven),

Lines 109–113. These lines appear to be only a fragment of a longer passage, now lost, which spoke of the second coming of the Christ.

Lines 114–126. This passage is cited in Theophilus, *ad Autol.*, ii, 31 [G., 6, 1101]; Josephus, *Ant.*, i, iv, 3. Comp. Eusebius, *Prœp. Evang.*, ix, 14 [G., 21, 702, 703]. See Gen. xi, 1–9. It is one of the oldest portions of the Sibyllines, and was probably once combined with the Proem, given on pp. 24–29.

(78–100.)

Straightway the Immortal added to the winds
120 A mighty force, and tempests from above
    Hurled down the huge tower, and among mankind
    Raised up confusion, wherefore mortals gave
    Unto that city the name of Babylon.
    But when the tower fell, and the tongues of men
125 Became discordant, all the earth was filled
    With mortals, and divided among kings.
        And then appeared the generation tenth
    Of mortal men, from the time when the flood
    Came on the earlier race.   And Kronos reigned,
130 And Titan and Japetus, whom men esteemed
    Fairest of Gaia and Uranus born,
    And gave them also names of earth and heaven,
    Because they were most excellent of men.
    Into three parts divided they the earth,
135 According to the inheritance of each,
    And each ruled his own portion, without strife;
    For they were bound by the paternal oath,
    And equal were their portions.   But old age
    Came on the father, and his time was full,
140 And he died; but the sons, infringing oaths,

Line 119. *Winds.*—"The idea that God threw down the tower by means of the winds was probably first written down by our poet, but it is really nothing but a subtile interpretation of Gen. xi, 7."—*Ewald*, p. 33.

Line 127. *Generation tenth.*—Cited by Athenagoras, *Legatio pro Christianis,* xxx [G., 6, 960], and Tertul., *ad Nationes,* ii, 12 [L., 1, 603]. In citing this passage Tertullian thus speaks of the Sibyl: "The Sibyl was earlier than all literature, that Sibyl, I mean, who was the true prophetess of truth.   In senarian verse she thus expounds the descent and exploits of Saturn."

Line 129. *Kronos.*—Greek name for the more familiar Latin title Saturn. The story of the Titans in the following lines (129-183) is familiar to students of Greek mythology, but the old myth exists with numerous minor variations, and, according to Hesiod (*Theog.*, 453-500), the birth and preservation of Dia (or Jove) were somewhat different from this story.

(101-118.)

Contended with each other in fierce strife,
Who should hold regal honor, and bear rule
Over all mortals.   Then did Kronos fight
And Titan with the rest.   But Rhea, and Gaia,
145 And garland-loving Venus, Demeter,
And Vesta, and Dione golden-haired
Brought them to friendship, and a council called
Of all the kings and brothers, and near kin,
And also others of ancestral blood,
150 And they decided Kronos should be king,
For he was oldest and of noblest form.
　　But Titan placed on Kronos mighty oaths
To rear no male posterity, that he
Himself might reign when age and fate should fall
155 On Kronos.   So whenever Rhea bore,
Beside her sat the Titans, and destroyed
All the male issue; but the female lived,
And were left to the mother's nursing care.
But when at the third birth the honored Rhea
160 Brought forth illustrious Juno, and they saw
With wondering eyes a race of females born,
The savage Titans took themselves away.
Then when a male child Rhea brought to birth
She sent him quickly into Phrygia,
165 There to be reared in secret, having bound
Three Cretans by an oath to do her will.
They called him Dia, for he was sent away.
Poseidon also secretly she sent;
And Pluto, third, by women's helping hand
170 Did Rhea, coming to Dodona, bear,

Line 170. *Dodona.*—The place of a most celebrated city and oracle, commonly supposed to be in Epirus, but according to this passage apparently in Thessaly. Its exact site is unknown.
(119–144.)

Whence flows Eurotas' moistened path away,
And, with Peneius mixed, pours in the sea
Its water, and men call it Stygian.
    But when the Titans heard of hidden sons
175 Begotten by King Kronos and his wife,
Straightway assembled Titan sixty youths,
Bound Kronos and his wife Rhea in chains,
Hid them in earth, and kept them under guard.
And then the sons of mighty Kronos heard,
180 And they stirred up a great tumultuous war.
And this was the beginning of dire war
Among all mortals, for it was indeed
With men the primal origin of war.
    Then God sent evil on the Titan race,
185 And all from Titan and from Kronos sprung
Died.   But as time rolled on these kingdoms rose;
Egyptian, Persian, Median, Ethiopian,
Assyrian-Babylon, and Macedon,
Egyptian yet again, then that of Rome.
190   And then a message of the mighty God
Pressed on my heart, and bade me prophecy
On all the earth, and in the minds of kings
Those things deposit which are yet to be.

Line 171. *Eurotas.*—Not the well-known river of Laconia in the Pelo-
ponnesus, but another name for the Titaresius, which flows into the Peneius in
the vale of Tempe.   Strabo (book ix, v, 19) says that the poets called the
river Eurotas, which is not far from the foot of Olympus, Titaresius; that
it rises in a part of Mount Olympus and enters the Peneius in the plain near
Tempe.   In this region he locates a Dodona, but does not specify its exact
location.   Comp. Homer, *Iliad*, ii, 750-755, who says, however, with Strabo,
that this river does not mingle with Peneius, but pours over the surface
like oil, for it is a broken-off portion of the terrible Styx.   This latter was
one of the streams of the lower world.
    Line 187. *Persian.*—Here probably meant for the Assyrian, while the
Median included in the writer's thought the later Persian.   So Ewald, p. 11.
(145-164.)

And first the only God delivered me
195 What kingdoms of mankind shall be raised up.
And first the house of Solomon shall rule
The horsemen of Phenicia and of Asia,
And those of other islands, and the race
Of the Pamphylians, Persians, Phrygians,
200 Carians, Mysians, and Lydians famed for gold.
And then the overweening Hellenes,
Impure, another Macedonian race,
Much mixed, shall rule, and they shall bring on men
A fearful cloud of war, but the God of heaven
205 Will utterly destroy them from below.
And then another kingdom will arise,
White, many-headed from the western sea,
Which will rule many a land, and many shake,
And afterward bring terror to all kings.
210 Much gold and silver will she take by force
From many cities, yet in the vast earth
There will be gold and silver and elegance.
And they will sore afflict mankind, and then
To those same men will come a ruinous fall,
215 When they attempt unrighteous insolence.
On them will be the bond of wickedness,
Male will consort with male, and they will set

Line 196. *House of Solomon.*—The kingdom of Solomon is here made to rule over nations which Old Testament history never mentions as subject to Israel. Comp. 1 Kings iv, 21. But the poet wishes to magnify that realm.

Line 201. *Hellenes.*—The Græco-Macedonian kingdom is here evidently intended.

Line 206. *Another kingdom.*—The Roman.

Line 207. *White.*—Probably an allusion to the white toga of the Roman magistrates. *Many-headed.*—Having a great number and variety of rulers. Competitors for office were called *candidati,* because of the white robe in which they presented themselves.

(165–185.)

Children in dens of shame.   And in those days
A great affliction among men will come,
220 And vex and wound and fill all things with evil
Through shameful covetousness, and gain ill-gotten
In many lands, but most in Macedon.
And hatred shall spring up, and all deceit,
Until the seventh kingdom, which a king
225 Of Egypt, but of Grecian birth, shall rule.
    And then the nation of the mighty God
Shall be again strong, and be guides of life
To all mankind.   But wherefore now should God
Lay it upon my spirit to declare
230 What evil first, what next, what last shall be
Upon all men, and how they shall begin?
    First on the Titans God will evil send,
For mighty Kronos's sons will vengeance take,
Because they bound the king and mother dear.
235 Again will tyrants rule the Hellenes,
And they will be proud, haughty, vicious kings,
Adulterous, and altogether bad;
And no more will there be a rest from war.
The dreadful Phrygians shall perish all,
240 And Troy will meet misfortune in that day.
    Evil will also to the Persians come,

Line 224.   *Seventh kingdom.*—Or seventh king (comp. line 726) of the
Greek-Egyptian dynasty.   This would point to Ptolemy Philometer if we
reckon Alexandre the Great as the first king, but Ptolemy Physcon if the
line of the Ptolemies alone are reckoned.   Ewald adopts this latter view,
Alexander the former.   All the Ptolemies were of Greek (or Macedonian)
origin.

Line 227.   *Again strong.*—The writer seems in the spirit and hope of Old
Testament prophets to conceive a triumph for the chosen people as following hard upon the evils of his own time.

Line 232.   Here the prophetess repeats herself, as if going back to the
subject of line 184.

(186–207.)

And to the Assyrians, and all Egypt too,
And Libya and the Ethiopians,
Carians, Pamphylians, and on mortals all
245 Shall evil be imposed. Why then of each
Do I speak? When the first comes to an end
Straightway the second falls upon mankind;
And yet I will the very first sound forth.
　　There will an evil come to pious men
250 Who dwell by the great temple of Solomon,
And are the progeny of righteous men.
Of these I also will declare the tribe
And line of fathers, and the home of all—
Do all with skill, O mortal full of guile.
255　　There is a city on the [Asian] soil,
Ur of the Chaldees, whence has come a race
Most upright, ever of good counsel fond
And noble deeds. For they seek not with care
The circling pathway of the sun and moon,
260 Nor monstrous deeds on earth, nor the blue depth
Of sea or ocean, nor the signs of sneezing,
Nor birds of augurers, nor soothsayers,
Nor wizards, nor enchanters, nor the frauds
And silly speeches of ventriloquists,
265 Nor studies of Chaldean astrologers,
Nor oracles they gather from the stars.
For all these things are errors, which vain men

Line 249. *Evil.*—What particular evil or calamity of the Jewish people is here intended is altogether uncertain.

Line 254. *Mortal full of guile.*—Comp. book i, 7.

Line 255. The passage is corrupt and the reading adopted in our version is to some extent conjectural, but has some support in manuscripts, and suits the context. The critical student should consult Alexandre's note in his edition of 1841, p. 111. On "Ur of the Chaldees" see Gen. xi, 31. Others, however, following another conjectural reading, understand the city to be Jerusalem. So Ewald, p. 21.

(208–228.)

4*

Search day by day, and exercise their souls
In labors void of profit, and then teach
270 Their error unto other thoughtless men.
Hence many evils have befallen men,
And turned them from good ways and righteous
　　deeds.
But they do seek with care for righteousness
And virtue, and have not the avarice
275 Which breeds unnumbered ills to mortal men,
Continuous war, and famine without end.
Just measure they observe in field and town;
They steal not from each other in the night,
Nor drive off herds of oxen, sheep, and goats;
280 Nor do they neighbors' landmarks take away;
Nor does the man of great wealth grieve the poor,
Nor oppress widows, but he rather aids,
Ever imparting wheat and wine and oil,
And always happy with those that have nought;
285 And to the destitute at harvest-time
He sends a share.　Thus they fulfill the word
Of the great God—a hymn enshrined in law.
For he who dwells in heaven completed earth
To be a common property for all.
290 　But when the people of twelve tribes·depart
From Egypt and with joy pursue their way,
With leaders sent of God, they will proceed
In a pillar of fire by night, and one of cloud
At morning of each day as they go on;
295 And for them God a leader will appoint,
A great man, Moses, whom a princess found
Beside a marsh, and carried off and reared
And called her son.　But when anon he came
As leader of the people whom God brought

300 Away from Egypt to the Sinai mount,
Then God delivered them the law from heaven,
And wrote upon two tables all things just,
Which he enjoined to do; and if, perchance,
One give no heed, he must unto the law
305 Make satisfaction, either at men's hands,
Or, if man's notice he escape, he shall
By ample satisfaction be destroyed.
    For he who rules in heaven completed earth
To be a common property for all,
310 And in all bosoms placed he noblest thought.
To them alone the bounteous field yields fruit,
A hundred-fold from one, and thus completes
God's measure. But to them shall also come
Misfortune, nor will they escape all plague.
315 And even thou, forsaking thy fair shrine,
Shalt flee away when it becomes thy lot
To leave the holy ground, and thou shalt be
Carried to the Assyrians, and shalt see
Wives and young children serving hostile men.
320 All means of life and wealth shall be destroyed,
And every land and sea be filled with thee,
And at thy customs all will take offense.
Thy land shall be all waste, and the fenced altar
And sacred temple and extended walls,
325 All to the ground shall fall, because in heart
Thou hast not kept the holy law of God;
But thou hast erred and served vain images,
And hast not feared the immortal Sire of gods
And of all men, nor willed to honor him,

Line 318. *Assyrians.*—Assyria and Babylon seem to have been often confounded together by the Sibylline authors. Comp. the expression "Assyrian-Babylon," line 188. Here the Babylonian captivity is referred to.
(256–279.)

330 But thou hast honored images of men.
　　　Therefore seven decades shall thy fruitful land
　　　And the wonders of the temple be a waste.
　　　And yet for thee a goodly end remains,
　　　And highest glory from the immortal God.
335 But wait thou, and confide in God's pure laws,
　　　When to the light he lifts thy wearied knee.
　　　　And then will God send out of heaven a king
　　　To judge each man in blood and light of fire.
　　　There is a royal tribe, whose progeny
340 Shall be unfailing, and in course of time
　　　Will it rule, and God's temple build anew.
　　　And all the kings of Persia will assist
　　　With gold and brass and well-wrought iron, and God
　　　Himself will give by night the holy dream,
345 And then the temple shall be as of old,

　　　　　＊　　　＊　　　＊　　　＊

　　　Now when my soul had ceased from hallowed song,
　　　And I prayed the great Sire to be released,
　　　Again a message of Almighty God

Line 331. *Seven decades.*—See Jer. xxv, 9–12.

Lines 337, 338. The king here referred to is best explained of Cyrus, and the description should be compared with Isa. xliv, 28; xlv, 1–4. Ewald (p. 32) understands the king to be the Messiah. See further on lines 777–781.

Line 339. *Royal tribe.*—Judah, which returned from Babylonian exile, and under Zerubbabel, a descendant of the house of David (Matt. i, 12; Luke iii, 27), rebuilt the temple.

Line 342. *Kings . . . assist.*—Comp. Ezra i, 4; vi, 8; vii, 15, 16, 22.

Line 344. *The holy dream.*—Perhaps alluding to the visions and prophecies of Zechariah and Haggai (comp. Ezra v, i).

Line 346. *When my soul had ceased.*—Comp. similar exordium in lines 1–10, 190–195, and 581–584. The passage beginning here and ending with line 580 forms a section by itself, and is regarded by Alexandre as an interpolation belonging to the times of the Antonines. Others, however, find in it evidences of a pre-Christian date.

(279–297.)

Rose in my heart, and he commanded me
350 To prophesy o'er all the earth, and place
In royal minds the things which are to be.
And to my mind God gave me first to tell
What bitter woes for Babylon he planned,
Because they God's great temple had destroyed.
355   Alas! alas! for thee, O Babylon,
And also for the Assyrians, when the clash
Of arms shall pass through all the sinful earth,
And shout of war shall ruin every land,
Even as the stroke of God, leader of hymns.
360 For it will come as from the air above,
O Babylon, and from the holy ones
Of the high heaven it will descend on thee,
And wrath eternal shall destroy thy children.
And then wilt thou be as thou wast at first,
365 Even as things which are not, and with blood
Shalt thou be filled, as thou before didst shed
The blood of many good and righteous men,
Whose blood yet cries out to the lofty heaven.
   To thee, O Egypt, a great plague shall come,
370 Dreadful to homes, and such as thou didst hope
Might never fall on thee; for through thy midst
A sword shall pass, and separation, death,
And famine shall prevail until of kings
The seventh generation, and then cease.
375   Woe, woe to thee, O land of Gog and Magog,

Line 353. *Babylon.*—Comp. how Jeremiah (**xxv**, 12) passes from the Jews' calamities to the penal visitation of Babylon.

Line 369. *Plague.*—The constant wars of the times of the Ptolemies.

Line 374. *Seventh.* See line 224, and note.

Line 375. *Gog and Magog.*—Names derived from Ezek. **xxxviii**, 2. Comp. Rev. **xx**, 8. Here apparently applied as symbolical names to the Ethiopians of the Upper Nile.

In the midst of the rivers of Ethiopia!
What pouring out of blood shalt thou receive,
And be called house of judgment among men!
And thy land of much dew shall drink black blood.
380   Woe, woe, to thee, O Libya, and woe, woe,
O sea and land!   Ye daughters of the West
How shall ye come upon a bitter day!
And ye shall come pursued by cruel strife
Dreadful and harsh; dire judgment will set in,
385 And by force ye will all to ruin come,
Because ye marred the Immortal's mighty house,
And with iron teeth ye chewed it terribly.
So shalt thou see thy land full of the dead,
By war, and every spirit of violence,
390 Famine, and pestilence, and barbarous foes,
Thy land all desert and the city waste.
     And there shall shine at evening-time a star
Which they will call a comet, baleful sign
To mortals of dire famine, sword, and death,
395 And ruin of great leaders and chief men.
     And among men great signs again shall be,
For the deep-flowing Tanais will forsake
Mæotis' marshy lake, and the deep stream

Line 380. *Libya.*—The northern coast of Africa immediately west of Egypt.

Line 381. *Sea and land.*—Comp. Rev. xii, 12.   *Daughters of the West.*—Roman cities, lying west of Egypt, and on or near the Mediterranean Sea, naturally so called by an Alexandrian writer.

Line 386. *Mighty house.*—This seems most naturally to refer to the overthrow of the temple in Jerusalem by the Romans.

Line 387. *Iron teeth.*—Comp. Dan. vii, 7, 19.

Line 393. *Baleful sign.*—Among most nations the appearance of a comet has been regarded by the superstitious as an omen of evil.

Line 397. *Tanais.*—Ancient classic name of the Don, which empties into the modern sea of Azof, the ancient Lake Mæotis.

(320–338.)

Shall flow along a fruitful furrow's mark,
400 And the vast flood a neck of land shall check.
And there will be wide chasms and yawning pits,
And many cities with their men shall fall.
In Asia—Iassus, Cebren, Pandonia,
Colophon, Ephesus, Nice, Antioch,
405 Tanagra, Sinope, Smyrna, Myrina.
In Europe—Cyagra, Clitos, Basilis,
Meropeia, Antigone, Magnesia,
Mykene, Pantheia, and most happy Gaza,
Hierapolis and Astypalia.
410　Know, then, Egypt's dread race is near its end,
And then unto the Alexandrians
Better the year gone by. Though Rome received

Line 402. *Cities . . . fall.*—Obviously a prophecy of a remarkable earthquake, which either overthrew or affected the cities named in the following lines. Earthquakes are not uncommon in these lands even at this day. There appears to be corruption of text and confusion in the order in which the twenty-two cities are named. The common text, followed in our translation, puts eleven in Asia, and eleven in Europe. But Gaza and Hierapolis were in Asia. Several of those here located in Europe are now unknown.

Lines 412–427. This prophecy of the subjugation of Rome by Asia is referred to by Lactantius, *Div. Inst.*, vii, 15 [L., 6, 787–790], who declares that "the Sibyls openly say that Rome shall perish, and that too by the judgment of God, because she held his name in contempt, was an enemy of righteousness, and slew a people that was a keeper of truth." Previously, in the same chapter, he says: "The Roman name by which the world is now ruled shall be taken from the earth, and the power will revert to Asia, and the East will again rule, and the West will be in subjection." The "virgin " addressed in line 419, being a " child of Latin Rome," cannot without unnatural violence be understood of "the virgin daughter of the true God, the community of Israel, which, while inflicting divine punishment also contributes to the true welfare " (Ewald, p. 19), but is rather a poetical name for Rome herself. Comp. the phrase "daughter of Zion," book viii, 404. The "haughty mistress," in line 424, is understood by Alexandre of the goddess Fortune, whom Horace (*Od.*, i, 35) addresses as able "in a moment either to lift a mortal body from the lowest place, or to turn the noblest triumphs into funeral scenes."

(339–361.)

Tribute of Asia, thrice as many goods
Shall Asia back again receive from Rome,
415 And savage insolence return to her.
Many from Asia served Italian homes,
But the Italians, twenty times as many,
Shall serve in Asia in great poverty.
O virgin, soft, rich child of Latin Rome,
420 How oft at thy much-courted wedding-feasts,
Drunken with wine, a servant, in the world
Thou shalt not become wedded, but how oft
Will haughty mistress cut thy pretty hair,
And taking vengeance cast upon the earth
425 The things of heaven, and from the earth again
Raise heavenward, for mortals are held fast
In miserable and unrighteous life.

And Samos shall be sand, and Delos dull,
And Rome a room, but all decrees fulfilled;
430 And Smyrna falls by no avenging word,
But by base plots and cowardice of leaders.

But calm peace into Asia's land shall go,
And Europe shall be happy—healthful air,
Full of years, strong, no winter and no hail;
435 Bearing all things, and birds and beasts of earth.
O happiest man who at that time shall be!
Or woman, free from care, in rural bliss!
For all good order from the starry heaven
Shall come on men, and justice, and with her

Lines 428, 429. These lines contain a notable play on the names Samos, Delos, and Rome. Comp. also book iv, 112, and viii, 207. Comp. also Tertullian, *De Pallio*, ii [L., 2, 1034]; Lactantius, vii, 25 [6, 812]; Palladius, *Lausiaca*, cxviii [G., 34, 1227].

Line 430. *Smyrna falls.*—See Herodotus's account (i, 150) of the artful capture of Smyrna by Colophonian exiles.

Lines 432-446. This passage reads like a fragment of Messianic prophecy, and a Jewish reader could scarcely understand it otherwise.

(362-374.)

440 The sober concord which with mortal men
    Surpasses all things, and affection, faith,
    And friendship for the stranger. Far from them
    Are lawlessness, blame, envy, folly, wrath.
    And want shall flee from men, and violence,
445 And murder, baneful strifes and bitter feuds,
    And theft, and every evil, in those days.
      But Macedonia shall to Asia bear
    A heavy woe, and greatest suffering
    Shall spring up over Europe from a birth
450 Of spurious Kronids and a race of slaves;
    And she shall subjugate fenced Babylon,
    And in all lands the sun looks down upon
    Call herself mistress, and then come to nought
    In bitter ruin, having not a law
455 For those late born, and wandering far away.
      And then shall come to Asia's happy land,
    Unknown, a man with purple garment clad,
    Ferocious, strange, unrighteous, fiery;
    For him a thunderbolt raised into light.
460 And Asia all shall bear an evil yoke,
    And many a murder will the damp soil drink.
    And he will court all the invisibles
    Of Hades, whose race he wills to destroy,
    And from whom his own race shall be destroyed.

Lines 447–455. This passage is most naturally explained as referring to the Macedonian rule of Alexander and his successors, who endeavored to appear as haughty world-ruling sons of Kronos (Saturn), but were, as a matter of fact, of heathen origin, ignoble, and really a bastard race. Perseus, the last of them, was truly a bastard. So Ewald, p. 12.

Lines 456–464. This passage seems best to describe Antiochus Epiphanes, but Alexandre understands it of Hadrian. The "thunderbolt," in line 460 (Greek κεραυνός,) is thought by Ewald (p. 13) to be a manifest allusion to Seleucus Ceraunus, one of the predecessors of Antiochus Epiphanes.

465 But there will be one root, perversely cut
From ten horns, and set by another plant;
The warlike father of the purple race
He will cut off, and be himself then taken
By sons of like mind in the chance of war;
470 And then the horn grown by his side shall rule.
    And straightway unto fruitful Phrygia
Shall be a sign, when Rhea's blood-stained race,
Growing and blooming in the god-like earth
Continually from roots that know no thirst,
475 Shall in one night be root and branch destroyed,
In a city of Neptune, shaker of the earth,
Antandrus, which thenceforward bears the name
Dorylæum, old Phrygia's much-wept town,
And therefore at that time *Earth-shaker* called.
480 It will scatter the secret places of the earth
And loosen walls.   And then no signs of good
But a beginning of evil will appear.
There will come on the well-known woes of war,
Among all tribes, and furnish Æneads

Lines 465–471. Here too the exact reference is uncertain, but the imagery
of being cut from ten horns is manifestly from Daniel (vii, 7, 8, 20, 24), and
favors the opinion that the writer had in mind one of the Syrian kings.
We must not suppose, however, that these Sibylline authors were always
accurate in their knowledge, or exact in their descriptions.

Line 471. *Phrygia.*—Comp. book i., 229, note.

Line 472. *Rhea.*—The wife of Saturn (Kronos) and mother of Jupiter,
Juno, Vesta, Ceres, Pluto, and Neptune.   Comp. line 155, *ff.*

Line 477. *Antandrus.*—A city of Troas on the bay of Adramyttium.
This seems to be identified in the next line with Dorylæum in Phrygia,
some two hundred miles east of Antandrus, which fact implies that the
writer had no exact knowledge of localities in the Phrygian land.   Such
inaccuracy, however, is perfectly compatible with a knowledge that this
whole region was injured by a fearful earthquake.   Such calamities seem to
have visited these regions many times.

Line 479. *Earth-shaker.*—A title of Neptune.   Comp. book i, 220.

Line 484. *Æneads.*—Generations of warlike heroes like Æneas, of whom
the Romans sprang.

(397–412.)

485 Sprung from the native soil and kindred blood;
But he again is prey to men beloved.
O Ilion, I pity thee! For Erinnys
In Sparta shall spring forth most beautiful;
A noble shoot and famous, she bequeaths
490 Asia and Europe a far-spreading wave.
But to thee chiefly wailings, toils, and groans
She will bear and award; but thou shalt have
Undying fame among those yet to be.
And then a certain old man will appear,
495 False writer and of doubtful native land,
And in his eyes the light will sink away.
But he will have large mind, and song immense
Of understanding, blended with two names.
Chios he will be called, and he will write
500 Of Ilion, not truthfully indeed,

Line 487. *Ilion.*—Lactantius, *Div. Inst.,* i, 6 [L., 6, 142], cites Apollodorus as affirming that the Erythræan Sibyl was his own country-woman, and that she foretold the destruction of Ilium. *Erinnys.*—The Greek name for the Furies, or deities of Vengeance, here applied to Helen, wife of Menelaus of Sparta, who was the occasion of the Trojan War, and called in Virgil (*Æn.*, ii, 573) "the common Erinnys of Troy and native land." Comp. also Pausanias, *Phoc.*, 12, and the parallel of this whole passage in book ix, 157, *ff.*

Line 494. *Old man.*—Homer, whose blindness is a well-known universal tradition, as well as the uncertainty of his birthplace.

Line 498. *Two names.*—If this refers to the song it may be understood of the *Iliad* and the *Odyssey.* Or does it refer to the two names so often applied to Homer: Melesigenes and Mæonides?

Line 499. *Chios.* A rocky island of the Ægean Sea, which some claimed as Homer's birthplace. So Thucydides understood the reference in the Homeric hymn, which he cites in his history, iii, 104:

"The blind old man who dwells in craggy Chios."

Line 500. *Not truthfully.*—This charge against Homer is referred to in Lactantius, i, 6 [L., 6, 142], and the Sibyl's claim that her verses would be appropriated by the great poet of the *Iliad* is recognized by Diodorus and other ancient writers. The charge is worthy of no serious consideration, and Gregory Nazianzen retorts on the Sibyl that she too has purloined material from various sources.

(412–423.)

But plainly, for my verses he will seize;
For he will be first to unfold my books.
And he war's helmed heroes will adorn,
Hector of Priam, and Achilles, son
505 Of Peleus, and the rest of warlike fame.
And with them he will make the gods to stand,
And by all arts deceive defenseless men.
And to those dying about Ilion
Shall be a glory widely spread abroad;
510 And he will celebrate their vengeful deeds.
    Also to Lycia will a Locrian race
Bring many evils. And thee, Chalcedon,
When thou the passage of the narrow sea
Hast taken, an Ætolian youth will slay.
515 And, Cyzicus, from thee the sea shall tear
Vast wealth away. And thou, Byzantium,
Shalt be in love with Asia, and receive
Sad wailings and immeasurable blood.
And Lycia's lofty mountain, riven at top
520 With rocky chasms, shall pour a murmuring stream,
Till Patara's prophetic signs shall cease.
O Cyzicus, that dwellest by Propontis,
City of wine, around thee Rhyndacus

Line 511. *Lycia.*—A province on the southern coast of Asia Minor. *Locrian.*—Three tribes of this name were known to antiquity; one on the eastern coast of Brittium, at the southern end of Italy, and two in Greece.

Line 512. *Chalcedon.*—Opposite Byzantium.

Line 515. *Cyzicus.*—City and island in the Propontis near the northern coast of Mysia.

Line 516. *Byzantium.*—Ancient name of Constantinople.

Line 521. *Patara* was a city of Lycia, and the seat of a celebrated oracle of Apollo.

Line 523. The river Rhyndacus flowed into the Propontis some distance to the east of Cyzicus, but the poet conceives the river as joined with the roaring sea, and dashing about the city.

(424–443.)

、Shall crash his crested wave.   And thou, O Rhodes,
525 Daughter of day, shalt long be unenslaved,
    And much prosperity shall yet be thine,
    And on the sea thy power shall be supreme.
    But later thou shalt be to greedy men
    A spoil, because of beauty and of wealth,
530 And on thy neck a dreadful yoke shall come.
    A Lydian earthquake shall again destroy
    The things of Persia, and most horribly
    Shall Europe's tribes and Asia's suffer woes.
    And Sidon's cruel king and shout of war
535 From others will show forth destruction dire
    Beyond the sea to Samos.   With the blood
    Of fallen lights earth murmurs to the sea,
    And wives together with the stately maids
    Their ignominious insults will bewail,
540 Some for the dead, some for the fallen sons.
    O sign of Cyprus, phalanxes shalt thou
    By earthquake overthrow, and many souls
    Shall gloomy Hades all at once receive.
    And Trallis, hard by Ephesus, shall fall
545 By earthquake, and walls built by cruel men;
    Boiling hot water shall rain on the earth,
    Which earth weighed down shall drink—a sulphurous
        smell.
    And Samos, in time, will royal houses build.

Line 524. *Rhodes.*—The famous island off the southern coast of Caria,
where now, as of old, it is said there is scarcely a day of the whole year in
which the sun is not visible.   Not mingling in the quarrels of Alexander's
successors, Rhodes enjoyed a considerable period of peace and prosperity,
and carried on extensive commerce with Egypt.   Its subsequent enslave-
ment and downfall were mainly due to the fact that it was such a tempting
spoil for greedy conquerors.

Lines 531–548. This passage is best understood of the wars and woes
which befell all the regions here named under the wars of Antigonus, who
(444–463.)

O Italy, to thee no foreign war
550 Shall come, but lamentable tribal blood,
Not easily subdued, and much renowned,
Wilt thou in reckless insolence destroy.
But thou thyself, beside hot ashes stretched,
As thou in thine own spirit didst foresee,
555 Shall slay thyself.   Not of the good shalt thou
The mother be, but of wild beasts the nurse.
   Another man shall come from Italy,
A spoiler; then, Laodicea, thou,
Beautiful city of the Carians,
560 By Lycus' wondrous water, creeping prone,
Shalt weep in silence for thy boastful sire.
Byzantine Thracians shall rise up on Hæmus.
To the Campanians quaking fear shall come
Because of wasting famine; Corsica
565 Weeps her old father, and Sardinia

---

became master of all Asia Minor and Syria, and whose son, Demetrius
Poliorcetes, conducted the famous siege of Rhodes.

Line 449. *No foreign war.*—But, as is immediately stated, terrible civil
wars.

Line 557. *Another man.*—L. Scipio, according to some; Nero, according
to others; but the reference is uncertain.   "The entire picture," says
Ewald (p. 38), "is so vast and so general that we cannot think of it as referring to an event that had already taken place."

Line 558. *Laodicea.*—Situated on the Lycus as here described, and on the
borders of Lydia, Caria, and Phrygia.   It suffered much by wars and
earthquakes.

Line 561. *Boastful Sire.*—Antiochus Theos, who named it in honor of his
wife Laodice.

Line 562. *Hæmus.*—A mountain range bounding Thracia on the north.

Line 563. *Campanians.*—Campania was the district of Italy south of
Latium, on the sea-coast.   Vesuvius was near its central part.

Line 564. *Corsica.*—Well-known island west of Italy, called in Greek
Cyrnus, from a hero of that name.   See Herod., i, 167.

Line 565. *Sardinia.*—A still larger island of the Mediterranean, west of
Italy and south of Corsica.

Shall by great storms of winter, and the strokes
Of a holy God, sink in the ocean depths—
Down in the waves with children of the sea.
Alas! alas! how many virgin maids
570 Will Hades marry, and the deep take charge
Of the unburied youths! Alas! alas!
Infants and vast wealth floating on the sea!
    O happy land of Mysians, suddenly
Shall cease thy royal race. Not long, indeed,
575 Will Carthage stand. But bitter grief shall be
To the Galatians. And to Tenedos
The last but greatest misery shall come.
And Sicyon with strong yells, and Corinth, thee
Boasting o'er all, an equal flute shall sound.
580   Now when my soul had ceased from hallowed song,
Again a message of Almighty God
Rose in my heart, and he commanded me
To utter prophecies upon the earth.
    Woe, woe, Phenician race of men and women,

Line 574. *Shall cease.*—Here we follow the conjectural emendation of Alexandre. Mysia and the kingdom of Pergamum were by the will of Attalus III. transferred to the Romans, B. C. 132. The mention of Carthage and Corinth in this passage, both of which cities were destroyed by the Romans B. C. 146, is thought by Ewald (pp. 16, 17) an evidence of the early date of this part of our poem. The whole passage (575–580), however, may have been based by the Sibylline writer on some compend of history without much regard for the order of time. Hence the mention of the other places in these lines. *Tenedos* was the name of the famous island just off the coast of Troy, though Alexandre imagines it is here meant for Rhodes. *Sicyon* was an ancient city some twenty miles north-west of Corinth, the ruins of which are evidence of its having suffered many times by earthquakes.

Lines 580–583 Here a new section begins, and has an exordium similar to those of lines 1–10, 190–195, and 347–355.

Line 584. *Phenician race.*—Famed for their extensive commerce. Ewald (p. 38) sees in this oracle an evidence of the bitter feeling of the author towards Phenicia chiefly on account of commercial rivalry.

(477–492.)

585 Also to all the cities by the sea;
    No one of you shall come to the sun's light
    In common light, no longer shall there be
    Number and tribe, because of unjust speech
    And lawless life and base which all indulged,
590 Opening a foul mouth, uttering fearful words,
    False and unrighteous; and they set themselves
    In opposition to the mighty God,
    And opened falsely a polluted mouth.
    Therefore shall they by dreadful strokes be slain
595 In all the earth, and bitter destiny
    Will God send on them, burning from the ground
    Their cities and foundations manifold.
        Woe, woe to thee, O Crete, burdened with pain,
    On thee shall come a stroke, and terribly
600 Shalt thou be made a ruin evermore.
    And every land shall see thee black with smoke,
    And fire shall never leave thee, but shall burn.
        Woe, woe to thee, O Thrace, for thou shalt bend
    Beneath a servile yoke; when the Galatians,
605 Mixed with the Dardans, hurriedly destroy
    Hellas, then will sore evil come on thee;
    In a strange land thou'lt give and yet receive.
        Woe, woe to thee, O Gog, and so with all,
    One by one, Magog, Marson, and Aggon;
610 How many an evil lot shall fall to thee!

Line 598. *Crete* was subjugated by the Romans under Metellus, B. C. 67, and never after rose to independence of foreign power.

Lines 604, 605. These *Galatians* are to be understood of those of the name in central Asia Minor, and the *Dardans* are probably the same as the Phrygians, who joined Galatia on the west.

Line 609. On *Gog* and *Magog*, see line 376. *Marson and Aggon* are unknown, unless they be a corruption of Mœsia and Dacia, provinces on both sides of the Danube. There was a tribe of Marsi in central Italy. Ewald (p. 38) reads for Aggon Dagon, and understands the Dahæ on the east of the Caspian Sea.   (493–513.)

Many shall also fall on Lycia's sons,
And those of Mysia and Phrygia.
And many nations of Pamphylia
And Lydia shall fall, and Maurians,
615 And Ethiopians and barbarous tribes,
And Cappadocians and Arabians.
How now may I, according to his lot,
Speak of each one? For unto all the nations,
As many as are dwelling on the earth,
620 Will the Most High send forth an evil plague.
When now a very barbarous nation comes
Against the Greeks, it will slay many chiefs
Of chosen men; and many fatted sheep
And horses shall be torn, and mules and herds
625 Of bellowing oxen, and in lawlessness
Shall they with fire the well-made houses burn.
And many shall as slaves be led by force
Into a foreign land, and children too,
And women from bed-chambers, girdled low,
630 Delicate, falling down with tender feet,
Will be seen chained and suffering all abuse
By hostile, barbarous men; nor shall they have
Helper in life, nor any help in war.
But they shall see their goods and all their wealth
635 Enriching foes; and trembling takes their knees.
A hundred fly, but one shall slay them all,
And five shall rouse an ambush heavy-armed.
But they among themselves mixed shamefully
In fearful war and tumult will bring joy
640 Unto the foes, but sorrow to the Greeks.

Line 614. *Maurians.*—In this name we most naturally recognize the people of Mauritania, on the west of Carthage, in northern Africa; but it seems strange to mention these and also *Ethiopians* and *Arabians* in connection, as here, with well-known provinces of Asia Minor.
Lines 636–637. Comp. Deut. xxxii, 30; Isa. xxx, 17.

(514–536.)

5

Then shall a servile yoke be on all Greece,
And all at once shall war and pestilence
With mortals yet remain. And God will make
The mighty heaven on high like brass, and drought
645 On all the earth, which itself will be iron.
And then will men all bitterly lament
The land uncultivated and unplowed.
And he who made the heaven and earth will place
High heaped on earth a fire, and of all men
650 The third part only shall remain alive.
O Greece, why hast thou trusted mortal men
As leaders, who cannot escape from death?
And wherefore bringest thou thy foolish gifts
Unto the dead, and sacrifice to idols?
655 Who put the wretched error in thy heart
To do these things and leave the mighty God?
Honor the All-Father's name and let it not
Escape thee. There have been a thousand years,
Yea, and five hundred more, since haughty kings
660 Ruled o'er the Greeks, who first to mortal men
Brought evils, making many images
Of gods that perish for such as are dead,
Whence ye were taught to think on vanities.
But when the anger of the mighty God
665 Shall come upon you, then will ye find out
The face of God the mighty; and all souls

Lines 641–647. This passage is best explained as the subjugation of
Greece by the Romans, B. C. 146.

Line 650. *Third.* Comp. Ezek. v, 2; Zech. xiii, 8; Rev. viii, 7–9.
Also Lactantius, *Div. Inst.*, vii, 16 [L., 6, 792].

Lines 651–657. Quoted (omitting one line) by Lactantius, *Div. Inst.*, i,
15 [L., 6., 196].

Lines 658–663.—Here the prophetess seems to forget her time and
place as the spouse of Noah, to which she pretends in the closing lines
of this book.

Of men, in great distress, will lift their hands
Up to the broad heaven and begin to call
On the great King, the Helper, and to seek
670 A rescuer from the mighty wrath to come.
    But come, learn this and lodge it in your hearts,
What troubles in the rolling years shall come.
When Hellas brings her sacrifice of oxen
And bellowing bulls, a whole burnt-offering
675 Unto the temple of the mighty God,
She shall escape the hateful sound of war,
And fear and famine, and go forth again
Away from underneath a slavish yoke.
But such a race of godless men shall be
680 Until that fatal day receives its end.
For ye shall not bring sacrifice to God
Till all things come to pass, whatever things
The one God wills to be not without end—
All shall be brought to pass; strong fate impels.
685   Of godly men there yet shall be again
A holy race, devoted to the mind
And counsels of the Highest; they shall honor
The great God's temple with drink-offerings,
Burnt-offerings, and holy hecatombs,
690 With sacrifice of well-fed bulls, choice rams,
Firstlings of sheep, and the fat parts of lambs,
Sacredly offering whole burnt sacrifice
On the great altar. But in righteousness,
Having obtained the law of the Most High,
695 Blest shall they dwell in cities and rich fields.
And prophets shall by the immortal One
Exalted be, and bring great joy to men.
For to them only has the great God given
His kindly counsel, and put in their hearts
700 Faith and most noble thought. Through vain deceit
                (558–585.)

They do not hold in awe the works of men,
Of gold, and brass, and silver, and ivory,
And wood, and stone, clay forms of feeble gods,
Besmeared with chalk, with figures painted o'er—
705 Whatever mortals with vain mind desire.
But they lift up their holy arms to heaven;
At daybreak from the couch they always cleanse
Their hands with water, and pay honors due
To God the immortal, who is ever great,
710 And then to parents. But above all men
They keep the bed of marriage undefiled,
And mix not boys with males in acts impure,
Like the Phenicians, Latins, and Egyptians,
And spacious Greece, and nations many more,
715 Persians, Galatians, and of Asia all,
Transgressing the immortal God's pure law.
Wherefore the Immortal will inflict on men
Delusion, famine, sufferings and groans,
And war, and pestilence, and mournful woes;
720 Because the immortal Father of all men
They did not wish to honor righteously,
But honored idols made with human hands,
Which things even men themselves will cast away
In clefts of rocks, concealing them from shame,
725   When a young king of Egypt seventh shall rule
His own land, reckoned from the Grecian power
Which Macedonia's mighty men shall rule,
Then shall there come from Asia a great king

Lines 701–710. Cited by Clem. Alex., *Cohort.*, vi [G., 8, 176].
Line 725. *Young king.*—Or *new* king; Ptolemy Philometer, the *seventh*
from Alexander, including the latter, as the poet evidently intends, by
"reckoning from the kingdom of the Greeks."
Line 728. *Great king.*—Antiochus Epiphanes, who invaded Egypt B. C.
170, and carried off Ptolemy Philometer as prisoner.
(586–611.)

With eagle's fire, who with his foot and horse
730 Shall cover all the land, break down all things,
And fill all things with evil; he will cast
The Egyptian kingdom down, seize on all goods,
And ride upon the broad back of the sea.
And then before the mighty God, the King
735 Immortal, they will bend the fair white knee
On the all-fostering earth, and all the works
Made with hands in a flame of fire shall fall;
And then great joy will God bestow on men.
For land, and trees, and countless flocks of sheep
740 Will yield mankind the genuine fruit of wine,
And of sweet honey, and white milk, and wheât,
Which is for men the very best of all.
　　But thou, O mortal versed in various arts
And evil-minded, shalt not be like this;
745 But turn back, and be reconciled to God.
Offer to God whole hecatombs of bulls
And lambs and goats, amid the circling hours.
Propitiate him, the immortal God;
Perchance he will show mercy.　For himself
750 Alone is God, and other there is none.
Hold righteousness in honor, wrong no man
As by oppression, for the immortal One
Enjoins these things on miserable men.
But thou, be on thy guard against the wrath
755 Of the great God, when to all men shall come
The height of famine, and, being overpowered,
They meet dire judgment.　King shall seize on king
And wrest his land away, and nations waste

Line 736.　*All the works, etc.*—Cited with slight change by Lactantius, *Div. Inst.*, vii, 19. [L., 6, 811.]
　Lines 739–742.　Cited by Lactantius, *Div. Inst.*, vii, 24 [L., 6, 811.]
　Lines 745–747.　Cited by Clem. Alex. and ascribed to Orpheus, *Cohortatio*,
vii [G., 8, 184].　　　　　　　(612–635.)

And plunder nations, and lords plunder tribes,
760 And leaders all flee to another land,
And earth itself be changed, and barbarous rule
Ravage all Greece, and the rich land of wealth
Become exhausted, and straight into strife
Shall they because of gold and silver come
765 In a strange land. (The love of gain will be
An evil guide for cities.) And they all
Shall be unburied, and their flesh shall be
By vultures and wild beasts of earth destroyed.
And when these things are finished, the huge earth
770 Shall all the remnants of the dead consume;
And all unsown shall it be, and unplowed,
Proclaiming woefully the abomination
Of countless men through many circling years,
And shields and javelins and all sorts of arms;
775 Nor will the forest wood be cut for fire.
    Then from the sunrise God will send a king,
Who will make all earth cease from evil war,
Killing some, others binding with strong oaths.
Nor yet will he by his own counsels do
780 All these things, but by excellent decrees
Of God persuaded. But again the people
Of the great God with wealth will be weighed down,
With gold and silver and purple ornament,
And of good things will earth and sea be full.
785 And then will kings begin again
To envy one another, and in heart

Line 761. *Barbarous rule.*—The Roman power, as line 622.

Lines 774, 775. Comp. a similar statement in Lactantius, *Div. Inst.,*
vii, 26 [L., 6, 814]. See also Isa. ix, 5, and Ezek. xxxix, 9, 10, and lines
865–869, where we have the fuller form of what seems here to be fragmentary.

Lines 777–781. This is best explained by Cyrus. See lines 338, 339.

(636–661.)

To cherish wicked projects. Envy brings
No good to wretched mortals. But again
Shall kings of nations rush upon the land
790 In masses, bringing doom upon themselves,
For they will purpose to destroy the shrine
Of the great God, and men most excellent.
What time they reach the land, polluted kings
Will sacrifice within the city's walls,
795 Each having his own throne and subject tribe.
    And then will God speak with a mighty voice
To all rude people of an empty mind;
And judgments from the mighty God shall come
Upon them, and they all shall be destroyed
800 By an immortal hand. And fiery swords
Shall fall from heaven on earth, and mighty lights
Shall come down flaming in the midst of men.
And mother earth shall be tossed in those days
By an immortal hand, and fish of the sea,
805 And all earth's beasts, and countless flocks of birds,
And all the souls of men, and all the sea
Shall shudder at the face of the Immortal,
And there shall be dismay. High mountain peaks
And huge hills he will rend, and Erebus
810 The dark and dismal will appear to all;
And misty gorges in the lofty hill
Shall be full of the dead; the rocks shall stream
With blood, and every torrent fill the plain.

Line 789. *The land.*—Of Judea.

Line 791. *Shrine.*—The Jewish temple at Jerusalem.

Lines 794, 795. Comp. Jer. i, 15.

Lines 798–828. A sublime apocalyptic passage, descriptive of the coming of God in judgment.

Line 800. *Fiery swords.*—Comp. Rev. xix, 15, 21, and Lactantius, *Div. Inst.*, vii, 19 [L., 6, 797].

(662–686.)

And well-built walls shall all fall to the earth
815 By hostile men, for they knew not the law,
     Neither God's judgment, but with senseless soul,
     All rushing to the temple, lifted spears.
     God judges all by war, and sword, and fire,
     And overwhelming flood; and there shall be
820 Brimstone from heaven, and stones and grievous hail;
     And death shall come upon the quadrupeds.
     Then shall men come to know the immortal God
     Who judges these things. Lamentation too,
     And uproar shall come on the boundless earth,
825 Because men perish, and in speechless woe
     Shall all be bathed in blood, and earth herself
     Shall drink the blood of them that are destroyed,
     And the wild beasts will glut themselves with flesh.
     All these things the eternal God himself
830 Gave me to prophesy; nor shall they be
     Without complete fulfillment, for he put
     Them only in the heart; for without guile
     The Spirit of God continues in the world.
     Again the children of the mighty God
835 Shall all about the temple live in peace,
     Delighting in those things which he shall give
     Who is Creator, righteous Judge, and King.
     For he alone, and standing wondrous near,
     Can shelter as a wall of flaming fire
840 From all around. And there shall be no wars
     In cities or in country; not the hand
     Of cruel war, but rather there shall be

Line 834–869. A glowing picture of Jewish prosperity and happiness, modeled largely after imagery found in the Hebrew prophets and the Psalms.

Line 839. *Wall of fire.*—Comp. Zech. ii, 5.

Line 840. *No wars.*—Comp. Mic. iv, 3.

With them the immortal Champion himself,
And the hand of the Holy One. And then the isles
845 And cities all shall speak, and tell how much
The Immortal loves those men, for he with them
Shares in all conflict and delivers them.
And heaven, and sun divinely formed, and moon,
And mother earth shall tremble in those days.
850 And a sweet word shall they lead forth in hymns:
" Come, falling on the earth let us all pray
To the immortal King, great God, most high.
Let us send to the temple, since sole Lord
He is, and let us all observe the law
855 Of God most high, who above all on earth
Is the most righteous One.   For we have strayed
Far from the path of the immortal One,
And have done reverence with a senseless soul
To works of human hands, to images
860 Carved out of wood, and of departed men."
These things souls of the faithful cry aloud:
" Come, let us with God's people, falling down
Upon our faces, gladden in our homes
With hymns God the Creator, and procure
865 The weapons of our foes in every land
For seven lengths of the revolving years—
Even shields and helmets and all sorts of arms,
And a great store of bows and harmful arrows,
For forest wood shall not be cut for fire."
870   But, wretched Hellas, cease thy arrogance,

Line 849. *Earth tremble.*—In such sense as Psa. xcviii, 7-9.
Line 851. *Come,* etc.—Comp. Psa. xcv, 1, 6, and lines 863–865.
Lines 856–860. Cited by Justin Martyr, *Chort. ad Græcos*, xvi [G., 6, 273].
Lines 865–869.   Comp. lines 774, 775, and note there.
Lines 870–884. The exact point and force of this exhortation to Hellas
are not easily determined.   Hellas is commonly believed to mean here
Egypt under the Greek dominion of the Ptolemies, and if with Ewald we

(711–733.)

5*

So willful, and entreat the immortal One,
Magnanimous, and be upon thy watch.
Send to this city the people ill-advised
Who from the Mighty's holy land have come.
875 Do not move Camarina, for 'tis best
She be unmoved—a leopard from the lair,
An evil which thou shouldst by no means meet.
But keep away, and do not in thy heart
Hold arrogance, an overbearing soul,
880 Ready for mighty contest. And serve God,
The mighty One, that thou mayst share with them,
Whenever this indeed shall have an end,
And on good men shall come the fatal day,
According as the mighty One ordains.
885   For earth, all-mother, shall to mortals yield
The best fruit, boundless store of wheat,

---

read a negative in line 873: "Send *not* to this city," etc., the passage becomes an exhortation to the Greeks of Egypt not to send to Jerusalem an
army of Alexandrine Jews, who might be excited by bad counsel to mix up
with the Palestinian wars so constantly raging between the Seleucids
and the Ptolemies. Such ill-advised action would be "moving Camarina," or provoking a fierce leopard in his lair. Another view is
that the oracle dates about the beginning of the rise of the Maccabees, and is
an exhortation to the Ptolemies to send to Jerusalem Jewish forces, numerous
in Alexandria, to help their brethren in the Holy Land. But all the at-
tempts to make the passage fit particular persons and events involve so
much of fancy and conjecture that one may well hesitate to adopt any of
them.

Line 875. *Camarina.*—The allusion is to the well-known story of draining
the marsh of Camarina, a city of southern Sicily. The inhabitants, disre-
garding the oracle, drained the neighboring marsh which was believed to
breed pestilence, and by so doing they opened a way for their enemies to
come and destroy their city. Hence the proverb, "Move not Camarina,"
was equivalent to: Do not seek to remove one evil which is likely to bring
on another and greater one. Comp. Virgil, *Æn.*, iii, 701.

Lines 885–905. Another picture of a golden future, much like the passage
835–870.

(734-745.)

And wine and oil.   And from the heaven a drink,
Delightful of sweet honey there shall be,
And trees, and fruits of trees, and fatted sheep,
890 And oxen, and young lambs, and kids of goats.
And forth shall burst sweet fountains of white milk,
And of good things the cities shall be full,
And fat the fields, and there shall not be sword
Nor uproar on the earth, nor shall the earth
895 Groan heavily and tremble any more.
Nor war nor drought shall longer be on earth,
Nor famine, nor the fruit-destroying hail,
But great peace shall be upon all the earth.
King will be friend to king until the end
900 Of time, and a new law on all the earth
Will the Immortal in the starry heaven
Perfect for men, touching whatever things
Have been by miserable mortals done.
For he alone is God, no other is,
905 And he will burn with fire man's grievous power.
    But now being quick to keep my thoughts in heart,
Shun godless worship, serve the living God,
Against adultery be on thy guard,
And all uncleanness ; thine own children rear,
910 And do no murder ; for the immortal One
Is angry with such as commit these sins.
    And then will he a kingdom for all time
Raise up for all men, and a holy law
Give to the pious to whom he has pledged
915 To open up the land, and the wide world,
And portals of the blessed, and all joys,
And mind immortal, and eternal bliss.
And out of every land unto the house

Lines 909–911. Cited by Lactantius, *de Ira Dei,* xxii [L., 7, 143].
(745–771.)

Of the great God will they bring frankincense,
920 And gifts, and there shall be no other house
To be inquired of by men yet to be ;
But whom God gave to honor faithful men,
Him mortals shall call Son of the great God.
And all paths of the field and the rough hills,
925 And lofty mountains, and the sea's wild waves,
Shall in those days be easy to pass over,
For all peace of the good shall come on earth.
And the sword shall God's prophets take away,
For they shall be the judges of mankind,
930 And righteous kings ; for of the mighty God
This is the judgment and the sovereignty.

Be of good cheer, O maiden, and exult ;
For the Eternal, who made heaven and earth,
Has given thee joy, and he will dwell in thee,
935 And for thee shall be an immortal light.
And wolves and lambs promiscuously shall eat
Grass in the mountains, and among the kids
Shall leopards graze, and wandering bears shall lodge
Among the calves, and the carnivorous lion
940 Shall eat straw in the manger like the ox,
And little children lead them with a band.
For tame will be on earth the beasts he made,
And with young babes will dragons fall asleep,
And no harm, for God's hand will be on them.
945 Now tell I thee a sign exceeding clear,
That thou mayst know when of all things on earth
The end shall be. When in the starry heaven

Line 919. Comp. Psa. lxviii, 29; lxxii, 10.
Lines 922, 923. Cited by Lactantius, *Div. Inst.*, iv, 6 [L., 6, 462].
Lines 932–935. Comp. Zech. ii, 10.
Lines 936–944. Comp. Isa. xi, 6–9. Cited also, with some verbal variations, by Lactantius, *Div. Inst.*, vii, 24 [L., 6, 811].
Lines 947–957. Comp. with this section Josephus, *Wars*, vi, v, 3.
(772–797.)

Swords shall be seen by night toward west or east,
Straightway shall there be a dark cloud of dust,
950 Borne downward from the heaven o'er all the earth,
And the sun's brightness in the midst of heaven
Shall be eclipsed, and the moon's beams appear
And come again on earth, and there shall be
The sign of blood-drops issuing from the stones,
955 And ye shall see a war of foot and horse
In a cloud, like a hunting of wild beasts,
Like a dark mist. This is the end of war
Which God who dwells in heaven shall bring to pass.
But all must sacrifice to the great King.
960   These things to thee say I, who madly left
Assyria's long Babylonian walls,
And prophesied to all men of the fire,
God's fury which on Hellas should be sent,
That I might unto mortals prophesy
965 Of mysteries divine. They say in Greece
That I am of a foreign fatherland,
Born of Erythres, shameless. Others say
I am a Sibyl and of Circe born
And father Gnostos, raving mad, and false.
970 But at the time when all things come to pass
Ye will make mention of me; no one more
Will call me mad, but God's great prophetess.
For God will show me whatsoever things
Belonged at first to my progenitors,
975 Those things God laid down in his plans for me.

Line 961. *Babylonian walls.*—Lactantius understood the Sybil to predict that she would be called Erythræan, "although she was born in Babylon." *Div. Inst.*, i, 6 [L., 6, 145].

Line 969. *Gnostos.*—Some have thought that *Glaucus* is intended, the sea-god and father of Deiphobe. See Virgil, *Æn.*, vi, 36.

Lines 970–973. Cited by Lactantius, *Div. Inst.*, iv, 15 [L., 6, 495].

(798–818.)

All future things God stored up in my mind,
That I might prophesy of things to come,
And things that were, and tell them unto men.
For when the world was deluged with a flood
980 Of waters, and one man alone was left,
A man of honor, sailing on the waves
In wooden house, along with beasts and birds,
His bride was I, and from his blood I came.
To him the first things were, and the last things
985 Were all made known ; and so from mine own mouth
All these things have I truthfully declared.

(819–828.)

BOOK IV.

CONTENTS OF BOOK IV.

Introduction, 1–26. Blessedness of the righteous, 27–53. The Assyrian kingdom, 54–71. The Medes and Persians, 72–80. Woes on Phrygia, Asia, and Egypt, 81–90. Asia against Greece, 91–96. Sicily burned by fire of Etna, 97–100. Strife in Greece, 101–104. Triumphs of Macedon, 105–124. Triumphs of Italy, 126–164. Italy's punishment, 165–176. Woes of Antioch, Cyprus, and Caria, 176–192. Wrath in reserve for the impious, 193–204. Exhortations and threatening, 205–224. Resurrection, judgment, and reward, 225–239.

BOOK IV.

HEAR, people of proud Asia, Europe too,
How many things by great loud-sounding mouth,
All true and of my own, I prophesy.
No oracle of false Apollo this,
5 Whom vain men called a god, though he deceived;
But of the mighty God, whom human hands
Shaped not, like speechless idols cut in stone.
For his house is no dedicated stone
Set for a temple, wholly deaf and dumb,
10 A great and sore dishonor to mankind;
For he, not formed by mortal hands, from earth
May not be seen, nor measured by men's eyes.
He looks on all, himself by no one seen.
His are the murky night, and day, and sun,
15 And stars, and moon, and seas that swarm with fish,
And land, and rivers, and perennial fountains,
Creatures designed for life, and rains that serve
To bring forth fruit, and tree, and wine, and oil.
The same has moved me in my inmost soul
20 As with a whip, how many and great things
Now and hereafter shall befall mankind,

This book appears to be of Jewish origin, and, for the reason stated in the Introduction, was probably written about A. D. 80.

Line 4. *Apollo.*—In the Greek *Phœbus.* Sometimes the two names are written together, Phœbus Apollo. He was the god of archery, prophecy, and music, and had temples at Delos, Delphi, Patara, Claros, Miletus, Grynium, and other places, in all of which he gave forth oracles of the future. His oracles were, according to Herodotus (i, 66, 75), often ambiguous and misleading.

Line 4–7. Cited by Clem. Alex., *Cohort. ad Grœcos,* iv [G., 8., 141].
(1–18.)

From the first generation to the eleventh,
Truly to tell. For all things he hath spoken
Who himself bringeth all things to an end.
25 But thou, O people, hear the Sibyl's words,
Who pours from hallowed mouth a truthful strain.
   Blessed of men shall they be on the earth
As many as shall love the mighty God,
Giving him praise before they eat and drink,
30 Trusting in piety. Such, when they see
Temples and altars, copies of dumb stones
Without worth, and polluted with the blood
Of living things and sacrifice of beasts,
Reject them all; but they shall look upon
35 One God's great glory, having not committed
Atrocious murder, nor acquired vast gain
By stealing, which things are most horrible;
Nor shameful longing for another's bed
Had they, nor vile and hateful lust of males.
40 Such mode of life and customs other men
Shall never imitate, as if they longed
For shamelessness; but children without sense
With jest and laughter ridiculing them—
Presumptuous deeds and vile—shall lie to them
45 In as many things as they themselves shall do;
For hard to trust is the whole race of men.

Line 22. Eleventh.—Or *tenth?* Comp. lines 55 and 106. The reckoning begins with the first generation after the flood. Comp. lines 60 and 61. By *generation* the author evidently means a long period, an age, but its duration is left indefinite.

Lines 27–35. Cited by Justin Martyr, *Cohort. ad Græcos*, xvi [G., 6., 273]; also by Clem. Alex., *Cohort. ad Græcos*, iv [G., 8., 161].

Lines 38, 39. Cited by Clem. Alex., *Pæd.*, ii, 10 [G., 8., 516].

Line 44. Comp. Lactantius, *Div. Inst.*, vii, 26 [L., 6., 816].

Lines 46–53. Cited with verbal variations by Lactantius, *Div. Inst.*, vii, 23 [L., 6., 807].

(19–41.)

But when the final judgment of the world
And mortals comes, which God himself shall bring,
Judging at once the impious and the just,
50 The ungodly under darkness he will send,
And they shall know what wickedness they wrought;
But in a fruitful land the just shall dwell,
God giving them breath, life, and sustenance.
   But all these things shall surely come to pass
55 In the tenth generation; and what things
From the first generation shall occur
I now declare. First shall the Assyrians rule
Over all men, and wield authority
During six generations of the world,
60 From the time when, the God of heaven being wroth,
Sea covered earth and cities and all men,
A whelming flood of waters breaking in.
The Medes shall overcome them, and exult
Two generations only on the throne,
65 At which time these events shall come to pass:
Dark night shall be at the mid-hour of day,
And from the heaven the stars and circling moon
Shall disappear, and earthquakes shake the land,
And many cities and the works of men

Line 53. Comp. Acts xvii, 25.
Line 57. *First . . . Assyrians.*—Comp. Gen. x, 11.
Lines 60–62. Cited by Lactantius, *de Ira Dei,* xxiii [L., 7., 144].
Line 63. *Medes shall overcome.*—Comp. Herod., i, 95 : " When the Assyrians had ruled over upper Asia five hundred and twenty years, first the Medes began to revolt from them, . . . and, having thrown off their slavery, became free."
Line 66. *Night . . . day.*—Probably to be understood of a notable eclipse of the sun. Herodotus (i, 74) relates that during the wars of the Medes and Lydians it happened that in the heat of battle the day was suddenly turned into night. This event, he observes, Thales had foretold, designating beforehand the very year in which it actually occurred.
(41–59.)

70 Hurl to the dust; and then out of the deep
   The islands of the sea shall peer aloft.
     But when the great Euphrates overflows
   With blood, then also both among the Medes
   And Persians shall arise the direful noise
75 Of battle, and the Medes, discomfited
   And falling underneath the Persian spears,
   Shall flee beyond the mighty Tigris' waves.
   The Persian power shall be of all the world
   The mightiest, and unto them shall be
80 One generation of most prosperous rule.
     But such foul deeds as men seek to avert—
   Battle-cries, murders, quarrels, banishments,
   Ruin of towers, and rising up of cities—
   Shall take place when proud, boasting Hellas sails
85 O'er the broad Hellespont, and carries doom
   To Phrygia and to Asia. But to Egypt,
   The land of many furrows and much wheat,
   Shall come a blasting famine twenty years,
   What time the Nile, corn-nourisher, shall hide
90 Somewhere beneath the earth his sable wave.

Line 71. *Islands . . . peer.*—The Greeks had a tradition that Delos and Rhodes were the first islands to emerge from the sea. Pliny (*Hist. Nat.*, ii, 89) mentions several islands that had appeared within historical times.

Lines 72–77. This statement of the fall of the Medes is not in strict accord with the best accredited history.

Line 83. *Rising up of cities.*—That is, in uproar and rebellion.

Lines 84–86. Reference to the Trojan War according to most critics, but according to Badt (*Das vierte Buch d. Sibyl. Orakel*, p. 10) to the beginning of the Persian War by the revolt of south-western Asia Minor, and the attack on Sardis by the Greeks.

Line 88. *Famine twenty years.*—Perhaps some allusion to the famine of seven years, as mentioned in Gen. xli, 27, was intended; but the statement has no historical verification.

Line 89. *Nile . . . hide.*—Comp. Horace, *Carm.*, iv, 14, 45; Tibullus, i, 7; Herod., ii, 19.

To Hellas there shall come a mighty king
From Asia, with innumerable ships,
Lifting his spear on high, and he shall walk
The wet paths of the deep, and sail alone
95 Where others tread on foot; him, fugitive
From battle, fearful Asia shall receive.
And Sicily the wretched shall a stream
Of powerful fire destroy, while Etna's flame
Breaks forth, and down into the molten stream
100 Shall Croton, great and powerful city, fall.
And strife shall be in Hellas; they shall rage
Against each other, and hurl to the dust
Numerous cities, and kill many men
Wrangling; but equal is the strife for both.
105   But when at length the course of time shall come
To the tenth generation of mankind,
Then shall there be a slavish yoke and fear
Upon the Persians.   And when Macedon
Shall boast the scepter, there shall come to Thebes
110 A terrible destruction; and the Carians
Shall dwell in Tyre, and Tyrians be destroyed.
And sand shall hide all Samos under shore;
Delos shall be no longer visible;

Lines 91–96. Reference to Xerxes's invasion of Greece.

Line 100. *Croton.*—No city of this name is known to have existed in Sicily, and the well-known Croton, or Croto, in southern Italy, cannot be thought of as perishing by lava streams of Etna. Another reading (βροτῶν) is, "the great city of men."

Lines 101–104.—Reference to the Peloponnesian War.

Lines 105–118.—Reference to the Macedonian power, which, under Alexander the Great, subdued the Persian Empire, and spread Greek colonies over its broad territory. The allusions are to be understood poetically, and were probably not designed to be altogether strict statements of fact.

Line 109. *Thebes*, in Bœotia, which was razed to the ground by Alexander before his expedition into Asia.

Lines 112, 113. *Samos . . . Delos.*—Comp. book iii, 429, and viii, 208, 209.

(76–94.)

And Babylon, magnificent to see,
115 But small to fight, shall stand with vain hopes walled.
Macedonians shall dwell in Bactria,
And those of Bactria and Susa all
Shall flee away into the land of Greece.
These things shall come to pass when Pyramus,
120 Pouring his silvery eddies on the shore,
Shall reach afar unto a sacred isle.
And Sybaris shall fall, and Cyzicus,
When earthquakes shake the land, and cities perish.
To Rhodes shall come the last but greatest woe.
125   Nor shall the Macedonians always rule;
But from the West a great Italian war
Shall blossom out, and under it the world,
Bearing a slavish yoke, shall subject be
To the Italians. Thou, O Carchedon,
130 Thy tower shall also to the ground be hurled.
Wretched Laodicea, thee some day
Shall earthquakes damage, leveling to the dust;
But a city of broad streets shall rise again.

Line 116. *Bactria.*—The north-eastern extreme of the Persian Empire, bordering on northern India.

Line 117. *Susa.*—The biblical Shushan, one of the capital cities of the Persian Empire.

Line 119. *Pyramus.*—A river of Cilicia flowing southward from Mount Taurus and emptying into the Mediterranean. Strabo (book i, chap. iii, 7) describes it and quotes these lines of the Sibyl as an ancient oracle.

Line 121. *Sacred isle.*—Referring probably to Cyprus, which word Strabo here reads.

Line 122. *Sybaris.*—Celebrated city of southern Italy, founded by Achæan colonists about B. C. 720, and totally destroyed by the army of the rural city Croton about B. C. 510. On *Cyzicus* and *Rhodes* see book iii, 516 and 525.

Lines 125-129. Rise, growth, and triumph of the Roman power.

Line 129. *Carchedon.*—Greek name for Carthage, which was destroyed by the Romans under Scipio, B. C. 146.

Line 131. *Laodicea.*—See book iii, 559.

(95-106.)

And also thou, O wretched Corinth, shalt
135 Some day behold thy utter overthrow.
O Lycian Myra, who art beautiful,
Thee also some time shall the heaving land
Hurl to the dust, and falling prone to earth,
Amid the din of battle thou shalt pray
140 To flee, an alien, to another land.
Then on the godless ones of Patara,
Along with thunders and with earthquake shocks
Another shall pour out a dark sea flood.
Also for thee, Armenia, there remains
145 A slavish fate, and then shall also come
To Solyma an evil blast of war,
From Italy, and God's great temple spoil.
But when they, trusting folly, shall forget
Piety, and foul murder consummate
150 Around the temple, then from Italy
A mighty king, even like a star, shall flee
Unseen, unknown, beyond Euphrates' ford.
Then shall he expiate the bloody crime
Of matricide, and many other deeds

Line 134. *Corinth.*—Destroyed by the Romans the same year as Carthage, B. C. 146.

Line 136. *Myra.*—Chief city of Lycia, on the southern coast, about a league from the sea. Its ruins witness to its ancient wealth and beauty.

Line 141. *Patara.*—See book iii, 522.

Line 144. *Armenia.*—There was Armenia Major, the vast territory south of the Caucasus Mountains and between the Euxine and Caspian Seas; and Armenia Minor, a small section on the west of Armenia Major, and east of Cappadocia. All these lands were subject to Alexander, then to the Syrian princes, and were made a Roman province under Trajan.

Line 146. *Solyma.*—That is, Jerusalem.

Line 151. *Mighty king.*—Nero, whose murder of his mother is notorious, and whose flight beyond the Euphrates and expected return as antichrist was a superstitious tradition long maintained. Comp. book v, 38. Instead of *like a star*, other copies read, *like a fugitive.*

(107-120.)

155 Which he with wicked hands will have performed.
    And many about Rome's sacred plain shall bleed,
    While he escapes beyond the fatherland.
      But into Syria Rome's great chief shall come
    And burn with fire the temple, and with spear
160 Shall slaughter many men of Solyma,
    And spoil the great broad country of the Jews.
    And then, too, shall an earthquake overthrow
    Both Salamis and Paphos, and dark floods
    Shall wildly dash on wave-washed Cyprus' shore.
165   But when from deep clefts of the Italian land
    Fire shall come whirling into the broad heaven
    And many cities burn and men destroy,
    And a vast mass of heated ashes shall fill
    The expanse of air, and the small drops of rain
170 Shall fall like a red mildew out of heaven,
    Then know the anger of the heavenly God,
    Because they slew the blameless godly race.
    And thereupon into the West shall come
    The wrangle of a newly wakened war,
175 And bearing a huge spear, Rome's fugitive
    Shall cross Euphrates with many myriads.

Line 156. *Many . . . bleed.*—By reason of the struggles for the imperial power.

Lines 158–161. This evidently refers to the destruction of Jerusalem and the temple, and the subjugation of all Palestine by the Romans under Vespasian and Titus.

Line 163. *Salamis and Paphos.*—Famous cities, one at the east and the other at the west end of Cyprus. "How often," says Seneca (*Epist.* 91), "has this calamity (earthquake) laid Cyprus waste? How often has Paphos fallen into ruin?"

Lines 165–172. The great eruption of Vesuvius, which destroyed Pompeii and Herculaneum, A. D. 79, is construed by the Sibyl as a sign of God's anger against the Romans for the slaughter of the Jews.

Line 175. *Rome's fugitive.*—Nero, referred to in lines 151–155.

O hapless Antioch, thee they shall call
No more a city, when thou fallest down
Through want of understanding round thy spears.
180 Then also famine and war's horrid din
Shall ruin Cyprus. Woe, wretched Cyprus, woe!
Thou shalt be hidden by the sea's broad wave,
Which by the wintry blasts is tossed on high.
But into Asia there shall come great wealth,
185 Which Rome herself, once plundering, put away
In her luxurious homes; and twice as much
Of other things shall she to Asia give;
And then there shall be an excess of war.
And Carian cities by Mæander's wave,
190 Which have been beautifully fenced with towers,
Shall by a bitter famine be destroyed,
When the Mæander his dark water hides.
But when from men shall perish piety,
And faith and righteousness, and they shall live
195 In recklessness profane, and insolence
Presumptuous, and full many other sins,
And of the pious no one makes account,
But from a want of understanding all
Like children utterly destroy themselves,
200 In violence exulting, and in blood
Holding their hands, then will it be discerned
That God is mild no longer, but surcharged

Lines 177–188. These lines depict a ruin which the Sibyl imagines will follow the return of Nero.

Line 186. *Twice as much.*—Comp. book iii, 413–419.

Line 189. *Mœander.*—This stream, having its sources in Phrygia, ran westward between Caria and Lydia, and was famous for its many windings. Comp. Ovid, *Metam.*, viii, 162–166.

(140–160.)

6

With fury, and by a great conflagration
Will utterly destroy the race of men.

205   Ah, miserable mortals, change these things,
Nor tempt the mighty God to wrath extreme ;
But letting go swords, wailings, homicides,
And insolence, wash in the flowing stream
The whole body, and with hands stretched out
        to heaven,

210 Seek pardon for the former deeds, and heal
Bitter impiety with piety,
And God will give repentance, not destroy.
And he will stay his wrath, if ye will all
Observe in your hearts precious piety.

215   But if, ill-minded, ye obey me not,
But loving wickedness, receive these things
With a base hearing, over all the world
Fire shall be, and the greatest omens, swords,
And trumpets, at the rising of the sun ;

220 All earth the mighty roaring sound shall hear.
The whole land he will burn, and the whole race
Of men shall perish, and he will consume
All cities, with the rivers and the seas ;
These all shall be reduced to smoky dust.

225   But when all things become an ashy pile,
God will put out the fire unspeakable
Which he once kindled, and the bones and ashes
Of men will God himself again transform,

Line 203. See lines 218–224, and comp. 2 Pet. iii, 7 ; Cicero, *de Natura Deorum*, ii, 49 ; Ovid, *Metam.*, i, 256–258. Justin Martyr refers to this passage in his first *Apology*, chap. xx.

Line 208. *Wash.*—Reference to Christian baptism.

Lines 225–239. This picture of resurrection, judgment, and awarding of punishments and rewards embodies the substance of familiar Christian doctrine. This passage is quoted in the *Apostolical Constitutions*, book v, 7 [G., 1, 844].

(161–186.)

And raise up mortals as they were before.
230 And then will be the judgment ; God himself
Will sit as judge, and judge the world again.
As many as committed impious sins
Shall Stygian Gehenna's depths conceal
'Neath molten earth and dismal Tartarus.
235 But the pious shall again live on the earth,
And God will give them spirit, life, and means
Of nourishment, and all shall see themselves,
Beholding the sun's sweet and cheerful light.
O happiest man, who at that time shall live !
(187–191.)

BOOK V.

CONTENTS OF BOOK V.

Introduction, 1–12. Rome's first emperors, 13–70. Grief of the Sibyl, 71–73. Inundation of Egypt, 74–80. Oracle against Memphis, 81–97. Idolatry and woes of Egypt, 98–142. Woes on various cities of the East and of Asia Minor, 143–162. Woe on Lycia, Phrygia, and Thessaly, 163–178. The vile and fearful king, 179–209. Oracle against Rome, 210–231. Lamentation over Egypt, 232–261. Britons and Gauls, 262–268. Ethiopians and Indians perish by conflict of the stars, 269–279. Doom of Corinth, 280–296. The dire destroyer, 297–320. The blessed Jews, 321–331. The heavenly Joshua, 332–336. Lovely Judea, 337–368. Woe on western Asia and Ephesus, 369–384. God's wrath on the wicked, 385–395. Woes on Smyrna, Cumæ, and Lesbos, 396–408. Woes of Corcyra, Hierapolis, and Tripolis, 409–418. Doom of Miletus, 419–423. Prayer for the land of Judah, 424–429. Wretched Thrace, Hellespont, and Italy, 430–445. Divine judgment and majesty, 446–465. Wars and woes of the last time, 466–497. Appeal to the wicked city, 498–512. Ruin of the temple, 513–532. Messianic day, 533–557. Fall of Babylon, 558–574. Woes of Asia, Crete, Cyprus, and Phenicia, 575–587. Vast armies in Egypt, Macedon, and Asia, 588–595. Destruction of the Thracians, 596–600. Mankind made few by woes, 601–609. Final darkness, 610–618. Ruin of Isis and Serapis, 619–630. The temple in Egypt, 631–646. Sin and doom of the Ethiopians, 647–657. Battle of the constellations, 658–681.

BOOK V.

BUT bring to me the lamentable time
Of the illustrious Latins, who were first,
After the kings of Egypt were cut off,
And had all been borne down into the earth;
5 And also after Pella's citizen,
Under whom all the Orient was subdued,
And the rich West, whom Babylon disgraced
And gave a corpse to Philip; not of Jove
Nor Ammon truly boasted to have sprung.
10 And they shall issue of the race and blood
Of great Assaracus, those born at Troy,
Even him who cleft the violence of fire.
  But after many kings and warlike men,
And after the twin children of the beast
15 That feeds on sheep, shall there come forth a king
Pre-eminent, who will sum up twice ten

This book appears, like the third, to contain compositions of different date, some of Christian and some of Jewish origin. In its present form it cannot be earlier than the close of Hadrian's reign, about A. D. 138.

Line 5. *Pella's citizen.*—Alexander, who was born at Pella, in Macedonia, B. C. 356.

Line 7. *Babylon disgraced.*—Alexander died at Babylon, and, according to common report, of a drunken debauch.

Line 9. *Ammon.*—A title given to Jupiter in Libya, from whom Alexander boasted a fabulous origin.

Line 11. *Assaracus.*—A Trojan prince, ancestor of Æneas.

Line 12. *Who cleft.*—That is, Æneas, who forced his way through the fire of Troy. Comp. book ix, 181–191, and x, 10–12.

Lines 14, 15. Allusion to Romulus and Remus, and the tradition of their being nursed by a she-wolf.

(1–12.)

With his initial letter.   He shall be
In war exceeding powerful; and of ten
Shall also his first letter be the sign.
20 After him rules who of the alphabet
Has the first letter.   Thrace and Sicily
And Memphis crouch and quail in dread of him—
Memphis, cast to the ground by wickedness
Of leaders, and a woman unsubdued,
25 Fallen on the wave.   And he will institute
Laws for the peoples, and subdue all things.
But after a long time will he transmit
The kingdom to another, who will have
The number of three hundred his first sign,
30 And of a river the beloved name.
The Persians he will rule and Babylon,
And then will smite the Medians with his spear.
Then one will rule who takes the number three.
Then shall one whose first letter marks twice ten
35 Become king, and to the remotest bounds
Of ocean shall he go, and sweep along
The refluent tide by the Ausonian shores.

Line 17. *Initial letter.*—On the use of letters and their numerical value as
designations of names see book i, 167, and comp. also lines 383–388 of the
same book.   The letter for twenty ("twice ten") is K, the first letter of the
Greek name for *Cæsar;* and the letter ten is I, the Greek initial of *Julius*
('Ιούλιος).

Line 21. *First letter.*—The letter *alpha,* A, initial of Augustus, who not
only became master of Thrace, Sicily, and Memphis, but attained the majesty and power of emperor.

Line 24. *Woman.*—Cleopatra, the last queen of Egypt, who committed
suicide to prevent falling into the hands of Octavius.

Line 29. *Three hundred.*—Represented by the letter T, the initial of Tiberius, as well as of the river Tiber.

Line 33. *Three.*—The letter Γ, Greek initial of Caius (Gaios) Cæsar, commonly known as Caligula.

Line 34. *Twice ten.*—As in line 16, but here designating Claudius (Greek,
Klaudios).

And one whose mark is fifty shall be lord,
A dreadful serpent, breathing grievous war ;
40 He will stretch out his hands against his kin,
And cut them off, and spread confusion wide,
Fight, kill the people, and dare countless things.
And he will cleave the isthmus, and with gore
Besprinkle it. But this destructive one
45 Shall pass from sight and then return again,
Presuming to be equal unto God ;
But he will sift him as if he were naught.
And after him will three kings be destroyed
By one another. Then a great destroyer
50 Of pious men shall come, and he shall show
Conspicuously the letter seven times ten.
His son, however, whose initial sign
Denotes three hundred, shall usurp the power.
And after him shall be a destined one,
55 A soul destroyer, of the number four.
And then an old man numbering fifty comes,
And next to him, whose first initial marks
Three hundred, is a Celtic mountaineer ;
Hastening away to battle in the East
60 He shall not miserable fate escape,

Line 38. *Fifty.*—The letter N, initial of Nero, the successor of Claudius.
His murders, flight to the East, and expected return are repeatedly referred
to in these oracles. Comp. book iv, 150–152 ; 175, 176.

Line 43. *Isthmus.*—Of Corinth, which Nero attempted to cut through.

Line 48. *Three kings.*—Galba, Otho, and Vitellius.

Line 51. *Seven times ten.*—The letter O, initial of the Greek form of the
name of Vespasian (Οὐεσπασιανός).

Line 53. *Three hundred.*—See on line 29. Here the name of Titus is intended.

Line 55. *Four.*—The letter Δ, initial of Domitian.

Line 56. *Fifty.*—See on line 38. Here Nerva is denoted.

Line 58. *Three hundred.*—See line 29. Here Trajan is intended, who,
however, was not of *Celtic* origin, but a Spaniard.

(28–44.)

6*

But sink in painful toils. Him foreign dust
Shall cover a dead corpse, having the name
Of Nemea's flower. And after him shall reign
Another man, with silver helmet decked,
65 And to him shall be given the name of a sea;
And he shall be a man of excellence,
And turn his mind to all things. And on thee
Thou excellent, most noble, dark-haired one,
And on thy branches all these days shall come.
70 Three shall reign, but the third one late shall rule.
  Thrice wretched I, sister of Isis, grieve
To place in heart an evil prophecy.
Even a sacred song of oracles.
First Mœnades shall rush around the base
75 Of thy sad temple, and in evil hands

Line 63. *Nemea's flower.*—Nemea in Argolis was the spot where triennial games were celebrated by the Greeks, and the victors were crowned with parsley, the Greek name of which is *selinon*. The emperor Trajan died in Selinus, a city of Cilicia in Asia Minor; hence the allusion of the Sibyl.

Line 65. *Name of a sea.*—The Adriatic (or Hadriatic), from which it is apparent Hadrian is referred to.

Line 70. *Three.*—The three Antonines, namely, Antonius Pius, M. Aurelius, and L. Verus. This last named, being only seven years old at the time of his adoption, was thought by the Sibyl to be likely to come late to the throne. Comp. book viii, 81.

Line 71. *Sister of Isis.*—The Sibyl, who elsewhere (book iii, 984) represents herself as the spouse of Noah, here assumes to be sister of the famous Egyptian goddess Isis, sadly prophesying the doom of Egypt, and especially of Memphis.

Line 74. *First*—Lactantius seems to have had this passage in mind when he says: "First of all, Egypt shall suffer punishment for her foolish superstitions, and will be covered with blood as if with a river." *Div. Inst.*, vii, 15 [L., 6, 786]. *Mœnades.*—A name applied to the priestesses of Bacchus, who were wont to work themselves into mad frenzy, and are here named as avenging furies, fit to execute judgment. Comp. line 621.

Line 75. *Thy sad temple.*—Or, *much lamented temple.* The temple of Isis is referred to. *Evil hands.*—Allusion perhaps to the tearing in pieces of Pentheus by the hands of his mother and aunts, to whom Bacchus made him appear as a wild beast.

(45–55.)

Shall it be in that day when the Nile whelms
All Egypt's land to sixteen cubits deep;
It shall flood all the land, and cover men
With water, and the beauty of the earth
80 And glory of her face shall disappear.
   Memphis, thou shalt for Egypt greatly mourn;
For though thou once didst rule the land in power,
Thou shalt become sad, and the Thunderer
Shall call from heaven with a mighty voice:
85 O mighty Memphis, who of old didst boast
So greatly o'er weak mortals, thou shalt wail
In sore distress, and wretchedness extreme,
So that thou truly shalt thyself discern
The eternal God, immortal in the clouds.
90 Where is thy gain in having among men
Prepared great power? Because thou hast against
My God-anointed children been enraged,
And hast stirred evil up among good men,
Thou shalt for such things have for penalty
95 This foster child. No longer openly
Shall there be right for thee among the blessed;
Fallen from the stars, thou shalt not mount to heaven.

Line 77. Sixteen cubits—The elevation of the Nile, in the vicinity of Memphis, is about twenty-three feet, according to Humboldt, which would be equivalent to the ordinary estimate of sixteen cubits. It is interesting to note that the famous piece of statuary in the Vatican, representing the Nile as a reclining human figure, has the child-like forms of sixteen genii climbing about it, as if to represent the sixteen cubits of the usual annual overflow.

Line 85. Memphis.—Ancient capital of lower Egypt. Comp. line 253.

Line 92. God-anointed children.—The Jewish people. Comp. Psa. cv, 15; Hab. iii, 13.

Line 95. Foster child—Rome, whose powerful help was sought by Egypt in the time of the wars with Syria.

Line 97. Comp. Isa. xiv, 12, 13; Matt. xi, 23.

(56–72.)

These things to Egypt God commissioned me
To utter touching the last time when men
100 Shall be all evil.   But the wicked toil
In sorrow, looking for calamity,
Wrath of the Immortal, Thunderer of heaven,
But worshiping false gods, and stones, and beasts,
And fearing many other things besides,
105 Which have no speech, nor mind, nor power to hear,
Which things for me to mention.is not right,
Dumb idols all, the work of mortal hands.
Of their own labors and their impious thoughts
Have men received gods made of wood, and stone,
110 And brass, and gold, and silver, soulless, vain,
Deaf, and they made them molten in the fire,
In such things having vainly put their trust.
Thmois and Xois are in sore distress;
Destroyed the counsel is of Hercules,
115 And Jupiter, and Hermes, and for thee,
O Alexandria, famed nourisher
Of cities, war shall never leave thee more.
For thy pride thou shalt give as many things
As thou hast done before.   Long time shalt thou
120 Be silent, even on the joyful day.
No more for thee shall flow the luxurious cup.

*   *   *   *

Line 113. *Thmois and Xois.*—Cities of Egypt, the former mentioned by
Herodotus (ii, 166), the latter by Strabo (xvii, 1, 19).

Line 114. *Counsel.*—Alexandre reads *house.* The one reading declares
that the oracular counsel of these deities is ruined, the other that their halls
or temples are destroyed.

Line 116. *Nourisher.*—Alexandria was, by her extensive commerce, a
source of supply for many cities. The Greek text as far as line 120 is imperfect, and after that is a lacuna.

Line 122. *Artful man.*—Alexandre understands this of Nero antichrist,
about to return from the East according to line 45 above. He also supplies
here a line found by him in a Paris codex, which, coming before this line,
reads : " And an ethereal (one) shall come upon thy soil like a hailstorm."

(73–92.)

And all thy land an artful man shall ruin
With blood, and corpses by the horrid altars;
Of barbarous mind, strong, very terrible,
125 Senselessly raging, hurrying on thy doom
With force innumerable as the sand.
Then wilt thou, happy city, suffer much.
All Asia falling on the earth shall wail
Because of gifts which she received from thee,
130 And with which, head encircled, she rejoiced.
   But he who had the Persians for his lot
Shall war on Egypt, and slay every man,
And plunder and destroy all means of life,
So that a third remains for wretched man.
135 But he from the West shall speed with nimble
      leap,
Invading all the land and wasting all.
But when he has obtained the height of power,
And odious dread, he will return, resolved
The city of the blessed to destroy.
140 And then a powerful king, sent forth from
      God,
Shall slay all mighty kings and noble men.
Then thus shall be a lasting end to men.
   Alas! alas for thee, unhappy heart!
Why dost thou move me Egypt's troubled state,
145 Beset by many rulers, to rehearse?
Go to the East, to Persia's thoughtless race,
And show them what is and what is to be.
Euphrates' river shall a deluge form,

Line 132. The Greek Codices here add a line—"A Cissian king sent
after him from God"—which is so obviously an error (probably a corruption of line 140 below), that we omit it from the text.

Line 135. *He from the West.*—This seems to refer to Vespasian.

Lines 140–142. A Messianic prophecy quoted by Lactantius, *Div. Inst.*, vii,
18 [L., 6, 796]. Lactantius's text differs somewhat from the one we follow.

(93–114.)

And Persians and Iberians destroy,
150 And Babylonians, and Massagetæ
That take delight in war, all armed with bows.
All Asia fire-consumed unto the isles
Shall drip.   And Pergamos, of old revered,
Shall wholly perish, and an utter waste
155 Shall Pitane appear to human eyes.
All Lesbos shall sink deep into the deep,
So as to perish ; Smyrna down the steep
Being rolled shall wail, she who was once revered
And famous shall be utterly destroyed.
130 And the Bithynians shall lament their land
Reduced to ashes, also Syria
The mighty, and Phenicia rich in plants.
    Woe, woe to thee, O Lycia, for thee
What evils are devised!   Of its own will
135 The sea has mounted on the troubled land,
So that the soil of Lycia, once replete
With fragrance sweet, shall wail for earthquake dire,
And bitter floods.   Fierce wrath shall also come
On Phrygia, on account of grief for which
170 Rhea, Jove's mother, came and tarried there.
The sea shall overthrow the Taurian race,

Line 149. *Iberians.*—Those north of Armenia, and between the Euxine and Caspian Seas, are probably intended; but they, as well as the *Massagetæ* mentioned in the next line, were in no contact with the Euphrates. The Massagetæ were east of the Caspian, in Scythia.

Line 155. *Pitane.*—A city on the east coast of Mysia, south-west of Pergamos.

Line 156. *Lesbos.*—Large island near the coast of Mysia.

Line 157. *Smyrna.*—Well-known city on the coast of Lydia, distinguished for its commerce in ancient and modern times.

Line 163. *Lycia.*—Province on the southern coast of Asia Minor, having Phrygia to the north.

Line 170. *Rhea.*—See book iii, 155–170.

Line 171. *Taurian race.*—A savage race in what is now the Crimean peninsula, who were wont to sacrifice strangers to the goddess Diana.

(115–131.)

A barbarous nation, and the Lapithæ
Shall to the earth be cast down and despoiled.
The land of Thessaly shall be destroyed
175 By the deep eddying river Peneus,
Deep-flowing, sweeping mortals from the earth.
Eridanus [the river that professed
To have begotten once the forms of beasts].
Greece the thrice wretched shall the poets weep,
180 When out of Italy a mighty king
Of mighty Rome shall smite the isthmus' neck,
A godlike man, whom they say Jove himself
And honored Juno bore, who, courting praise
For his sweet songs with a melodious voice,
185 Will with the wretched mother many slay.
From Babylon shall flee the fearful king
And shameless, whom all mortals justly hate;
For he slew many, and laid violent hands
Upon the womb; against his wife he sinned,
190 And of flagitious parents was he born.
But he will come unto the Medes and kings
Of Persia whom he first sought, and for whom
He wrought renown, and, with these wicked ones,
Will lurk against a nation not beloved.
195 He seized the God-made temple, and he burned
The citizens and people going in,
Who have been justly eulogized in song.

Line 172. *Lapithæ.*—A tribe in the mountains of Thessaly, famous in Greek mythology for their contest with the Centaurs.

Line 175. *Peneus.*— Chief river of Thessaly.

Line 177. *Eridanus.*—Another name for the Padus, or Po, in Italy. The words in brackets are omitted from the text of Alexandre.

Lines 180–201. This whole passage obviously refers to Nero. Comp. lines 40–45.

Lines 194–197. The Jewish War, which, in the ruin of Jerusalem and the temple, was begun under Nero.

(132–150.)

On his appearing the creation shook,
Kings perished, but among them yet remained
200 Authority, until they had destroyed
The mighty city and the righteous people.
But when in the fourth year a star shall shine,
Which alone shall destroy the entire land,
Because of honor first to Neptune paid,
205 Then there shall come from heaven a mighty star
Into the dreadful sea, and burn the deep,
And Babylon itself, and Italy,
For which full many faithful Hebrew saints
And also the true temple were destroyed.
210   Thou shalt among base mortals suffer wrongs,
But shalt remain whole ages all a waste,
Hating thy soil, for thou didst long for drugs,
Adulteries were with thee, and with boys
Thou didst indulge in lawless acts of shame,
215 Effeminate, unjust, and wicked city,
Ill-fated above all. Woe, woe to thee,
Thou unclean city of the Latin land!
Mad woman, fond of serpents, by thy banks
A widow thou shalt sit, and over thee
220 The river Tiber shall weep as for a spouse.
  O thou of murderous heart and impious soul,

Line 202. *Fourth year.*—Perhaps in allusion to the time, times, and dividing of time (three and a half years) in Dan. vii, 25, a symbolic number for a period of woe.

Line 205. *Star into the…sea.*—Comp. Rev. viii, 8; xvi, 3. This whole passage is an apocalyptic prophecy of judgment to come on Rome, and is so interpreted by Lactantius, *Div. Inst.*, vii, 15 [L., 6, 790].

Line 207. *Babylon.*—Here used as a symbolic name for Rome.

Line 210. *Thou.*—Direct address to Rome.

Line 211. This line is in substance repeated in the codices and editions of the Greek text, but is so evidently a corruption that we omit the repetition from our text.

Lines 214, 215. Cited by Clement of Alex., *Pæd,* ii, 15 [G., 8, 516].

Line 219. *Widow.*—Comp. Lam. i, 1.

(151–170.)

Dost thou not know what God has power to do,
And what his purpose is? But thou didst say,
"I am alone, and none shall plunder me."
225 But now thee and all thine shall God destroy,
The ever-living One, and in that land
No longer shall a trace of thee remain,
As when of old thy honors God procured.
Remain thou then alone, O lawless one,
230 And, mixed with burning fire, dwell in the realm
Of Hades, the Tartarean lawless land.
    And now again, O Egypt! I lament
Thy sorrow. Memphis, leader thou of toils,
Filled with the dead, in thee the pyramids
235 Shall utter forth a shameful sound of woe.
Python of old, twin city rightly called,
Be still forever, that thou mayest cease
From wickedness. Thou basely insolent,
Store-house of sorrows, Mænad, full of woe,
240 Terrible sufferer, and full of tears,
Thou shalt remain a widow through all time.
Thou didst become old ruling the world alone.
But when a white dress Barca round herself
Shall put on over that which is defiled,
245 O may I not be, might I not have been!
    O Thebes, where is thy great power? A rude man

Line 232. *Again, Egypt.*—Comp. lines 71–97.

Line 236. *Python.*—This name seems to be here applied to Memphis as a symbolical name, equivalent to "oracle city," in allusion to the famous Delphic oracle in Greece.

Line 239. *Mænad.*—A raving priestess of Bacchus. Comp. line 74.

Line 243. *White dress.*—According to Alexandre the nomad population of Barca, in the northern part of Africa, were wont to put on a white garment over their sun-burned and filthy bodies when about to go into battle.

Line 246. *Thebes.*—The ancient and famous capital of Upper Egypt, as Memphis was of Lower. The *rude man* of this line and the *great man* of line 253 are both understood by Alexandre to refer to antichrist, but it is better perhaps to understand this whole passage as apocalyptic in the broad, general way, and so no particular person known in history need be supposed.

(171–188.)

Shall slay the people; but thou, throwing on
Gray garments, wretched one, shalt weep alone.
And thou shalt make atonement for all things
250 Which thou hast done, because of lawless deeds,
And they shall look upon thee in distress
As one that did possess a shameful soul.
    Syene a great man shall overthrow,
And Tentyris of the Ethiopians
255 Shall swarthy Indians occupy by force.
Pentapolis, a man of mighty power
Shall make thee weep. O Libya, much bewildered,
Who shall explain thy woes? And who of men
Cyrene, shall bewail thy miseries?
260 Thou shalt not from thy hateful weeping cease
Until the time of thy destruction comes.
    Among the Britons and the wealthy Gauls

Line 253. *Syene.*—City of Upper Egypt near the equator, and famous for the quarries whence the obelisks were dug.

Line 254. *Tentyris.*—Situated on the Nile some distance north of Thebes, and near the modern Denderah.

Line 256. *Pentapolis.*—A name applied to Cyrenaica, in northern Africa, because of the five cities, Cyrene, Barce, Ptolemais, Berenice, and Tauchira.

Line 257. *Libya.*—Extensive region of northern Africa, of which Cyrenaica was but a part.

Line 259. *Cyrene.*—One of the cities of the Pentapolis mentioned in line 256.

Lines 262–268. In these verses the Sibyl foretells punishment on the Britons and Gauls, who are supposed to have furnished soldiers for the legions led by Vespasian against the Jews. These last are to be understood by the "sons of God" in line 264. The "Phenician king" (verse 265) is Vespasian, who led his forces out of Ptolemais in Syria to carry the war into Galilee. See Josephus, *Wars*, iii, vi, 2, 3, and Tacitus, *Hist.*, iv, 39; v, 1. Ravenna, the great naval station of the Romans on the Adriatic, comes in for its share of the curse, for it was a chief city of Cisalpine Gaul, and naturally associated with the military operations of Rome in the time of the Cæsars.

(189–199.)

Shall ocean, filled with much blood, loudly roar,
For they did evil to the sons of God,
265 When a Phenician king from Syria led
With the Sidonians a vast Gallic force;
And thee thyself, Ravenna, he will slay,
And in the work of murder be a guide.
O Indians and great Ethiopians,
270 Be not presumptuous, for when Capricorn
Around the pole, and Taurus in mid heaven
Among the Twins shall have encircled these,
And Virgo rises, and about his front
The sun a girdle fastening leads all heaven—
275 A great ethereal fire shall be on earth,
And in the conflicts of the warring stars
Shall nature become new, and all the land
Of the Indians and the Ethiopians
Shall perish in the midst of fire and groans.
280   Weep also thou, O Corinth, the sad doom
Of thy destruction, when with twisted threads
The Fates, three sisters, spinning, lead on high
The one who fled by guile beside the voice

Line 270. *Be not presumptuous.*—The common text reads, *fear not;* but
the sentiment is not in harmony with what follows, according to which the
Indians and Ethiopians are doomed to perish amid a conflict of the constellations. Hence instead of ταρβεῖτε, *fear,* Alexandre reads θαρσεῖτε, *be presumptuous,* or impudently bold, and we adopt this conjectural emendation.
Comp. lines 498, 499. On the war of the stars, comp. lines 660–681, at the
close of this book.

Line 282. *Fates.*—These, according to popular mythology, were three
sisters, named Clotho, Lachesis and Atropos, who are continually spinning
out the destiny of mortals. Clotho, it was said, held the distaff, Lachesis
spun out the thread of existence, and Atropos cut it off.

Line 283. *The one who fled.*—The reference seems to be to Nero and his
cleaving the isthmus (comp. line 43). His return from the East as antichrist
was a superstitious apprehension prevalent for some time after his death.
Comp. book iv, 150–162.

(200–215.)

Of the isthmus, until all shall gaze on him
285 Who once cut off the rock with beaten brass;
And he thy land will ruin, and will smite
As it has been appointed; for to him
Has the only God given to accomplish what
Not one of all the former kings could do.
290 For standing there in power he will give others
To pluck off with a sickle from the root
Three heads, so that unholy kings shall eat
Their parents' flesh.   For unto all mankind
Murder and terrors are laid up in store
295 Because of the great city and just people
Saved through all time by special providence.
    O thou unstable one, and ill-advised,
By evil fates surrounded, unto men
Both a beginning and great end of woe,
300 A creature harmed and saved again by fate,
Excess of evils, woe, and man's great end,
Who among mortals ever longed for thee?
Who is not angry with thee in his heart?
In thee cast forth, what king his honored life
305 Lost?   All things evilly hast thou disposed,
And deluged all with evil, and by thee
Have beautiful portions of the world been changed.
Into our strife these last, perchance put forth:
And how dost thou say, "I will thee persuade,
310 And if in any thing I blame thee, speak!"
    There once was among men the sun's bright light,

Line 292. *Three heads.*—Comp. Dan. vii, 8, 24; 2 Esdras xi, 23; xii, 22. Hippolytus, *de Christo et Antichristo*, lii [G., 10, 772].

Line 295. *City . . . people.*—Jerusalem and the Jews.

Lines 297–320. A prophetic curse against Rome as the greatest source of misery to men.

Lines 308–314. In these lines we may understand a strife of words between Roman and Jew.

(216–237.)

And prophets' common rays were wide diffused,
And language, dripping fair drink for all men,
Appeared, developed, and day dawned on all.
315 Because of this, O thou of narrow mind,
Author of greatest evils, both a sword
And sorrow will be coming in that day.
Beginning and great end of woe to men,
A creature harmed and saved again by fate,
320 Hear the harsh sound of sharp words, bane of men.
　　But when the Persian land is free from war
And pestilence and woe, then in that day
There shall be of the blessed heavenly Jews
A race divine, who in the midst of the land
325 Shall round God's city dwell; and with great walls
Even as far as Joppa circled round,
They lift themselves up to the dusky clouds.
No longer will the trumpet sound abroad
War's murderous tones, nor shall men be destroyed
330 By the mad hands of foes; but there shall stand
Forever monuments of wicked men.
　　But there shall come from heaven a wondrous man,
Whose hands were stretched out on the fruitful wood,
The noblest of the Hebrews, who once caused
335 The sun to stand still, when he gave command
With admirable speech and hallowed lips.

Line 321. *Persian land.*—All western Asia, which the Roman and other wars destructive to the Jews had long ravaged, and which was also often visited with pestilence. In the midst of this land, namely, at Jerusalem, the restored Jewish race, according to the Sibyl, are to dwell in peace and glory.

Line 323. *Heavenly Jews.*—This line is cited by Lactantius, *Div. Inst.*, iv, 20 [L., 6, 516].

Lines 332–336. *Wondrous man.*—In this passage the Messiah is conceived as both Moses and Joshua coming down out of the heavens. The allusions are to Moses stretching out his hands with the wonder-working rod (comp. Exod. vii, 17–20, and xvii, 9–12), the rod that put forth buds and fruit (Num. xvii, 8), and Joshua commanding the sun to stand still (Josh. x, 12).

(238–258.)

No longer vex thy soul, nor put a sword
Unto thy bosom, O thou child of God,
Rich, only longed-for flower, thou goodly light,
340 Thou consummation noble, longed-for, pure,
Lovely Judea, city beautiful,
Inspired by hymns.   No longer on thy soil
Will the Greeks revel with unhallowed foot,
But have within their hearts a similar law.
345 But thee shall noble children reverence,
And at the table stand with holy songs,
With offerings of all sorts and worthy prayers.
As many as endure the weariness
Of light affliction, and are just, shall come
350 To greater good and excellent delights;
But those who sent to heaven foul, lawless speech
Shall against one another cease to speak,
And hide themselves until the world shall change.
But from the clouds a rain of gloomy fire
355 Shall come, and mortals shall no longer reap
From earth the splendid corn; wild and untilled
Shall all things be, till mortal men shall know
The God who rules all, the immortal One,
Existing ever; mortal things no more
360 Shall grow old, neither dogs nor carrion birds,
Such as the Egyptians taught should be revered
By tender youthful mouths, and foolish lips.
But all these things the Hebrews' holy land
Alone shall bear; from honey-dripping rock

Line 340. By two slight changes in the Greek, Alexandre makes this line
read:

"O venerable branch, O longed-for plant."

Line 343. *Greeks revel.*—Comp. Joel iii, 17; Isa. lii, 1.

Lines 363–366. These lines are cited by Lactantius, *Div. Inst.*, vii, 42
[L., 6., 811]; comp. Joel iii, 18.

(259–280.)

365 And from a spring there shall a rivulet
And milk ambrosial flow to all the just;
For in our glorious Maker, God alone,
Having great faith and piety, they hoped.
But why does the wise mind grant me these things?
370 Yet thee, O wretched Asia, I deplore
In pitying sorrow, and the Ionian race
And Carians, and the Lydians rich in gold.
Woe, Sardis; woe, woe, Trallis, greatly loved;
Woe, woe, Laodicea, city fair,
375 How shalt thou perish by the earthquake shock,
Fall into ruin, and to dust be changed!
In gloomy Asia of the rich Lydians
Shall Dian's temple, fixed at Ephesus,
Some day by yawning chasms and earthquake shocks
380 Come headlong down into the dreadful sea,
Even as ships are overwhelmed by storms.
And Ephesus, quite overthrown, shall wail,
Lamenting by her banks, and searching out
Her temple, no more to be occupied.
385   And then, incensed, shall God, the imperishable,
Who dwells on high, send lightning from the heaven
Down on the power of him that is impure.
And in that day, instead of winter's storms
There shall be summer; and to mortal men
390 This shall then be, for the great Thunderer
Will utterly destroy all shameless ones
With thunders, lightnings, and terrific flames
Against malicious men, and ruin them

Lines 370–384. The Sibyl here pronounces woe on several well-known provinces and cities of Asia Minor, all which have been repeatedly shaken by earthquakes. Especially interesting is the mention of the famous temple of Diana at Ephesus. Comp. Acts xix, 24–28.

Lines 382–384. These lines are cited by Clem. Alex., *Cohort.*, iv [G., 8, 141]. (281–303.)

As godless, so that bodies of the dead
395 Shall lie on earth more numerous than the sand.
    And Smyrna also, weeping for Lycurgus,
    Unto the gates of Ephesus shall come,
    And yet herself the rather come to naught.
    And foolish Cumæ, with her inspired streams,
400 By hands of gods and lawless men hurled down,
    Shall offer up her joy into the air
    No more, but lie a corpse by Cumæ's streams.
    And then those left shall suffer ills together.
    Cumæ's rude populace, a hateful tribe,
405 Having a sign, shall know for what they suffered.
    And then when they shall have their wicked land
    Reduced to ashes, Lesbos, situate
    By Eridanus, shall perish evermore.
    Woe, woe to thee, Corcyra, city fair,
410 Cease from thy revel. Hierapolis,
    Thou also, only soil with riches mixed,
    Shalt have what thou hast longed to have, a land
    Of many tears, having been enraged against
    A country by the streams of Thermodon.

Line 396. *Smyrna.*—Already mentioned in this book, line 157. The mention
of Lycurgus is difficult to explain, except as a false reading. Alexandre
substitutes the conjectural emendation *Samornos* and cites Strabo (book xiv,
i, 4) to show that this was another name for Ephesus, and that these two
cities were once in the most intimate relationship with each other.

Line 399. *Cumæ.*—Or *Cyme*, some fifteen miles north of Smyrna. Its "rude
populace" (line 404) is said by Strabo (book xiii, iii, 6) to have been ridi-
culed for stupidity.

Line 407. *Lesbos.*—Large island off the coast of Mysia (see line 156),
but not by the Eridanus of line 177. The name Eridanus is perhaps a
corruption of *Adramyttium*, written also *Adrymon* and *Adramytan;* for the
island of Lesbos was by the bay of Adramyttium.

Line 409. *Corcyra.*—City on island of the same name off the coast of Epirus, identical with the modern Corfu.

Line 410. *Hierapolis.*—In Phrygia, not far from Laodicea and Colossæ.

Line 414. *Thermodon.*—River of Pontus, emptying in the Euxine.

(304–319.)

415 And rocky Tripolis, beside the waves
Of the Mæander, filled up by the shore
With mighty waters, thou shalt be destroyed
Utterly, by God's will and providence.
   I do not wish to take the neighboring land
420 Of Phœbus, yet a thunderbolt from heaven
Wanton Miletus some day shall destroy,
Because she took up Phœbus' crafty song
And the wise care and prudent plans of men.
Be merciful, All-Father, to the land .
425 Of Judah, wanton, fruit-abounding, great,
That we may live to see thy purposes.
For this thou knewest at first, O God, in love,
That to all men it might appear thy gift,
And that they might see what God will bestow.
430   I long thrice wretched Thracia's works to see,
And the wall trailed in dust between two seas,
Even like a river for the swimming fish.
   O wretched Hellespont, some day a child
Of the Assyrians shall throw a bridge
435 Across thee.   Against thee will Thracians fight
And of thy power exhaust thee utterly;
And on the Macedonian land shall seize

Line 415. *Tripolis.*—North-west of Hierapolis, on the Mæander.

Line 421. *Miletus.*—Said to have been founded by, and named after, a son of Phœbus (that is, Apollo; see note on book iv, line 4), and hence called land of Phœbus, as in this passage. According to Strabo (book xiv, i, 6) the Milesians invoke Phœbus as the dispenser of health and healer of diseases.

Line 430. *Thracia's works.*—Reference probably to the wall, mentioned in next line, built by Miltiades across the isthmus of the Thracian Chersonese. See Herodotus, book vi, 36.

Line 434. *Assyrians.*—Here put for Persians, who occupied the Assyrian territory. The reference is manifestly to Xerxes, who bridged the Hellespont, as described by Herodotus, book vii, 34-36.

(320–337.)

7

A king of Egypt, and a barbarous clime
Will cast the prowess of the leaders down.
440 Lydians, Galatians, and Pamphylians,
With the Pisidians, being armed for war,
With all the people conquer in fell strife.
　　Thrice wretched Italy, thou shalt remain
Unwept, deserted, in a blooming land,
445 The deadly serpent fully to destroy.
　　But far above along the ethereal sky
God's voice like rolling thunder shall be heard,
And the sun's own imperishable flames
Be no more, and the moon's brilliant light
450 Shall not again be in that latest time,
When God shall rule. All things shall be in gloom,
Darkness shall be on earth, and blinded men,
And evil beasts, and a long time of woe;
So that it will be seen that God is king,
455 And looks down from the heavens on all below.
Himself will not then pity hostile men,
Who sacrifice the herds of lambs and sheep,
And bellowing calves, great calves with gilded horns,
To lifeless Hermes and to gods of stone.
460 But let the law of wisdom take the lead,
The glory of the righteous, lest, anon,
The imperishable God be filled with wrath,

Line 438. *King of Egypt.*—Lysimachus seems to be referred to, and is thought of as being Egyptian because of his marriage with Ptolemy's daughter. The provinces of Asia Minor named in lines 440–442 were all involved in the wars of Lysimachus.

Line 445. *Serpent.*—The meaning is unintelligible. For *serpent* Alexandre reads *plain.*

Line 459. *Hermes.*—Called also Mercury, the god of arts and eloquence; messenger of the gods and conductor of souls to Hades. The reference in the text is to statues of Hermes.

Lines 461–465. Cited by Lactantius, *de Ira Dei,* xxiii [L., 7, 144].

(338–357.)

And every race and tribe of men destroy;
For it is binding on us to love God,
465 The wise Creator, who forever lives.
　　There shall be at the last time, when the moon
Comes near its end, a world-disputing war,
And it will be in cunning and in guile;
And from the earth's extremity shall come
470 A matricidal man, a fugitive,
Revolving sharp devices in his mind;
He every land will seize, and conquer all;
Wiser than all men, he will know all things.
　That on account of which he himself perished
475 Forthwith he will seize. And he will destroy
Many men and great tyrants, and consume
All of them as none other ever did.
And such as fell he will restore through zeal.
But from the West shall come much war to men,
480 And hills of blood shall to the rivers flow.
But in the plains of Macedonia
The rage drops, and alliance from the West
Is offered, but destruction for the king.
And then a wintry blast shall blow on earth,
485 And evil war shall fill the land again.
For fire on mortals from the heavenly plains

Line 470. *Fugitive.*—Reference to Nero, here conceived as returning from his flight beyond the Euphrates (see book iv, 150) and embodying the traits of the vile king described in Dan. viii, 23–25. This passage (lines 469–470) is quoted by Lactantius, *de Morte Persec.*, ii [L., 7, 197], and he says that some persons of his own time understood it of Nero, who was supposed to be still living in some distant region whither he had been secretly conveyed.

Line 474. That for which he perished, and which the returning Nero would again seize, was the sovereignty.

Lines 480–483. The exact import of these lines is quite unintelligible, except that by various concurring forces the Nero antichrist is to be destroyed.

(358–376.)

hall be rained down in showers, fire, and blood,
Water and lightning, darkness, awful night,
Wasting in war, and on the slaughter gloom;
390 And it will bring destruction to all kings,
Even those then best; and thus shall terminate
The lamentable ruin of dire war.
No longer will one fight with swords, or iron,
Or darts, which things shall not again be right.
495 And prudent people, such as have survived,
Will have peace, having tested wickedness
In order that at last they might have joy.
Ye matricides, leave off the impudence
Of bold effrontery and wicked works,
500 Ye who have basely furnished couch for boys,
And in the brothel harlots made of those
Who once were pure, by means of insolence,
And punishment, and forced indecency.
For in thee lawless mother with her child
505 Held carnal intercourse, and with her sire
The daughter was united as a bride.
Also in thee have kings their ill-starred mouth
Polluted, and in thee have wicked men
Found couch with beasts.   O city full of grief
510 And evil, given to reveling, be still.
For virgins will no longer find with thee
The sacred fire of the love-kindling grove.
By thee the loved house was of old put out,

Line 498. *Matricides.*—The Romans are thus addressed, as if they were conceived in the Sibyl's mind as so many Neros. Comp. line 470.
Line 512. *Sacred fire.*—This was kept burning in the temple of Vesta at Rome, and attended by six virgin priestesses known as Vestal virgins. The safety of the city was believed to depend on keeping this fire ever burning.
Line 513. *Loved house.*—The temple in Jerusalem, laid waste first by the Chaldeans (2 Kings xxv, 8–11) and a second time by the Romans under Titus.

When I saw it a second time laid waste,
515 And wrapped in fire by an unholy hand,
House always blooming, temple watched of God,
Brought forth by saints, imperishable ever,
A ground of hope for soul and body too.
For without burial rites none will praise God
520 Out of the hidden earth, nor will the wise
Artificer prepare a stone for such,
  Nor did he reverence gold, the cheat of souls
And of the world; but they with sacrifice
And holy hecatombs adored the God
525 And mighty Maker of all breathing things.
But now an unseen and unholy king
Rose, cast this down, and let it go unbuilt,
With a great multitude and famous men.
But having gone up to the immortal land
530 He himself perished. Such a sign no more
  Was ever wrought on men; so it seemed good
That others the great city should destroy.
    For from the heavenly plains there came a man,
A blessed one, who held within his hand
535 A scepter with which God intrusted him,
And all things he ruled nobly, and restored
To all the good the wealth which former men
Had taken; and all cities with vast fire

Line 519. The ancient Greeks believed that no soul could enter the abode of the blessed, or be at peace, until the body had received due burial rites.

Line 530. *Himself perished.*—This was not true of either Vespasian or Titus, who were personally engaged in the Jewish war which destroyed Jerusalem and the temple. Perhaps the author referred to Nero, under whom this war was begun, and who died before its termination. The epithets "unseen and unholy," in line 526, are better descriptive of Nero.

Lines 533–557. A Messianic passage, depicting with prophetic ardor the restoration and glorification of the Jews.

Line 536. *Restored.*—Comp. book iii, 414–419; iv, 184–188.

(397–417.)

From the foundations he destroyed and burned,
540 The towns of men who had wrought wicked deeds.
And that same city which God loved he made
More radiant than the stars, and sun and moon,
And put on ornament, and made in flesh
A sanctuary very beautiful,
545 And formed for miles a great and boundless tower
Touching the very clouds, and seen by all,
So that the faithful and the just might all
Behold the glory of the eternal God,
A longed-for sight.   Morning and evening hymned
550 The praise of God.   For there shall no more come
Dire evils upon miserable men,
Adulteries and lawless lust of boys,
Nor murder, nor confusion, but with all
A righteous rivalry.   Last is the time
555 Of the saints, when the lofty Thunderer,
God, who is founder of the mighty temple,
Brings to their consummation all these things.
    Alas! alas for thee, O Babylon,
For golden throne and golden sandal famed,
560 Thou ancient kingdom, sole lord of the world;
Once mighty and all-potent, thou shalt lie
No more in golden mountains, and the streams
Of the Euphrates; thou shalt be laid low
In time of earthquake.   But the dreadful Parthians
565 Made thee rule all things.   Hold thy insolent mouth,
O vile race of Chaldeans!   Do not speak
Nor be concerned how thou shalt rule the Persians,

Lines 541, 542. Cited by Lactantius, *Div. Inst.*, vii, 24 [L., 6, 809].
Line 558. *Babylon.*—Here put for Ctesiphon on the Tigris, the metropolis
of the Parthian Empire. This empire was one of the great powers of the
East, and, after long conflict with the Syrian king, spread its dominion over
western Asia, and very successfully resisted the Romans until the third
century of our era.

(417–440.)

Or how thou shalt be conqueror of the Medes.
For on account of thy power which thou hadst,
570 Having sent hostages to Rome, and served
In Asia, thou shalt as a prudent queen
Into the judgment of the unrighteous come,
For whom thou hast sent ransoms.   Thou shalt give
Instead of puzzling words keen wrath to foes.
575   And in the last time shall the sea be dry,
And ships no longer sail to Italy;
But great and fruitful Asia and the plain
Of Crete shall be all water.   And great woe
Shall Cyprus have, and on a dreadful fate
580 Shall Paphos rush, so that one shall behold
Salamis, great city, suffering mighty woe.
Now waste and fruitless shall she be again
Upon the coast; and locusts not a few
The Cyprian land shall ruin.   Look at Tyre
585 And weep, O hapless mortals!   Fearful wrath
Waits thee, Phenicia, until thou fall
A vile corpse, so that sirens truly weep.
    In the fifth generation, when the ruin
Of Egypt shall have ceased, and shameless kings

Line 570. *Hostages to Rome.*—A little while before the beginning of the
Christian era, the Parthian king Phraates sent four of his sons to Rome, and
the Roman writers speak of them as hostages to Augustus.   See Rawlinson,
Sixth Oriental Monarchy, chap. xiii.

Line 572. Comp. book ii, 70, 71.

Lines 575–587.   Malediction on western Asia and the Mediterranean
islands.

Line 578. *Crete.*—Comp. book iii, 599.

Line 579. *Cyprus.*—Comp. book iv, 181.

Lines 580, 581. *Paphos . . . Salamis.*—Comp. book iv, 163.

Line 586. *Phenicia.*—Comp. book iii, 585.

Lines 588–595. *Fifth.*—Alexandre understands this passage to refer to
the fifth generation after Ptolemy Philometer, and the time of Cleopatra.
(440–458.)

590 Mingle together, nations of all tribes
    Shall camp in Egypt, and in Macedonia,
    And Asia, and among the Lydians
    Shall rage a cruel world-oppressing war
    Of much blood and dust, which the king of Rome
595 And rulers of the West shall cause to cease.
        When wintry storm comes dropping like the snow,
    And the great river and vast lakes are frozen,
    Straightway into the Asian land shall go
    A barbarous multitude, and the dire race
600 Of Thracians like a feeble thing destroy.
    And then will wretched mortals, hunger-worn,
    Devour their parents, and gulp down all food,
    And wild beasts in all dwellings eat their food,
    They and the birds devour all mortal men.
605 And with the wicked ocean shall be filled,
    Being blood-red from the river—flesh and blood
    Of foolish men.   Then thus a littleness
    Shall be upon the earth, that of mankind
    And womankind the number one may see.
610   But myriad things shall a dire race bewail
    At the end, when the sun sets not to rise,
    But to remain submerged in ocean's wave,
    Because it saw the baneful wickedness
    Of many mortals.   And a moonless night

Line 592. *Lydians.*—Instead of this Alexandre conjectures the emendation
Libyans, and so fits it to the times of Cleopatra and the Roman conquest of
Egypt and the contiguous lands.

Line 596. *Wintry storm.*—Comp. line 484 and what follows there.

Line 597. *Great river.*—Not the Nile, as Alexandre, but a general reference to the great rivers and lakes of northern Europe and Asia.

Line 599. *Barbarous multitude.*—Probably a reference to the invasion of
some barbarous tribe from northern Europe, but the whole passage bears an
apocalyptic cast, and no definite historical allusions need be sought.

Line 611. *Sun sets.*—Comp. line 466.

(459–478.)

615 Shall gather round the mighty heaven itself,
    And no small mist shall hide the world's ravines.
    But then a second time shall God's light rule
    The good men, even as many as praise God.
      Isis, thrice wretched goddess, thou alone
620 Shalt by the waters of the Nile remain,
    A lawless Bacchanal upon the sands
    Of Acheron, and over all the earth
    No more shall memory of thee remain.
    And thou, Serapis, sitting on the stones,
625 Shalt be in trouble about many things.
    Thou shalt in thrice unhappy Egypt lie
    An immense corpse; all that in Egypt bore
    A love toward thee shall wail thee bitterly.
    But such as praise God, having in their minds
630 Unimpaired reason, know that thou art naught.
      And then a linen-vested priest shall say :
    " Come, let us raise a beautiful temple of God
    In truth; come, let us change the fearful laws
    Of our forefathers, by which they required
635 Processions, and performed their mystic rites
    To gods of stone and clay that had no sense.
    Let us our souls turn and give praise to God
    The imperishable, who himself is sire,
640 Who always has been, who is Lord of all

Line 619. *Isis.*—Comp. lines 71–80, and notes there.

Line 624. *Serapis.*—Another Egyptian deity like Isis, to whom a great number of temples were erected throughout Egypt.

Line 631. *Priest.*—Commonly supposed to refer to Onias, who, according to Josephus (*Ant.*, xiii, 3) obtained of Ptolemy Philometer permission to build a temple like that in Jerusalem. But see below on verse 644.

Line 635. *Processions. . . . mystic rites.*—The Jewish priest, if Onias be understood, speaks as a representative of the Egyptians, whom he would fain hope to turn from their idolatries to the worship of the true God. This accords with the spirit of Onias's epistle to Ptolemy, as given in Josephus.

(479–498.)

The true one, king, and soul-sustaining sire,
The mighty God, existing evermore.
     And then in Egypt there shall be a great
And holy temple, and their sacrifices
645 Into it shall the God-made people bring,
And God shall give to them eternal life.
     But when the Ethiopians forsake
The shameless tribes of the Triballians,
And cultivate their Egypt, wickedness
650 They will begin, that afterward all things
May come to pass.   For they shall overthrow
The mighty temple of the Egyptian land,
And on earth will God rain a fearful wrath
Upon them, and all base and lawless men
655 Shall be destroyed.   And in that land no more
Will any one receive forbearing grace,
Because they did not guard what God had given.
     The threatening of the shining sun I saw
Among the stars, and in the lightning flash
660 The dire wrath of the moon.   The stars travailed
With battle; God permitted them to fight.

Line 644. *Temple.*—Commonly supposed to refer to the Jewish temple at Leontopolis in Egypt. See Josephus, *Wars*, vii, 10, 2, 3; *Ant.*, xiii, 3. Alexandre, however, controverts this explanation, and maintains that this writer, being subsequent to the closing of the temple at Leontopolis, and the abolishing of its worship by order of the Roman emperor (Josephus, *Wars*, vii, x, 4), could not have thus spoken of this temple, nor prophesied its overthrow by Ethiopians (lines 651 and 652). Hence the plausible supposition that the entire passage about a temple in Egypt is a poetical amplification of the prophecy of Isa. xix, 18–22.

Line 648. *Triballians.*—These were a powerful and savage tribe near the Danube in Europe (comp. book x, 91), and are here strangely associated with the Ethiopians. But probably both names are here used symbolically, like Gog and Magog, in book iii, 376.

Lines 658–681. Comp. lines 270–279 and book viii, 237. Also Lactantius, *Div. Inst.*, vii, 16 [L., 6, 792].

For in the sun's stead long fire-flames arose;
The morning star made fight and trod upon
The Lion's back, and the moon's double horn
665 Changed its face; Capricorn smote Taurus' neck,
But Taurus took away from Capricorn
Returning day; Orion would no more
Abide the yoke, and the lot of the Twins
Did Virgo change to Aries; no more shone
670 The Pleiads, and the Dragon left his zone.
Pisces went down into the Lion's belt;
The Crab remained not, for he feared Orion;
Scorpio approached the dreadful Lion's tail,
And from the sun's flame slipped the Dog away;
675 Aquarius kindled to a flame the might
Of the strong shining one. The flame itself
Was roused up till it shook the warring ones,
And in a rage hurled them headlong to earth.
Then quickly smitten down upon the waves
680 Of ocean, it set all the earth on fire,
And the high heaven remained without a star.
(514-530.)

BOOK VI.

CONTENTS OF BOOK VI.

Pre-existence, incarnation, and baptism of the Son of God, 1–9. His teaching and his miracles, 10–25. Miseries in store for the guilty land, 26–32. The blessed cross 33–36.

BOOK VI.

THE Immortal's mighty Son, renowned in song,
Proclaim I from the heart, to whom a throne
The most high Father gave for a possession
Ere he was born; and then he was raised up,
5 In flesh given him, and washed in Jordan's stream,
Which bears with gleaming foot the waves away.
He having fled from fire first shall behold
The blessed Spirit of God descending down
With white wings of a dove.   And he shall bloom
10 A blossom pure, and all things shall burst forth.
And he will show to men the ways, will show
The heavenly paths, and with wise words teach all.
And he will lead to righteousness, and win
The hostile people, boasting a descent
15 From a celestial Father.   He will tread
The billows, and men's maladies destroy.
He will raise up the dead, and many woes
Drive far away; and from one root shall come
Enough of bread for men, when David's house
20 A scion shall bring forth, and in his hands

This book is scarcely entitled to a place among the Sibylline Oracles, or to be called a book. It is a brief hymn in honor of Christ and the cross, and probably of later date than any other portion of the present collection.

Lines 2–4. Comp. John xvii, 5.
Line 9. Comp. Matt. iii, 16.
Line 10. *Blossom pure.*—Cited by Lactantius, *Div. Inst.*, iv, 13 [L., 6, 486], and comp. Isa. xi, 1, 2, where the Septuagint reads *blossom.*
Line 15. *Tread.*—See Matt. xiv, 25.
Lines 15–19. Cited by Lactantius, *Div. Inst.*, iv, 15 [L., 6, 494].
Line 18. *Root.*—For this Lactantius reads *wallet.*
Line 20. *Scion.*—Comp. Isa. xi, 1.

(1–16.)

Shall be the whole world—land and heaven and sea.
He will flash lightning on the earth, as once
The two born from each other's sides beheld
The light appear.   And this shall come to pass
25 When earth rejoices in hope of a son.
     But for thee only, Sodomitic land,
Are miseries in store, for with fell mind
Thou didst not give attention to thy God,
Who laughs at mortal schemes, but out of thorns
30 Didst plait for him a crown, and fearful gall
In wanton insolence of spirit didst mix.
This shall bring on thee bitter miseries.
     O wood most blessed, on which God was stretched,
Earth shall not hold thee, but a heavenly house
35 Shalt thou behold, when the new form of God
Shall flash forth as the lightning into view.

Line 23. Comp. Gen. ii, 21–23.
Line 26. *Sodomitic land.*—Judea, so called on account of her wickedness.
Comp. Isa. i, 10 ; Ezek. xvi, 48, 49.
Lines 27–31. Cited by Lactantius, *Div. Inst.*, iv, 18 [L., 6, 507].
Line 33. Cited by Sozomen, *Hist. Eccl.*, ii, 1 [G., 67, 933].

(17–28.)

BOOK VII.

CONTENTS OF BOOK VII.

Woes of Rhodes, Delos, Cyprus, and Sicily, 1–8. The deluge, 9–14. Ruin of Phrygia, Ethiopia, and Egypt, 15–27. Woe of Laodicea, 28–30. Signs and powers of Messiah, 31–46. The new shoot, 47–50. Persian wars, 51–64. Fall of Ilias, 65–69. Doom of Colophon, Thessaly, Corinth, and Tyre, 70–82. Cœle-Syria accursed, 83–98. Rules for sacrifice and alms-giving, 99–125. Doom of Sardinia, Mygdonia, the Celtic land, Rome, Syria, and Thebes, 126–155. The devouring fire, 156–173. False prophets, 174–181. Long night followed by a better time, 182–196. Confession and doom of the Sibyl, 197–211.

BOOK VII.

O RHODES, thou wretched one, thee first I mourn.
Of cities first, first shalt thou be destroyed,
Bereft of men and of all means of life.
And Delos, thou shalt sail upon the sea,
5 And be unstable on the watery way.
Cyprus, a billow of thy bridal sea
Shall some time ruin thee. Thee, Sicily,
The burning fire within thee shall consume.
    *   *   *   *
Nor heed God's terrible and pleasant water.
    *   *   *   *
10 Noah, sole fugitive of all men came.
    *   *   *   *
The land shall swim, the mountains and the air
Shall also swim, all things shall water be,
And all things shall by water be destroyed.
The wind shall cease, and a second age begin.
15   O Phrygia, from the upper water first

This book is of Christian or Jewish-Christian origin, and probably belongs to the close of the second, or the early part of the third, century, A. D.
Line 1. This line is wanting in several manuscripts; in some it is appended to book vi, together with some lines of the acrostic beginning with book viii, 269. *Rhodes* is mentioned in book iv, 124. Comp. also iii, 525-531.
Line 4. *Delos.*—Comp. book iii, 429, and reff.
Line 6. *Cyprus.*—Comp. book iii, 542.
Line 7. *Sicily.*—Comp. book iv, 97.
Lines 9-14. This passage, evidently referring to the flood of Noah, is fragmentary, and closely parallel with book v, 215, 225, 228.
Line 15. *Phrygia.*—Comp. book i, 229, and note there. Comp. also iii, 164, and v, 168-170.

(1-12.)

To break forth, thou thyself shalt be the first
To deny God, being pleased with other gods,
Who shall destroy thee, miserable one,
When many rolling years shall be complete.
20 The wretched Ethiopians, suffering
By pitiable woes, and crouching down
In terror, shall be smitten by the sword.
Rich Egypt, ever caring for the corn
Which the Nile underneath his floating waves
25 Makes seven times drunk, shall perish by the strife
Of tribes with one another.   Quickly then
Will men drive Apis out, no god for men.
Woe, woe, Laodicea, daring one,
Thou shalt be false, God having never seen;
30 And Lycus' surges shall wash thee away.
  He himself, who is born the mighty God,
Shall work great signs, and in the midst of heaven
Shall hang an axle, and shall place on high
A mighty terror to be seen by men,
35 Measuring a column with an immense fire,
Whose drops shall slay the races of mankind
That have done evil.   For a time will come
When men may God appease, but put no end
To bitter sorrows; but through David's house
40 Shall all things be fulfilled.   For unto him
Has God himself given and confirmed a throne;
And messengers beneath his feet repose,
Some in the fire, some in the streams appear,
Others save cities, and some send forth winds.

Line 27. *Apis.*—The sacred bull, worshiped by the Egyptians.
Line 28. *Laodicea.*—Comp. book iii, 559–562.
Lines 33–35. *Axle . . . column.*—This idea of a column, axle, or pillar, to
be reared on high in connection with the final judgment, is peculiar to the
Sibyl. Comp. book ii, 293, 344, and 355.

45 And unto many men shall life be hard,
   Entering in souls, and changing minds of men.
      But when a new shoot from the root shall spring,
   The vast creation which he once to all
   Spread forth abundantly for nourishment,
50 And all things with the times shall be complete.
   But when strange Persians, warlike tribe, shall rule,
   The bridal chambers shall be full of fear
   Because of lawless tribes.   For her own son
   Will mother have as husband, son will harm
55 His mother, daughter couching by her sire
   Shall sleep according to barbarian law.
   But afterward to them the Roman Mars
   Shall shine forth from a multitude of spears,
   And they shall mix much land with human blood.
60 But then the chief of Italy shall flee
   From the power of the spear, and they shall leave
   Upon the land a shaft engraved in gold,
   Among the foremost fighters, evermore
   Bearing a symbol of necessity.

Line 47.   Comp. book vi, 20.

Line 51. *Persians.*—The reference is most probably to the Parthians, under the rule of the Arsacidæ.   Ewald, however, understands *Persians* here as a symbolical name for the incestuous Romans.

Line 57. *Roman Mars.*—Roman military expeditions against the Parthians.

Line 60. *Chief of Italy.*—Imperial commander of the army.   Alexandre understands the reference to be to Alexander Severus, who warred with the Parthians.

Line 62. *Shaft.*—The manuscripts read *a flower*, but without sense.   We follow the emendation of Alexandre.   The idea seems to be that the Roman forces suffered some defeat, the royal commander withdrew from the conflict, but they left upon the field and among the foremost combatants the imperial standard or ensign, ever after to be a sign of the dire necessity that forced the warlike legions of Rome to retreat.   It would, perhaps, be well to read ἀρχῆς, *dominion,* instead of ἀνάγκης, *necessity.*

(36–50.)

65   But then shall Ilias sink into the tomb,
Wicked and piteously starred by fate,
No wedding there, and brides shall deeply grieve,
Because they knew not God, but ever gave
The echo to the cymbal and the drum.
70   Consult the oracle, O Colophon;
For over thee is hanging fearful fire.
Ill-wedded Thessaly, the earth no more
Shall see thee, nor thy ashes, and alone
Escaping from the main-land thou shalt sail;
75 So, hapless one, thou shalt be war's vile filth,
Falling by means of rivers and sharp swords.
And thou, O hapless Corinth, shalt receive
Around thee heavy war, thou timid one,
And by each other ye shall be destroyed.
80 O Tyre, how much shalt thou alone receive?
For the small number of the pious men
Within thy land will scatter thee afar.
O Cœle-Syria, thou towerest high
Above Phenician men, for whom the sea
85 Of Berytas lies pouring forth abroad;
O wretched one, thou hast not known thy God,
Who once in Jordan's waters bathed himself,

Line 65. *Ilias.*—Here apparently put for all the region round about ancient Ilium or Troy, or perhaps for Perganum in the neighboring province.

Line 70. *Colophon.*—Situated a little to the north of Ephesus, and the seat of an ancient oracle of Apollo (Strabo xiv, i, 27).

Line 72. *Ill-wedded.*—Unfortunate in the marriages of the inhabitants. Comp. line 67.

Line 74. *Sail.*—Go into exile over the sea.

Line 77. *Corinth.*—Comp. book iii, 575, note; also book iv, 134.

Line 83. *Cœle-Syria.*—That part of Syria which lies between the Libanus and Antilibanus mountain ranges.

Line 85. *Berytas.*—On the Phenician sea-coast north of Zidon, the modern Beyrout. The sea of Berytas is the Mediterranean along this coast.

(51–67.)

And over whom the Spirit spread his wing;
Who, ere the earth and starry heaven were formed,
90 Was made a ruler of his Father's word,
And by the Holy Spirit put on flesh,
And quickly flew unto his Father's house.
Three towers for him the mighty heaven has fixed,
In which God's noble stewards shall abide,
95 Hope, piety, and longed-for reverence,
In gold and silver having no delight,
But in the holy reverence of men,
And sacrifices, and most righteous thoughts.
    But thou to the immortal, mighty God,
100 The lofty One, shalt offer sacrifice,
Not melting grains of frankincense in fire,
Nor smiting with the sword the shaggy lamb.
But with all such as bear thy blood, take thou
Wild fowls, and, having prayed, send them away
105 And turn thy eyes to heaven ; and thou shalt pour
On the pure fire the water, and thus cry :
"O Father, thou who didst beget the Word,
A bird have I sent thee, swift messenger
Of words, O thou Word, sprinkling thy baptism
110 With holy waters, through which from the fire
Thou didst make thyself manifest to light."
    Thou shalt not shut the door when unto thee
A stranger comes in need to keep away

Line 93. *Three towers.*—Corresponding with the three virtues named in line 95. Comp. Hermas's vision of the one tower which was explained to him as a revelation of the Church. *Hermæ Pastor*, book i, vision iii [G., 2, 899–909].

Lines 99–125. This passage contains a series of precepts which are strictly neither Jewish nor Christian. Some of the precepts suggest certain doctrines of the Essenes (comp. Josephus, *Ant.*, xviii, i, 5) ; others bear a manifest Christian character, and lines 107–111 contain allusions to the baptism of Jesus, as lines 87, 88.

Hunger of poverty, but taking hold
115 Of that man's head, and sprinkling it with water,
Pray thrice, and cry unto thy God such things :
"I ask not riches. Suppliant I received
Once openly a suppliant. Father, thou
Provider, hear; thou wilt give him that prays."
120 Then, when the man has gone, say : "Press me not,
God's sacred service, righteous, holy, free,
By which Gehenna was reproved . . .
O Father, strengthen thou my wretched heart.
To thee I look, to thee, the Undefiled,
125 Who wast not fashioned by the hands of men."
    Sardinia, weighty now, thou shalt be changed
To ashes. Thou shalt be no more an isle,
When comes a decade round. Amid the waves
Shall sailors seek thee when thou art no more,
130 And the king-fishers for thee shall lament.
    Mygdonia, rugged, inaccessible,
A watch-fire o'er the sea, thou boastest age,
And of age thou shalt perish altogether
With the hot wind, and rave with many woes.
135   O Celtic land, on thine own mountain heights,
Along the Alps so inaccessible,
Deep sand shall altogether cover thee.
Tribute shalt thou no longer give, nor corn,
Nor pasture; but thou shalt forever be
140 Deserted by the nations, frozen thick
With chilling ice, and shalt atone the wrongs
Which thou, unholy one, didst not discern.

Line 122. Lacuna in the Greek text at the end of this line.
Line 126. *Sardinia.*—Comp. book iii, 566.
Line 131. *Mygdonia.*—The well-known provinces of this name, one in Macedonia and one in Mesopotamia, do not agree well with the import of the Sibyl's language here. Perhaps it is an erroneous reading.

(87–107.)

Great-hearted Rome, thou to Olympus shalt
Flash lightning after Macedonian spears;
145 But God shall make thee utterly unknown,
When yet thou seemst more firmly to remain.
Then to thee such things I will cry aloud.
Being ruined thou wilt speak aloud, once bright
And clear. A second time to thee, O Rome,
150 Again a second time I'll speak to thee.
    And now thee, wretched Syria, piteously
Do I bewail. O Thebans ill-advised,
In you there is an evil noise, flutes play,
The trumpet sounds for you an evil note,
155 And ye shall see the entire land destroyed.
    Woe, woe to thee, thou wretched, ugly sea!
Thou shalt be utterly consumed by fire,
And thou wilt ruin people with thy brine.
For there shall be such raging fire on earth
160 As flows like water, and it shall destroy
The whole land; mountains it will set on fire,
Burn up the rivers, empty out the springs.
The world shall be disordered, men destroyed.
Then sorely burned, the wretched ones will look
165 Toward heaven, not with stars, but fire inwrought.
Not quickly do they perish, but destroyed

Line 143. *To Olympus.*—The reference seems to be to the decisive battle of Pydna on the Macedonian coast, just north of Mount Olympus, where the Romans defeated the Macedonians, and put an end to their kingdom.

Line 145. Comp. book iii, 413–428, note.

Line 150. *Again.*—Rome is repeatedly made the subject of the Sibyl's song. Comp. book viii, 45 ; ix, 325; xii, 252.

Line 152. *Thebans.*—Comp. book iv, 109. Here, however, the reference may as well be understood of Thebes in Egypt.

Line 156. *Sea.*—Comp. book v, 205. The whole passage should be compared with 2 Pet. 6, 7, 10–12.

Line 163. Cited by Lactantius, *Div. Inst.*, vii, 16 [L., 6, 792].

(108–126.)

8

Under the flesh and burning in the spirit
For endless years, they will know that God's law
Is hard to prove, and cannot be deceived.
170 And then earth shall be taken by violence,
Whatever god she daringly set forth
Upon the altars, and shall be deceived
By the smoke through the air, producing woes.
　But they shall bear much longing, who for gain
175 Prophesy shameless things and lengthen out
The evil time ; who, clothed in shaggy skins
Of sheep, themselves as Hebrews falsely pass,
Which race they have no part in, but with words
Constantly talking, misers in their woes,
180 They will change customs, and will not persuade
The just, who through the heart propitiate God.
　But in the third lot of revolving years,
The eighth, first shall another world appear.
And there shall be a long unyielding night.
185 And then shall pass around a dreadful stench
Of brimstone, messenger of homicides,
When men by night and hunger shall be killed.
Then a pure mind will he beget in men,
And will establish thy race as it was
190 To thee aforetime.　No more shall one cut
Deep furrows with the plow, nor oxen sink
The guiding iron downward; nor shall vines
Nor ears of corn be seen, but all shall eat
The dewy manna with their fair white teeth.
195 With them then also God himself shall be,

Lines 182, 183. *Third lot . . . eighth, first.*—The idea intended by these
peculiar designations of time is not apparent.

Line 184. Lacuna in the Greek text of this line.

Line 189. *Thy race.*—Jewish race ; a millennial conception of Jewish
restoration and glory.

(127–150.)

And teach them, as he taught me, doleful one.
For O, how many evils once I did
Knowingly! Also many other things
I wickedly and carelessly performed.
200 Countless my couches, but no marriage bond
Concerned me, and to all a savage oath
I rashly brought. The needy I shut out,
And among those who went to the like glen
I went, and did not heed the voice of God.
205 Therefore did fire devour me, and shall gnaw,
For I myself shall not live, but a time
Of evil shall destroy me. Then will men
Make me a grave, passing me by the sea
And killing me with stones. For with my sire
210 A dear son share I. Stone me, stone me, all;
For thus shall I live, and fix eyes on heaven.

Line 207. *Destroy me.*—Had Arnobius this passage in mind when he
wrote: "If the Sibyl, when she was uttering her prophecies and oracular
responses, and was filled with Apollo's power, had been cut down and slain
by impious robbers, would Apollo have been slain in her?" *Adv. Gentes,*
book i, 62 [L., 5, 802]. Comp. the conclusion of book ii.
(151–162.)

.

BOOK VIII.

CONTENTS OF BOOK VIII.

Introduction, 1–6. Oracle for Italy, 7–20. Lust of gain, 21–44. Doom of Rome, 45–60. The gray-haired prince, 61–80. The three rulers, 81–90. Misery of Rome, 91–110. Final judgment of Rome, 111–134. Dirge over Rome, 135–166. The sixth race of Latin kings, 167–175. Fifth appearance of the phenix, 176–179. Fall of Rome, 180–189. The destroyer destroyed, 190–201. Woes of Rhodes, Thebes, Egypt, Rome, Delos, Samos, and the Persians, 202–210. The Messianic king, 211–213. The day of evil and of doom, 214–240. The Sibyl's wish, 241–246. The end of all things, 247–267. Christian acrostic concerning the last day, 268–309. Moses a type of the Messiah, 310–316. The Messianic Saviour portrayed, 317–356. The crucifixion, 357–387. Entrance into Hades and resurrection, 388–403. Exhortation to honor the Messianic king, 404–421. Another picture of the day of doom, 422–447. Self-declaration of the Creator, 448–493. His appeal to idolaters, 494–508. Christian precepts, warnings, and promises, 509–544. The heavenly Ruler, 545–553. Creator of man and of all things, 554–577. The incarnation of the Word, 578–610. Additional Christian precepts, 611–635.

BOOK VIII.

God's revelations of great wrath to come
In the last time upon the faithless world,
I make known, prophesying to all men
According to their cities, from that time
5 When the great tower fell, and the tongues of men
Were parted into many dialects.
First of the Egyptian kingdom did I speak,
Then that of Persians, Ethiopians, Medes,
And also of Assyrian Babylon,
10 Then the great pride of Macedonia;
Now am I into the dominion sent
Of celebrated lawless Italy.
At last unto all mortals will it show
Manifold evils, and exhaust the toils
15 Of men of every land. And to the West
Will it the warrior king of nations lead,
Give laws to peoples, and subdue all things.
Late will the mills of God grind the fine flour.
Fire then will ruin all things, and to dust
20 Reduce the summits of the leafy hills,
And all flesh. Love of gain and want of mind
Of evils a beginning are to all;

This book is obviously of Christian origin, composed of various fragments, and probably not earlier than the beginning of the third century.

Lines 1–4. Cited by Lactantius, *de Ira Dei*, xxiii [L., 7, 143].

Line 5. *Tower.*—Comp. book iii, 114–126, notes.

Lines 7–9. Comp. book iii, 186–189, 197–205, 240–245, 356–359.

Line 18. A proverb found also in Plutarch, *de Sera Num. Vind.,* and Sextus Empiricus, *Contra Mathem.,* i, 13.

Lines 21, 22. Comp. 1 Tim. vi, 10.

(1–17.)

For of deceitful gold and silver springs
Longing desire, for nothing mortals deem
25 Better than these, not the sun's light, nor heaven,
Nor sea, nor the broad earth whence all things grow,
Nor God who gives all things, Maker of all;
Nor faith, nor piety do they prefer.
Source of impiety, confusion's guide,
30 A means of wars, an enemy of peace,
Is want of understanding, setting fathers
At enmity with sons, and sons with fathers.
And marriage in comparison with gold
Will have no honor. Borders land will have,
35 And guards each sea, divided craftily
For all that have gold, so that evermore
Those wishing it possess the nursing earth.
They waste the poor, that they themselves more land
Procuring may enslave them by deceit.
40 And if the huge earth from the starry heaven
Held not her throne afar, even light to men
Had not been equal, but, being bought with gold,
Had by the rich been owned, and for the poor
God must have then prepared another world.
45 On thee some day shall come, O haughty Rome,
A fitting stroke from heaven, and thou the first
Shalt bend the neck, be leveled to the earth,
And fire shall utterly consume thee, beat
Upon thy pavements, and thy wealth shall perish,
50 And on thy site shall wolves and foxes dwell.
And then shalt thou become all desolate
As though thou hadst not been. Where then will be
Palladium ? What God will keep thee safe,
Whether of gold or stone or brass ? Or then
55 Where the decrees of thy assembly ? Where

Line 53. *Palladium.*—Image of Minerva in the temple of Vesta at Rome.
(18–45.)

Rhea, or Kronos, or the race of Jove,
And all those whom thou didst once hold in awe,
Demons without life, phantoms of the dead,
The boast of whose tomb ill-starred Crete shall have,
60 Worshiping thrones of the unconscious dead ?
    When thou hast had thrice five voluptuous kings,
And hast enslaved the world from east to west,
A gray-haired prince shall rise, bearing the name
Of the near sea, and with polluted foot
65 Will he survey the world, and gifts obtain,
And have vast sums of gold, and gather up
Of hateful silver more, and having stripped
[The peoples], he will then again return.
And in all mysteries will he partake
70 Of Magian shrines, show forth a child as god,
Abolish all things sacred, and disclose
To all from the first the mysteries of deceit.
Sad then will be the time when he himself,
Sad one, shall perish. And the populace
75 Some time will say: " O city, thy great power
Has fallen, knowing that an evil day
Staightway is coming." Then shall weep together
Fathers and infant children, when they see
Before them thy most lamentable fate.
80 Woe, woe, they wail by Tiber's mournful banks.
    After him at the last shall three bear rule
And fill the name out of the God of heaven,

Lines 58, 59. Cited by Lactantius, *Div. Inst.*, book i, xi [L., 6, 179].
Line 61. *Thrice five.*—Emperors from Julius to Hadrian; a round number, but inexact. Comp. the first part of book v.
Line 63. *Gray-haired prince.*—Hadrian. Comp. book v, 65.
Line 70. *Child as god.*—Reference to the beautiful youth Antinous, whom Hadrian sought to deify.
Line 81. *Three.*—The Antonines. See book v, 70.
Line 82. *Name.*—Allusion probably to the Hebrew name *Adonai*, which it was thought to resemble.

(45–66.)

8*

Whose power now is and shall be evermore.
And one, an old man, very long will wield
85 The scepter, a most pitiable king,
Who all the treasures of the world shall guard,
And shut up in his houses, that when comes
The matricidal fugitive again
From the earth's ends, having given these things to all,
90 Vast wealth on Asia he will then bestow.
   And then shalt thou weep, having put aside
The glory of the ruler's purple robe,
And put on mourning garments, O proud realm,
Offspring of Latin Rome. No more to thee
95 Shall be the glory of thy lofty mien,
Nor shalt thou, hapless, ever be raised up,
But prostrate shalt thou lie; for even the glory
Of eagle-bearing legions shall fall down.
Where then thy power? What land will be ally,
100 O thou who hast been lawlessly enslaved
By thine own follies? For through all the earth
There will be then confusion of mankind,
When the Almighty, coming to the throne,
Shall judge the souls of living and of dead,
105 And all the world. And parents will not be
Dear to their children, nor will children be
To parents, on account of wickedness
And unexpected trouble. Then to thee
Shall gnashing, capture, and dispersion come,
110 Cities shall fall and earth be rent in chasms.
   When thus upon the billows there shall come
A dragon bearing fire, and full within,
And shall afflict thy children, there shall be

Line 84. *Old man.*—Antoninus Pius.
Line 88. *Fugitive.*—Nero. Comp. book v, 38.
Line 112. *Dragon.*—Allusion to Rev. xii, 17; xiii, 1.
(67–89.)

Famine and tribal war, and near at hand
115 Is the end of the world, and the last day
And judgment of the immortal God for such
As are both called and chosen. First of all
Inexorable wrath shall fall on Rome;
A time of blood and wretched life shall come.
120 Woe, woe to thee, O land of Italy,
Great, barbarous nation; thou didst not perceive
Whence naked and unworthy thou didst come
To the sun's light, that to that place again
Naked thou shouldst return, and then come forth
125 To judgment, as one who unjustly judged.
With hands gigantic coming from on high
Alone through all the world, thou shalt abide
Under the earth. By naphtha and asphalt
And sulphur and much fire thou utterly
130 Shalt disappear, and be as burning dust
Forever, and all who behold shall hear
From Hades an exceeding mournful wail,
And gnashing of teeth, and with thine own hands
Thou wilt forever beat thy godless breast.
135   To all alike there shall be equal night,
To rich and poor; naked they came from earth
And naked into earth again they go.
They grow, complete their time, and cease from life.
No slave, nor lord, nor tyrant will be there,
140 Nor king, nor leader, filled with vain conceit.
No legal advocate, nor magistrate
Judging for money; nor do they pour out
The blood of sacrifices in libations
Upon the altars. Not a drum will sound,
145 Nor cymbal, nor the perforated flute

Line 125. Lacuna in Greek text after this line.
Lines 135, 136. Comp. Job i, 21.
(90–114.)

Of frenzied tone, nor sound of pipe like that
Of crooked dragon; nor the barbarous trumpet
The harbinger of wars, nor drunken men
In lawless revels, nor in choral dances,
150 Nor sound of lyre; no instrument of evil,
Nor strife, nor wrath of various kind, nor sword
Is with the dead, but unto all alike
Eternity is keeper of the key
Of the great prison for God's judgment-seat.
155 With images of gold and silver and stone
Be ready, that unto the bitter day
Ye may come, thy first punishment, O Rome,
Even a gnashing anguish to behold.
And no more under slavish yoke to thee
160 Will either Greek or Syrian put his neck,
Barbarian or any other nation.
Thou shalt be plundered and shalt be destroyed
For what thou didst, and wailing loud in fear
Thou shalt give until thou shalt all repay.
165 And thou shalt be a triumph for the world,
Also a matter of reproach for all.
   And then the sixth race of the Latin kings
At last end life, and lay the scepter down.
From the same race another king shall reign,
170 Rule the whole earth and hold the scepter firm;
And he shall govern with untrammeled power
And by the counsels of the mighty God.

Line 154. Lacuna after this verse in Greek text; some think it may be supplied from book iii, 67–69.

Line 167. *Sixth race.*—That of the Antonines, best reckoned probably as Alexandre: (1) The Cæsars, (2) the Flavii, (3) Nerva, (4) Trajan, (5) Hadrian, (6) the Antonines.

Line 169. *Another king.*—The exact reference here is doubtful, but probably Septimius Severus is intended, as sprung from the same Latin race. Alexandre suspects this and the four following lines as an interpolation.

(115–135.)

Sons and a race of stable sons are his,
For thus it is decreed, as time rolls on,
175 When there shall be of Egypt thrice five kings.
　　Thence when the phenix the fifth time appears,
He will come pillaging a race of people,
A countless tribe, the nation of the Hebrews.
　　Then Mars will plunder Mars, and he himself
180 Shall the presumptuous threats of Rome destroy.
Perished the power of Rome, once flourishing,
Along with ancient kings of neighboring cities.
No longer will the plain of fertile Rome
Prevail, when out of Asia comes with Mars
185 One bearing rule; and having wrought all this
He afterwards will in the city come.
　　And thrice three hundred eight and forty years
Shalt thou in full complete, when ill-starred fate
Shall seize upon thee, finishing thy name.
190 　　Alas for me, me, the thrice wretched one!
When shall I see that day of thine, O Rome—
Thine, but most for all Latins? Honor him
If thou wilt, who ascends the Trojan car,
As by a secret birth from Asia's land,

Line 175. *Thrice five.*—The same as those referred to in line 61.

Line 176. *Phenix.*—Fabulous Egyptian bird, said to appear once in five hundred years. See Herod., ii, 73; Pliny, *Nat. Hist.*, x, 2; Clem. Rom., 1 *Cor.*, xxv [G., 1, 261–275]. According to Tacitus (*Annal.*, vi, 28) the fourth appearance of the phenix occurred in the reign of Tiberius.

Line 185. *One bearing rule.*—The matricidal fugitive of line 88, returning as antichrist. This whole passage is apocalyptic, and no exact conformity to history need be sought.

Line 187. The number 948 is the numerical value of the Greek letters in the name Rome (ρ—100, ω—800, μ—40, η—8,— $P\acute{\omega}\mu\eta$). Nine hundred and forty-eight years after the founding of Rome extends to about 196 of our era, and the reign of Septimius Severus.

Line 190. *Wretched.*—Comp. book v, 71, and the close of book vii.

Line 194. *From Asia's land.*—Another allusion to Nero. His ascending the Trojan car is metaphorical of his supposed coming with war chariots from the east, and all the force and fury of Mars. Comp. lines 179–186.

(136–154)

195 Having a soul of fire. But when he smites
The isthmus, peering eagerly around,
Going to all and passing through the sea,
Then will black blood go after the great beast,
And a dog chase the lion which destroys
200 The shepherds. But his scepter they will take,
And into Hades he will pass away.

   The last but greatest ill shall come to Rhodes.
And base captivity yet waits for Thebes.
Egypt shall perish by her ruler's baseness.
205 But those men who escaped the utter ruin—
Thrice blessed, four times blessed, was each man!
And Rome shall be a room, and Delos dull,
And Samos sand. . . .
Later shall evil on the Persians come
210 For their pride, and all insolence shall perish.

   And then a holy king o'er all the earth
And to all ages shall the scepter wield,
Having risen from the dead. A piteous fate
Will then the Most High bring on those at Rome,
215 And on all men, and all within these bounds
Shall perish. But they will not be persuaded
Of what much better is. But when for all
The evil day of famine and of plague
Shall come on, and of uproar hard to bear,

Line 196. *Isthmus.*—Comp. book v, 43, 181.

Line 199. *Dog chase lion.*—Comp. book xii, 19, 20. The meaning is not clear, owing, probably, to the corrupt condition of the Greek text.

Line 201. *Into Hades.*—Comp. Rev. xvii, 8, 11.

Line 202. *Rhodes.*—Comp. book iv, 124; and iii, 525–531.

Line 203. *Thebes.*—Comp. book v, 246–252.

Line 204. *Ruler's baseness.*—Comp. book v, 23, 24.

Lines 207, 208. Comp. book iii, 429, 430. Lacuna in last line.

Line 209. *Persians.*—Put for Parthians, as in book vii, 51.

Line. 211. *Holy King.*—The Messiah.

(155–175.)

220 Even then again that former daring prince,
Having convened the council, shall forthwith
Take counsel with them how he may destroy.

    *   *   *   *   *

Blight shall appear along with flowers and leaves,
And heaven's base shall display on the firm rock
225 Rain-storm and fire, and much wind on the land,
And over all the earth a multitude
Of poisonous sowings. Yet again they'll work
With shameless soul, nor fear the wrath of God,
Nor that of man. Forsaking modesty
230 They will choose shame, become tyrannical
And violent transgressors, liars too,
Lovers of unbelief, evil-doers,
Untrue, faith-killers, pouring out foul speech
In false words; no sufficiency of wealth
235 Will they have, but will basely gather more.
Subject to tyrants, they will be destroyed.

    The stars shall all fall down into the sea,
Many stars one by one, and the bright star
Men call a comet is a sign of evil,
240 Of much war and calamity to come.

    Let me not live when the gay one shall reign,
But then, when heavenly grace shall rule within,
And when a holy child the murderous guile   -
Of all shall utterly destroy with chains,

Line 220. *Former daring prince.*—Same as the one referred to in lines 193–197.

Line 222. After this verse there seems to be a lacuna.

Lines 223–236. A dark picture of the last times, and quite parallel with such Scriptures as 1 Tim. iv, 1, 2; 2 Tim. iii, 1–9.

Line 237. *Stars . . . fall.*—Comp. Matt. xxiv, 29, and book ii, 249, v, 681, and Lactantius, *Div. Inst.*, vii, 16 [L., 6, 791, 792].

Line 241. *Gay one.*—The same probably as the woman described in lines 248–251, and also in book iii, 89–95, where see note.

Lines 243, 244. *Holy child . . . with chains.*—Apparent allusion to Rev. xx, 1–3.   (176–197.)

245 Opening the baleful deep and suddenly
The house of wood shall cover mortals round.
But when the tenth generation shall go down
To Hades, then shall come the mighty power
Of one of female sex; and God himself
250 Will permit many evils to increase,
When she with royal honor crowns herself;
And all the year will be how like an age!
The parched sun running onward nightly shines,
The stars will leave the heaven; and rushing on
255 With a strong tempest, he will waste the earth.
And there shall be a rising of the dead;
The lame shall swiftly run, the deaf shall hear,
The blind shall see, those who spoke not shall speak,
And life and wealth shall be alike to all.
260 The land the same for all, divided not
By walls or fences, shall more fruits produce,
And fountains of sweet wine, and of white milk,
And honey he will give . . .

   *   *   *   *

And judgment of the immortal God. . . .
265 But when the seasons God shall change, . . .
Winter producing summer, then oracles [will all be fulfilled].
But when the world has perished. . . .

Line 247. *Tenth generation.*—Supposed by the Sibyl to be the last. Comp. lines 167–189.

Line 249. *Female.*—The woman symbolically portrayed in Rev. xvii, 1–6. Comp. book iii, 89, note.

Lines 257, 258. Comp. book i, 414, 415.

Lines 261–263. Comp. book iii, 740–743, and Lactantius, *Div. Inst.*, vii, 24 [L, 6, 811]. What follows between these lines and the acrostic is fragmentary. The remaining words, translated in our text, show that the general subject was that of judgment of God and the end of the world.

Line 266. *Winter . . . summer.*—Cited in Lactantius, *Div. Inst.*, vii, 16 [L, 6, 792]. *Oracles.*—This line appears in full, book xii, 363–364.
(197–216.)

JESUS CHRIST, SON OF GOD, SAVIOUR, CROSS.

Earth will sweat when the judgment sign appears,
And the eternal King will come from heaven
270 In person to judge all flesh and all the world.
The faithful and the faithless shall see God
Exalted with the saints at the end of time.
The souls of fleshly men upon his throne

Lines 268–309. This passage is celebrated as being an acrostic of thirty-four lines in the Greek text, the first letters of which lines form the title given above, namely, JESUS CHRIST, GOD'S SON, SAVIOUR, CROSS. It is quoted in full by Eusebius in his report of Constantine's Oration to the Assembly of the Saints, xviii [G., 20, 1288, 1289], and, excepting the seven lines representing the word CROSS, by Augustine, *de Civitate Dei*, xviii, 23 [L., 41, 579], we give in our text a faithful translation of the Greek without any attempt to transfer it into a corresponding English acrostic. The English reader, however, may be pleased to compare the following version found in Dodd's translation of Augustine's *City of God*, vol. iii, pp. 242, 243 (Edinb., 1878).

I   Judgment shall moisten the earth with the sweat of its standard,
H   Ever enduring, behold the king shall come through the ages,
Σ   Sent to be here in the flesh, and judge at the last of the world.
O   O God, the believing and faithless alike shall behold thee
Υ   Uplifted with saints, when at last the ages are ended,
Σ   Sisted before him are souls in the flesh for his judgment.

X   Hid in thick vapors, the while desolate lieth the earth,
P   Rejected by men are the idols and long hidden treasures;
E   Earth is consumed by the fire, and it searcheth the ocean and
      heaven;
I   Issuing forth, it destroyeth the terrible portals of hell.
Σ   Saints in their body and soul freedom and light shall inherit;
T   Those who are guilty shall burn in fire and brimstone forever.
O   Occult actions revealing, each one shall publish his secrets;
Σ   Secrets of every man's heart God shall reveal in the light.

Θ   Then shall be weeping and wailing, yea, and gnashing of teeth;
E   Eclipsed is the sun, and silenced the stars in their chorus.
O   Over and gone is the splendor of moonlight, melted the heaven.
Υ   Uplifted by him are the valleys, and cast down the mountains.
(217–222.)

He will judge, when the whole world is laid waste,
275 And thorns spring up.   And men will cast away
Their idols and all wealth.   And searching fire
Will burn the land, the heaven and the sea;
And burn the gates of Hades' prison-house.
Then to the free light of the saints shall come
280 All the flesh of the dead, but lawless ones
The fire will try forever.   Every thing
One did in secret will he then declare,
For dark breasts God will open to the light.
Wailing will come from all, and gnashing of teeth;
285 The brightness of the sun will be eclipsed,
And the dances of the stars; the heaven shall whirl.
And the moon's beaming luster be destroyed.
He will exalt the valleys and destroy
The heights of hills, and no more shall appear
290 A gloomy height among men.   With the plains
The mountains will be level, and no more
Will there be any sailing on the sea.
For earth with springs shall be by thunder parched,
And dashing streams shall fail.   The trump from heaven
295 Shall send a woful sound, and bellow forth

Υ   Utterly gone among men are distinctions of lofty and lowly.
Ι   Into the plains rush the hills, the skies and oceans are mingled.
Ο   O, what an end of all things! earth broken in pieces shall perish;
Σ   Swelling together at once shall the waters and flames flow in rivers.

Σ   Sounding, the archangel's trumpet shall peal down from heaven,
Ω   Over the wicked who groan in their guilt and their manifold
       sorrows.
Τ   Trembling, the earth shall be opened, revealing chaos and hell.
Η   Every king before God shall stand in that day to be judged.
Ρ   Rivers of fire and brimstone shall fall from the heavens.
Lines 275-276.   Cited by Lactantius, *Div. Inst.*, vii, 19 [L, 6, 798].
Lines 294-295.   Cited by Lactantius, *Div. Inst.*, vii, 16 [L, 6, 792].
(223-239.)

Approaching pest and sorrows of the world.
And then the widely-yawning earth will show
Tartarean chaos, and all kings shall come
Unto God's judgment-seat. From heaven shall flow
300 A stream of fire and brimstone. But the Wood
Shall then be to all mortals for a sign,
Among the faithful a distinguished seal,   ˙˙
The longed-for horn, the life of pious men,
But the world's stumbling-block, bestowing light
305 On the elect by water in twelve streams.
And then the shepherd-rod of iron shall rule.
This one now in acrostics written down
Is our God, Saviour, and immortal King,
Even the one who suffered for our sake.
310   Whom Moses typified, when he stretched out
Holy arms, conquering Amalek by faith,
In order that the people may know him
To be elect and honored before God,
The rod of David, and the very stone
315 Which he indeed once promised, and in whom
He who believes shall have eternal life.
For not in glory, but as mortal man

Lines 297–299. Cited by Lactantius, *Div. Inst.*, vii, 20 [L., 6, 798].

Line 300. *Wood.*—The cross. Comp. book vi, 33–36.

Line 301. *Sign.*—According to Chrysostom, Cyril, Hilary, Augustine, Jerome, and other fathers, "the sign of the Son of man" in Matt. xxiv, 30, was a cross appearing in the heavens.

Line 302. *Seal.*—Comp. line 379 and note.

Line 303. *Horn.*—Comp. Psa. cxxxii, 17; Luke i, 69.

Line 304. *Stumbling-block.*—Comp. Gal. v, 11.

Line 306. *Rod.*—Comp. Psa. ii, 9; Lev. ii, 27; xii, 5.

Line 310. *Moses.*—See Exod. xvii, 8–12.

Line 314. *Rod of David.*—Same as shepherd-rod in line 306. *Stone.*—Comp. book i, 406; Isa. xxviii, 16; Zech. iii, 9; Matt. xxi, 42.

Line 316. Comp John iii, 36.

Line 317. *Not in glory.*—Obvious reference to the first advent of Christ, his incarnation. Comp. John iii, 18–21.

(240–256.)

Shall he come unto judgment, pitiable,
Dishonored, without beauty, that he might
320 Give hope to them that mourn; and he will give
Form to corruptible flesh, and heavenly faith
To those without faith, and entirely change
Man who was fashioned by the hand of God,
And whom the serpent craftily deceived
325 To go away unto the fate of death,
And gain a knowledge of the good and bad,
And so, forsaking God, serve mortal ways.
For taking him at first as counselor,
From the beginning, the Almighty said:
330 "O child, forthwith let us make, both of us,
Forming from our own image, mortal tribes;
I with my hands and thou then with the Word
Shalt serve our form, that we may give to it
A common origin. Keeping in mind
335 This purpose, into judgment he will come:
And to a holy virgin he will bear
An antitypal copy, giving light
By water through the elder's hands, by word
Doing all things, and healing all disease.
340 His word shall stay the winds, and with his feet
He'll calm the raging sea, and walk thereon
In peace and faith. And with five loaves of bread
And one fish of the sea, in a desert place
Will he of men four thousand satisfy;
345 And taking all the fragments which remain,

Lines 318–320. Cited by Lactantius, *Div. Inst.,* iv, 16 [L., 6, 498].

Line 328. *Counselor.*—Comp. Prov. viii, 14, 22–31, and Lactantius, *Div. Inst.,* iv, 6 [L., 6, 463].

Line 330. *Let us make.*—Allusion to Gen. i, 26.

Line 338. *Elder's hands.*—Allusion probably to John iv, 2, where it is said that Jesus himself did not baptize, but left that to his disciples.

Lines 340–346. Comp. book i, 417–420.

(256–277.)

Twelve baskets he will fill for the people's hope.
And he will call the souls of blessed ones,
And love the sorrowful, who being mocked
Will render good for evil, beaten, scourged,
350 Yet ever longing after poverty.
Knowing, beholding, hearing every thing,
The heart he will discern, and lay it bare
Unto conviction. For of all things he
Is hearing, mind, and vision, and the Word,
355 Who made all forms, to whom all things give ear;
The dead he saves, and healeth all disease.

At last into the hands of lawless men
And faithless he will come, and they will give
With hands unholy blows as against God,
360 And poisonous spittle from polluted mouths.
And he will give his holy back to scourges
[For he himself shall give unto the world
A holy virgin], and silent he remains
Under the scourge, lest any one should know
365 Who or of whom he is, or whence he came,
In order that he may speak to the dead.
And he will also wear a crown of thorns,
For out of thorns shall ever come the crown
Of holy ones elect. And with a reed
370 According to their laws they'll pierce his side,
For from reeds by another spirit moved
Was he brought up for judgments of the soul,
And wrath and recompense. But when these things
Which I have spoken shall all be fulfilled,
375 Unto him then shall every law be loosed,
Which from the first by the decrees of men

Line 348. *Sorrowful.*—Others read *enemies.*

Lines 357-361. These lines, and also 363-367, are cited by Lactantius,
Div. Inst., iv, 18 [L, 6, 506].

(278-303.)

Was given because of disobedient people.
He will spread out his hands and all the world
Will measure.   Gall for food, and vinegar
380 For drink, they gave him ; they shall dearly pay
The price of this inhospitable board.
The temple's veil is rent, and in midday
For three hours shall a monstrous night prevail.
For when the eternal Ruler came on earth,
385 It was again shown, what had been concealed
From the thought of the world, that men no more
Should serve the secret temple and the law.
And he shall come to Hades, and announce
To all the saints hope, the end of the ages,
390 And the last day ; and death's lot he will end,
The third day sleeping, and then from the dead
Freeing himself he will come into light,
First having shown the power of the resurrection
To the elect, washed from their former sin
395 By means of water from the immortal spring,
That, being born again, they might no more

Line 379. *Measure.*—"In his suffering," says Lactantius, "he stretched
forth his hands and measured out the world, that even then he might show
that a great multitude, collected out of all languages and tribes, from the
rising of the sun even to the setting, was about to come under his wings
and to receive on their foreheads that great and lofty sign." *Div. Inst.*, iv,
26 [L., 6, 530].

Lines 382, 383. Cited by Lactantius, *Div. Inst.*, iv, 19 [L., 6, 511].

Line 388. *To Hades.*—This doctrine of Christ's descent into Hades is found
in the well-known clause of the Apostles' Creed, and claims for its biblical
support the language of Psa. xvi, 9 (comp. Acts ii, 25–27); Rom. x, 7;
Eph. iv, 8–10; 1 Pet. iii, 18–20.   It is found also in Justin Martyr, *Trypho*,
72 [G., 6, 645]; Irenæus, *Adv. Hær.*, iii, xx, 4 [G., 7, 945]; and iv, xxvii, 2
[G., 7, 1058]; Clem. Alex., *Strom.*, vi, chap. vi [G., 9, 265–275]; Tertullian,
de Anima, chaps. vii [L., 2, 657] and lv [L., 2, 742–745]; Origen, *adv. Celsus*,
ii, 43 [G., 11, 864].

Lines 390–393. Cited by Lactantius, *Div. Inst.*, iv, 19 [L., 6, 513].

Line 396. *Born again.*—Comp. John iii, 5.

(304–316.)

Serve the unlawful customs of the world.
First to his own will then the Lord appear
In the flesh as he was before, and show
400 In hands and feet four marks fixed in his limbs,
As if for east and west, and north and south ;
For even so many kingdoms of the world
Shall consummate this lawless, blameful deed.
    Daughter of Zion, holy one, rejoice.
405 Thou who hast suffered many things, thy King,
Mounted upon a foal is entering in,
Appearing meek to all, that he may wrest
The slavish yoke so heavy, under which
We are enthralled, and which lies on our neck,
410 And loose the godless laws and powerful bonds.
Know thou thy God, him who is Son of God,
Giving him glory, and within thy breast
Holding him cherished; love him from the soul
And bear his name.   The former deeds put off,
415 And loose them by his blood, for by thy songs
And by thy prayers he will not be appeased.
Nor unto perishable sacrifices
Will he give heed, being imperishable,
But rather he delights in sacred song
420 Of holy mouth, proceeding from the soul.
Know who he is, and thou shalt see thy Maker.
    Then shall the elements of all the world
Be desolate, air, earth, sea, flaming fire,
And sky and night, and all days to one fire
425 And to one barren, shapeless mass shall come.

Line 401. Comp. book iii, 30, note.
Line 404. *Rejoice.*—Comp. Zech. ix, 9; Matt. xxi, 5; John xii, 15.
Lines 407–409. Cited by Lactantius, *Div. Inst.*, vii, 18 [L, 6, 796].
Lines 422–440. Comp. similar passage in book ii, 242–260, and book iii, 96–108; and also Lactantius, *Div. Inst.*, vii, 16 [L, 6, 791, 792].   All these prophecies are obviously derived from corresponding Scripture passages.
(317–340.)

For all the luminous stars shall fall from heaven ;
No more will winged birds fly through the air,
Nor footstep be on earth ; for all wild beasts
Shall perish, voices of men, beasts, and birds
430 Shall be no more. The world, being disarranged,
Shall hear no useful sound, but the deep sea
Shall echo back a mighty threatening noise,
And swimming, trembling creatures of the sea
Shall all die ; and no longer on the waves
435 Will sail a freighted ship. The earth shall groan
Blood-stained by wars ; and all the souls of men
Shall gnash their teeth—the souls of lawless men,
Wasted by lamentations and by fear,
By hunger, thirst, and pestilence and murders—
440 And they shall call it beautiful to die,
And death will flee from them, for death no more
Nor night shall give them rest. And many things
Will they in vain ask God who rules on high.
And then he will turn openly his face
445 Away from them. [For he gave seven ages,
Days of repentance unto mortal men,
Fashioned by means of a holy virgin's hand.]
    All these things to my mind did God reveal,
And all that has been spoken by my mouth
450 Will he fulfill. The number of the sands,
And measured spaces of the sea I know.
I know the secret places of the earth,
And gloomy Tartarus, and men who are,

Line 441. *Death will flee.*—Comp. Rev. ix, 6.
Lines 445–447. Comp. book ii, 371, 372.
    Line 450. At this point the Sibyl assumes to represent God himself as speaking, and continues this strain to line 544, throwing in occasional observations of her own, as if forgetful of the part she holds. Lines 350, 351, and 472, 473, are identical with two lines attributed to the oracle of Delphi by Herodotus, i, 47.

And who shall be hereafter, and the dead.
455 I know the numbers of the stars and trees,
    And all the species of the quadrupeds,
    And swimming things, and birds that fly aloft.
    For I myself the forms and mind of men
    Have fashioned, and right reason have bestowed,
460 And taught them knowledge. I who see and hear
    Formed eyes and ears ; and I observe each thought,
    And have myself a knowledge of all things,
    Silent a while, and afterward reproving,
    And punishing whatever any man
465 Has done in secret. On God's judgment-seat
    I also come to speak with mortal men.
    Also the dumb I understand, and hear
    The one who speaks not, and I know how great
    The entire height from earth to heaven is.
470 And the beginning and the end I know,
    Who am Creator of the heaven and earth.
    [For all is from him, first and last he knows.]
    For I alone am God, and other God
    There is not. They my image deify,
475 Obtained from wood and fashioned by the hand
    Into dumb idols, which they glorify
    With supplications and unholy rites.
    Forsaking the Creator, they become
    Servants of insolence. But holding still
480 To him, they sacrifice their useless gifts,
    And as if honoring him, they deem these things
    All useful, filling feasts with smell of flesh,
    As if to their own dead. For they burn flesh
    And marrow bones, on altars sacrifice,
485 To demons pour out blood, and kindle lights
    For me who give light; and men pour out wine,

Line 473. Cited by Lactantius, *Div. Inst.,* i, 6 [L., 6, 148].
(363–387.)

9

As to a thirsty god !   Unto no purpose
They become drunken over useless gods.
   I have no need of your burnt offerings,
490 Nor your libations, nor polluted smoke,
Nor odious blood.   For these things will men do
In memory of tyrants and of kings
Unto dead demons as though they were heavenly,
Performing godless and destructive rites.
495 And, godless, they their images call gods,
Forsaking the Creator, and from them
Imagine they derive all hope and life,
Though they are deaf and without power to speak,
Faithful for evil, ignorant all of good.
500 Two ways have I myself before them placed,
Of life and death, and counsel I have given
A good life to prefer; but they themselves
Laid hold on death and on eternal fire.
   Man, having upright reason, is my image
505 For him a table pure and without blood
Make ready and with good things fill it up.
Give to the hungry bread, to the thirsty drink,
And to the body that is naked clothes,
From thine own labors and with holy hands
510 Providing.   Raise up the afflicted, stand
Beside the weary, for the living One
Provide and bring this living sacrifice.
Sow thou in piety that I may give
These things to thee ; immortal fruits and light
515 Eternal thou shalt have, and fadeless life,
When I put all things to the proof with fire.
For I will melt down all things and select
For purity.   I will roll up the heaven,

Line 501. *Life and death.*—Comp. Deut. xxx, 15, 19, and also the opening
words of the "Teaching of the Twelve Apostles."
   Lines 518–523. Cited by Lactantius, *Div. Inst.*, vii, 20 [L., 6, 799].
(388–413.)

And open wide the caverns of the earth.

520 And then will I raise up the dead, and loose
The lot and sting of death ; and afterward
For judgment I will come and judge the life
Of pious and of impious men, and place
Goat opposite to goat, and shepherd to shepherd,

525 And calf to calf, convicting one another.
Whoever will exalt themselves shall be
By proofs condemned, and those who stopped each
mouth,
That they themselves, being full of jealousy,
Might thus enslave such as were doing right,

530 Commanding silence, urged by love of gain. ˙
And then the approved shall all have place by me.
No longer in affliction wilt thou say,
" To-morrow shall be, and yet it is not ;
Yesterday has been." No long days of care,

535 Nor spring, nor summer, nor the winter cold,
Nor autumn, nor the sunset and sunrise.
For I will make a long day, and the light,
The great and longed-for light of Jesus Christ,
Shall be forever and for evermore. . . .

540   The Self-begotten, Undefiled, Eternal,
Dwelling in heaven and measuring with his power
The fiery blast, who also holdeth fast
The clashing scepter with ferocious fire,
And calms the rolling thunder's crashing noise,

545 He shakes the earth and holds the rushing [winds],
And blunts the lightning's whip of fiery flame,
The vast outpour of storms, and vernal hail,

Line 524. Comp. Matt. **xxv**, 33.

Line 539. Lacuna here in manuscript.

Line 545. *Winds.*—Lacuna here. We supply *winds;* Alexandre sug·
gests *sea;* Friedlieb, *sun.*

(413–436.)

And chilling stroke of clouds, and winter's shock.
For these were every one marked out in thought,
550 As many as seemed good to thee thyself,
And to whose movements thou didst nod assent ;
Who, ere yet any creature had been formed
Wast with thy Son as bosom counselor,
Former of mortal men, and judge of life.
555 Him with the first sweet utterance of mouth
Thou didst address and say : " Let us make man
According to our likeness and our form,
And give him vital breath, to whom though mortal
All worldly things shall be subordinate,
560 And to whom, dust-formed, we subject all things."
  Thus spakest thou to the Word, and by thy mind
All things occurred, and all the elements
At once obeyed thy order, and a creature
Eternal was in mortal image formed;
565 Heaven also, air, fire, earth, and the sea's wave,
Sun, moon, chorus of stars, mountains and day,
Night, sleep, awaking, spirit and emotion,
Soul and intelligence, art, voice and strength,
And the wild tribes of living things, of fish,
570 And birds, land animals, amphibia,
And also creeping things, and double natures;
For he himself arranged all things for thee,
Under thy rule.   But in the latest times
The earth has changed itself, and there has come
575 A humble one, from the Virgin Mary's womb;
A new light rose, and coming from the heavens
He entered mortal form.   And therefore first
Did Gabriel show his strong and holy frame,

Line 553.   *Counselor.*—Comp. line 328.
  Lines 561–573.   This passage is a free poetical expansion of the main
thoughts of Psalm viii.
  Line 578.   *Gabriel.*—Comp. Luke i, 26–28.
              (437–460.)

And second to the virgin he by voice
580 Spoke, being himself a messenger, and said:
"Virgin, receive God in thy holy breast."
So speaking God breathed grace.   But as for her,
Always a virgin, terror and surprise
Seized her at once as she heard, and she stood
585 In trembling, and her mind was filled with fear,
Her heart leaped at the messages unknown.
But she again was gladdened, and her heart
Was by the voice cheered, and the maiden laughed,
And her young cheek blushed, merry with the joy;
590 And she was spell-bound in her heart by awe.
But confidence came to her, and the Word
Flew in her womb, and became flesh in time,
Was gendered and was made a human form,
And came to be a youth, of virgin born,
595 This was a mighty wonder to mankind,
But it was nothing greatly wonderful
To God the Father, and to God the Son.
    And the glad earth received the new-born babe,
The heavenly throne laughed, and the world exulted.
600 The new appearing and prophetic star
Was honored by the wise men, and the babe
In the manger and wrapped in his swaddling-clothes
Was shown to those obedient unto God.
And of the Word was Bethlehem fatherland
605 Called by the keepers of herds, goats and sheep.

*   *   *   *

To be of lowly mind, to hate base plans,

Line 600.   Star.—See Matt. ii, 2.

Lines 606–630.   These lines are a fragment, which may have once been
naturally connected with what now precedes by intervening lines no longer
extant.   As they now stand they have no natural connection with the preceding passage, and appear mutilated both at beginning and end.

(461–481.)

Wholly to love one's neighbor as himself,
And from the soul to love God and to serve him.
Therefore we, from the holy heavenly race
610 Of Christ sprung, shall be called of common blood,
And in our service have a sense of joy,
Following the paths of piety and truth.
Let us not venture in the inmost shrine
Of temples, nor to graven images
615 Pour out libations, nor revere with prayers,
Nor with the pleasant perfume of the flowers
Nor light of lamps, nor yet with votive gifts
Adore them, nor with smoke of frankincense
Upon the altar sending forth its flame,
620 Nor with the sacrifice of bulls to send
The cruel gory slaughtering of sheep,—
Those mysteries of recompense on earth,—
Nor with the smoke of flesh-consuming fire
And odors foul pollute the light of heaven ;
625 But, joyful with pure minds and cheerful soul,
With love abounding, and with generous hands,
With soothing psalms, and songs that honor God,
We are commanded to sing praise to thee,
Imperishable and without deceit,
630 All-Father God, of understanding mind. . . . .

*   *   *   *

(482–501.)

BOOK IX. (XI.)

CONTENTS OF BOOK IX. (XI.)

Introduction, 1–21. Egyptian kings and judges, 22–35. The exodus and giving of the law, 36–43. A notable Egyptian king, 44–49. The Persian domination, 50–65. Ionian domination, 66–75. Woes of the Medes, 76–84. Rule of the Indian prince, 85–99. The great Assyrian king, 100–116. Numerous subject-kings, 117–135. Origin of Rome, 136–152. The fall of Ilion, 153–180. Escape of Æneas and founding of the Latin race, 181–205. The wise old minstrel, 206–215. Wars of the nations, 216–223. The terrible invader of Greece, 224–234. Philip of Macedon, 235–245. Alexander the Conqueror, 246–281. The kings of Egypt, 282–296. Egypt an asylum for the Jews, 297–303. The eight kings and treacherous queen of Egypt, 304–324. Rise of the Roman Cæsars, 325–338. Fall of Cleopatra, 339–372. Subjection of Egypt, 373–399. The Sibyl's testimony of herself, 400–411.

BOOK IX. (XI.)

O WORLD of widely scattered men, long walls,
Insatiate cities, and unnumbered nations,
Of the east, and west, and south, and also north,
Divided into various languages
5 And kingdoms, of you what is worst I speak.
  For from the time when on the earlier men
The flood came, and a miserable race
Destroyed by many waters, he who rules
Over all things produced another race
10 Of tireless men, who stood up against heaven
And built a tower of height unspeakable.
From others then came tongues, and upon them
Came hurled along the wrath of God most high,
And the huge tower fell. But against each other
15 They stirred up bitter strife. Then the tenth race
Of mortal men lived when these things occurred,
And then the whole earth was distributed
Among strange men and various dialects,
Whose numbers I will mention and by name

The following four books are numbered xi–xiv in the manuscripts and in Alexandre's edit'on. It has seemed to us better, in the absence of intervening books, to number them consecutively in order after t! e eighth book, ix–xii. To prevent misunderstanding, however, we print both numbers at the top of the page, placing the manuscript number in parentheses. On the discovery and first publication of these four books see the Introduction. This book ix (xi) is probably the work of an Egyptian Jew, who wrote in the earlier part of the second century, A. D.

Line 1. *Widely scattered men.*—Homeric phrase, *Iliad,* 2, 804; *Od.,* 11, 365.

Lines 6–18. Comp. book iii, 114–126.

20 Celebrate in acrostics, and by means
   Of the initial letter make them known.
     First Egypt shall receive a royal power
   And eminently just; but then in her
   Shall many counsel-bearing men arise
25 And there shall reign a formidable man,
   A very powerful warrior; he shall have
   The letter of the acrostic for his name,
   And against pious men will draw the sword.
   And a great sign shall he have while he rules
30 In the Egyptian land, which, famed afar
   For great things, shall with plenteous corn provide
   Souls perishing with hunger, and the judge,
   Himself in bonds, child of Assyrian men,
   The eastern land shall nourish, and his name
35 Know as the measure of the number ten.
     But when the ten plagues from bright heaven
      shall come
   On Egypt, then again to thee I'll cry.
   Woe, woe, thou Memphis, woe, thou mighty
      kingdom !
   The Red Sea shall much people of thine slay. `
40 But when the twelve-tribe people, by command
   Of the Immortal, leave the fertile plain

Line 20. *Acrostics.*—In the sense illustrated in the first portion of book v, where the Roman emperors are designated by the initial letters of their names.

Line 22. *First Egypt.*—Comp. book i, 229, note.

Line 27. *Letter of the acrostic.*—Meaning the letter which begins the next line of the Sibyl's song, φάσγανα, *sword*, and so designates the name *Pharaoh.*

Line 33. *Assyrian.*—The Sibyl thinks of the Hebrews as emigrants from Assyria, or the far East.

Line 35. *Ten.*—The Greek letter for ten is I, the initial of the Greek form of the name *Joseph.*

(17–36.)

A wasted ruin, then unto mankind
Will God himself, sole ruler, give a law.
  Then for the Hebrews shall a mighty king
45 Of lofty spirit over Egypt reign,
Whose name resembles sand, but falsely called
As to his fatherland a Theban man.
But Memphis he, dread serpent, will admire,
And many things will he protect in wars.
50 And when twelve rolling decades of the kingdom
Shall have passed round, and in addition seven,
And also the tenth hundred in the East,
Of others all things being left behind,
Then shall the Persian domination come.
55 And then shall darkness be upon the Jews,
  Nor shall they famine in that day escape,
Nor pestilence most unendurable.
  But when the Persian shall rule, and the son
Of his son's son shall lay the scepter by,
60 And years roll round until they reach five fours,
A hundred add to these, and so complete
Nine hundred, and all things thou shalt repay.

Line 46. *Sand.* — The name Psammiticus best answers this, but the reference may be to Psammenitus, who was defeated by Cambyses, the Persian. See Herodotus, iii, 10–15. But how either of these reigned over Egypt for the Hebrews does not appear. The periods of time denoted are equally uncertain.

Line 54. *Persian.*—The Persian domination at the time of Cambyses was a time of trouble to the Jews, who were just struggling to rally from their Babylonian exile. But we need not be surprised that a writer who calls Joseph an Assyrian (line 33) should also confound Persians and Assyrians, Parthians and Medes. The allusion to Persians and Medes in lines 63 and 64 favors the idea that the Assyrians are intended. Comp. 2 Kings xvii, 6.

Line 59. *Son of his son's son.*—A doubtful reading. Friedlieb takes it as a proper name: *son of an Ionian*, as in line 70.

Line 62. *Shalt repay.*—Addressed to Jews or Israelites, who must make atonement for their misdeeds.

Then thou shalt to the Persians be a slave,
Given over to the Medes, by plagues destroyed
65 And also by the impetuous battle-fray.
   Then to the Persians and the Assyrians
Shall evil come, and to the whole of Egypt,
And unto Libya and the Ethiopians,
And the Pamphylians and all other men.
70 And unto the Ionians shall be given
The royal power, and they again shall waste
The nations, plundering all the earth for spoil.
Sad dirges will the doleful Persians sing
Beside the Tigris; Egypt will shed tears
75 Sufficient many a land to irrigate.
   And then to thee, O Media, many evils
Will one in India born, a rich man, do,
Until thou hast made recompense for all
Which thou hast done before with shameful soul.
80 Woe, woe to thee, O nation of the Medes,
Hereafter thou to Ethiopian men   .
Shalt be enslaved; beyond the meridian land
Shalt thou seven and a hundred years complete,
Wretched, and place thy neck beneath the yoke.
85   And then an Indian prince of sable skin,
Gray hair, and mighty soul, shall come to power,
Who shall lay many evils on the East
By reason of impetuous battle-frays.
   And he shall injure thee and lay thee waste
90 Much more than all.   But when he shall have reigned

Line 70. *Ionians.*—Here probably intended for the Macedonians, the Javanic kingdom of Dan. viii, 21.

Line 77. *India born.*—By India the Sibyl appears to mean Ethiopia, which names are used interchangeably. See lines 80–85, below. This India-born rich man seems to designate Shebek, or Sebacon.

Line 85. *Indian prince.*—The Ethiopian Tirhakah, mentioned in 2 Kings xix, 9, belonging to the same dynasty as Shebek.

(51–71.)

Twenty and ten years, yet seven more and ten,
Then shall each nation be in furious rage
Against the king's dominion, and make known
Their freedom, leaving for three single years
95 Their slavish blood.   But he will come again
And put their necks beneath the servile yoke,
Each nation of strong men, even as before
Serving the king, and willingly they'll yield.
And there shall be great peace through all the world.
100   And then to the Assyrians there shall be
A mighty man for king, and he shall rule
And persuade all to speak what he desires,
Whatever things God in the law enjoined.
And then will all the long-haired kings fear him,
105 Timid, and mute, and strong, of lovely mien.
Him by the counsel of the mighty God
Will they serve, for he will persuade all things
By reason, and all things will he subdue.
And he a temple of the mighty God
110 And lovely altar will himself erect
In his might, but will hurl the idols down.
But having gathered into one the tribes
And race of fathers, and the infant children,
He will include them as inhabitants.
115 His name shall have two hundred for its number,
And of the eighteenth letter show the sign.
     But when at the tenth revolving period
He shall wield power, and at an end of time
Come to the two and five, then shall the kings

Line 100. *Assyrians.*—Here again put for Hebrews, or Israelites.

Line 115. *Two hundred.*—Represented by Σ, the eighteenth letter of the Greek alphabet, and the initial of Solomon.

Line 119. *The two and five.*—The reference is to us unintelligible. Alexandre suggests twenty-five years after the completion of the temple, but that is incorrect.

(72–94.)

120 Be numerous as the plants of mortal men,
    Even numerous as the tribes, cities, and isles,
    Lands of the blessed, and the fruitful fields.
    But one of these shall be a mighty king,
    Leader of men, and many great-souled kings
125 Shall under him have rule, and unto him
    And to his sons and grandsons opulent
    Will parts be given because of royal power.
    Decades of decades, eight ones add to these,
    Of years of rule, and to the last they come.
130 But when the strong beast with fierce war shall come,
    Then, O ye noble kings, shall wrath spring forth.
    Woe to thee, Persian land!   How many streams
    Outpoured of human blood shalt thou receive,
    When that strong-minded man shall come to thee !
135 Then to thee I again will cry these things.
        But when the Italian land puts forth its growth,
    Great wonder to men, shall a child-like moan
    Be heard with unmixed stroke, in shadowy cave,
    Offspring of the wild beast that feeds on sheep,
140 Who, grown to manhood, on seven mighty hills,
    Shall hurl down many with a shameless soul;
    Both of them have the number of one hundred,
    And their names will of things which are to come
    Show forth a great sign.   On the seven hills

Line 123. *Mighty king.*—Probable reference to Cyrus.

Line 128. *Decades of decades.*—If we take this to mean twice ten decades, and add eight more, we have two hundred and eight, a near approximation of the duration of the Persian monarchy.

Line 130. *Strong beast.*—Reference to Alexander the Great.

Lines 136–140.   Comp. book v, 14, 15.

Line 142. *One hundred.*—Represented by the Greek letter P, initial of Romulus and Remus.

Line 144.   *Great sign.*—Probably in the thought that the first letter of these names is also the initial of Rome, the eternal city, the symbol of power.

145 Will they build mighty walls, and around them
Will men wage heavy wars.   And then again
Around thee will be rising up of men,
O thou great land that hast the beautiful corn,
Bold Egypt—but again I'll cry these things.
150 Against thee in thy house a mighty stroke
Shalt thou receive, and yet again to thee
Shall be a rising up of thine own men.
        Now over thee, O wretched Phrygia,
I weep in pity, for to thee shall come
155 Capture from Hellas, tamer of fleet steeds,
And fearful war through mighty battle fray.
Ilion, I pity thee, for on thy roofs
From Sparta shall the avenging Furies come,
Conjoined with evil star, and bring thee toils,
160 Distresses, groans and sobs, when well-trained men,
By far the noblest heroes of the Greeks,
And dear to Ares, shall begin the fight.
Of these one shall be king, a spearman famed,
And with his brother plan the basest deeds.
165 And they shall overthrow the famous walls
Of Phrygian Troy, and in ten rolling years
Complete the bloody work of the time of war.
But suddenly a wooden artifice
Shall cover men, and this upon thy knees
170 Thou wilt receive, not knowing it replete
With Grecian treachery and heavy woe.
Alas, alas, how many in one night
Will Hades gather in, and how much spoil
Of tearful old men will be led away!
175 But in the generations that shall come
Fresh and undying shall the glory be.

Lines 153–180.   These lines rehearse the familiar story of the Trojan War.
Comp. book iii, 488–494, notes.
(116–140.)

And the great king, a hero sprung from Jove,
Of the first letter of the alphabet
Shall have a name ; and homeward he will march,
180 And then fall by a treacherous woman's hand.
    But of Assaracus's race and blood
A child will reign, a hero of renown,
A strong and valiant man ; and from this [race]
Made desolate by mighty fire, shall come
185 A fugitive, by the dread toil of war
Without a fatherland ; upon his shoulders
Bearing his aged sire, and in his hand
Holding his only son, a pious deed
Will he accomplish.   Looking all around,
190 He put aside the onset of the fire
Of burning Troy, and hastening through the crowd
In terror, crosses fearful land and sea.
And he shall have a trisyllabic name;
And the first letter of the alphabet
195 Will not obscurely show this highest man.
Then the strong Latin city he will build,
And in the fifteenth year, by waters slain,
Come to his end in the depths of the sea.
But him, though dead, the nations of mankind
200 Shall not forget, for his race over all
Hereafter shall rule, far as the Euphrates,
And to the middle of the Tigris stream,
The Assyrian land, and where the Parthian dwells.

Line 178. *First letter.*—Initial of Agamemnon, who on his return from Troy was slain by his wife, Clytemnestra.

Line 181. *Assaracus.*—Comp. book v, 11.

Line 185. *Fugitive.*—Æneas. See lines 193, 194.

Line 187. *Sire.*—Anchises.

Line 188. *Son.*—Ascanius.

Line 197. *By waters slain.*—According to one tradition Æneas was drowned in the river Numicus.

This in the generations yet to come
205 Shall be, when all these things shall come to pass.
But there shall be a certain wise old man,
A minstrel, whom all mortals call most wise,
By whose great understanding all the world
Shall be instructed; for with power and thought
210 Will he his chapters write, and clearly write
At times with beauty inexpressible,
Seizing my words, my measures, and my verse,
For he himself will first my books unfold,
And after these things hide them, and to men
215 Show them no more till life and death shall end.
But when these things which I spoke are fulfilled,
The Greeks again will fight with one another;
Assyrians, Arabs, quiver-bearing Medes,
Persians, Sicilians, and the Lydians
220 Will then revolt; Thrace and Bithynia,
And those that dwell along the streams of Nile,
Land of the beautiful corn—at once on all
Will God, the Eternal, set the din of war.
But terribly will an Assyrian man,
225 A base-born Ethiopian, quickly come,
Having a wild beast's soul, and every isthmus
Will he cleave, prying timidly around,
Going to all and sailing through the sea.
And then, O faithless Greece, shall many things
230 Befall thee. Woe, woe to thee, wretched Greece;
How many things must thou aloud bewail!
For during seven and eighty rolling years
Thou shalt the miserable refuse be
Of fearful battle among all the tribes.

Line 206. *Old man.*—Homer. See book iii, 495–511, and notes there.
Line 224. *Assyrian man.*—The reference seems to be to Xerxes, but the epithets Assyrian and Ethiopian seem designed to puzzle.
(162–185.)

235   And then again a Macedonian woe
       Shall come on Greece and lay all Thracia waste,
       And bring the toil of war upon the isles
       And mainlands; with war-loving champions
       Will he be foremost, and the name he bears
240 Is by the sign of ten times fifty shown.
       He shall be short-lived in his government,
       But leave a mighty monarchy behind,
       And a boundless land.   But he himself shall fall
       By an ill-minded spearman, while he lives
245 In plenty as no other leader lived.
          But after him a great-souled son of his
       Shall reign, whose name begins the alphabet;
       But he shall be the outgo of his race.
       Not truly shall all call him son of Jove,
250 Or Ammon, nor yet Kronos' bastard son,
       As they would feign.   And he will plunder cities
       Of many mortal men, and there will rise
       In Europe sore distress; and he himself
       With pestilence will ravage Babylon,
255 And every land the sun looks down upon;
       And he alone will sail the eastern world.
       Alas, alas, for thee, O Babylon,
       Being captive led in triumph, thou shalt serve—
       Thou who of Asia wast the mistress called.
260 And Mars shall come, shall surely come and slay
       Thy many children.   Then shalt thou send forth

Line 240. *Ten times fifty.*—Represented by Φ (= 500), the Greek initial
of Philip, the famous Macedonian king, and father of Alexander the Great.
   Line 244. *Spearman.*—Pausanias, one of the royal guards, who assassi-
nated Philip on his way to the theater.
   Line 246. *Great-souled son.*—Alexander the Great.
   Line 248. *Outgo of his race.*—Comp. Dan. xi, 4.
   Line 250. *Ammon . . . Kronos.*—Comp. book v, 5–9.
                          (196–206.)

Thy royal man, with name of the number four,
Wielding the spear and fearful with the bow;
Along with powerful warriors he will go.
265 And then Cilicia's and Assyria's midst
Famine and war shall hold. But great-souled kings
Will arm for bitter strife a dreadful band.
But do thou flee and leave the former king;
Desire not thou to stay nor be a slave.
270 For a dread lion shall upon thee come,
Flesh-eating beast, ferocious, strange to law,
With mantle cast upon his shoulders round.
Flee thou that man of thunder; there shall come
On Asia a base yoke, and all the land
275 Shall drink a shower of murder. But when Mars
Of Pella shall a great, rich city found
In Egypt, bearing his name, he shall meet,
Betrayed by treacherous comrades, fate and death.
For, leaving India, and to Babylon
280 Returning, there around the festal board
Shall barbarous murder bring him to his fall.
　　Thereafter a few years shall other kings,
Cruel and insolent and faithless, rule
According to each tribe. And then shall rise
285 A great-souled, valiant hero, who shall glean

Line 262. *Four.*—This number is denoted by the fourth letter of the Greek alphabet, Δ, the initial of Darius, the last Persian monarch. He was defeated at Issus and Arbela by Alexander.

Lines 270–273. *Dread lion . . . man of thunder.*—Descriptive of Alexander.

Line 276. *Pella.*—Comp. book v, 5. *City.*—Alexandria in Egypt.

Line 281. *Murder.*—This does not accord with the current tradition, which is that he died of a drunken debauch; Plutarch, however, mentions suspicions that he had been taken off by poison.

Line 285. *Hero.*—Referring most probably to Antigonus, the most famous of Alexander's immediate successors, who certainly gleaned all western . Asia, if not Europe.

(207–226.)

All Europe naked, and each land shall drink
The blood of every tribe. But having filled
Of life his portion, he shall disappear.
And other kings, twice four men, there shall be
290 Of this race, and the same name to them all.
And Egypt then shall be a regal bride,
And the great city of the Macedonian king,
Rare Alexandria, famous nourisher
Of cities, and in beauty radiant,
295 Shall be the sole metropolis.
And then let Memphis blame those in command.
     And peace profound shall be through all the world,
And more fruit will the black-soil land then have.
And then shall be disaster to the Jews,
300 Nor shall they famine in that day escape,
Nor grievous pestilence ; but wandering men
And many will the black-soil land receive,
Ambrosial land, of fine corn, the new world.
     But eight kings of the Egyptian marshy soil
305 Shall fill two hundred three and thirty years.
Yet of them all, the race shall perish not,
But there shall issue forth a female root,

Line 289. *Twice four men.*—The eight famous Ptolemies of Egypt, who
were of Macedonian origin.

Line 296. *Let Memphis blame.*—Because overshadowed and superseded by
the Ptolemies, who made Alexandria the sole metropolis.

Line 299. *Disaster.*—Reference to the capture of Jerusalem by Ptolemy
I. and the transportation of a great number of Jews to Egypt. See Josephus, *Ant.*, xii, 1.

Line 301. *Wandering men.*—Scattered by famine and seeking a new and
better country. Alexandre reads *ruined men*.

Line 305. The period of the eight Ptolemies is commonly reckoned from
Ptolemy I. (Soter), B. C. 323, to Ptolemy VIII. (Soter II.), B. C. 81, or about
242 years.

Line 307. *Female root.*—The famous Cleopatra would seem most obviously
intended, but the associated events (lines 309–315) appear to be those of the
(227–246.)

A bane of men, betrayer of her kingdom.
But then they wickedness and evil deeds
310 Shall perpetrate, and one destroy another.
The son that wears the purple robe will smite
His warlike sire, and he by his son falls,
And ere he shall beget another child
He shall cease.   But again the root shall sprout
315 Spontaneous ; of it is a neighboring race.
For of the land beside the streams of Nile
Which travel on by seven mouths to the sea
She shall be queen, and her beloved name
The number twenty tells.   And she shall ask
320 Ten thousand things, and gather up all goods
Of gold and silver ; but from her own men
Shall treachery befall her.   Then on thee,
O fair and happy land, again shall come
Battles and fights and slaughter of mankind.
325   But after many shall o'er fertile Rome
Have borne rule, not indeed of happiness
Precursors, but despotic lords and chiefs
Of thousands and of countless myriads,
Then, overseers of the lawful assemblies,
330 Shall the most mighty Cæsars bear the rule,
And every day keep making their demands.
The last of these shall rule the number ten,
The highest Cæsar, who upon the earth

---

disorders and crimes of the times following the reign of the eighth Ptolemy.
Hence, perhaps, this "betrayer of her kingdom" may best refer to the
mother of the eighth Ptolemy (Soter II.), who expelled him from Egypt and
placed the crown on the head of her favorite son, Alexander.

Line 319. *Twenty.*—The letter K, initial of the Greek form of the name
Cleopatra.   Here, without doubt, the last queen of Egypt, the famous
daughter of Ptolemy Auletes, is intended.

Lines 332, 333. *Last . . . highest.*—In the sense of loftiest, noblest.   *Ten.*
—Greek initial of Julius.   Comp. book v, 17, note.
(247-267.)

Shall stretch his limbs, cast down through fearful Mars
335 By a hostile man ; whom, bearing in their hands,
The sons of Rome shall bury piously,
And round about him heap a monument
For love of him, in memory of his grace.
But when there comes an end of passing time,
340 And thou hast filled out twice two hundred years.
And also twice ten, from the time when ruled
Thy founder, child of the wild beast, no more
Shall there be a dictator of short rule,
But there shall be a king, a godlike man.
345 And when the king is going into Egypt,
Against him horrid Mars shall surely come
With glittering helm, and then shall conquest dire
Come to thee ; for around the walls of the land
Shall be foul works of dire and violent wars.
350 But suffering pitiable things in war
Over the freshly wounded she will flee
In wretched plight ; and then unto the couch
Of that dread man will she come ; and the end
Is but the nuptials and the marriage-bed.
355 Woe, woe to thee, ill-wedded woman, thou
Shalt give the Roman king thy royal power ;

Line 340. *Twice two hundred.*—Comp. book x, 15. Alexandre emends by
reading *twice three hundred;* but this differs from the common chronology
by more than one hundred years.

Line 343. *Dictator of short rule.*—The Roman dictators were appointed
only for extreme emergencies, and clothed with unlimited power, but only
for a term of six months at most.

Line 345. *The king.*—Octavius (Augustus) seems here referred to, who
carried the war to Egypt and effected the utter overthrow of that kingdom.

Line 348. *Thee.*—Egypt is addressed.

Line 351. *She will flee.*—Here Cleopatra's flight to Julius Cæsar seems to
have been in the mind of the writer; and throughout this passage the Sibylline poet appears to confound events of different periods, part of which
occurred with Antony, part with Julius Cæsar, to whom Cleopatra bore a son.

(268–286.)

And thou shalt make atonement for all things
Whatever thou hast done to men in wars.
. . . For all the land . . . unto a mighty man,
360 As far as Libya and the dark-skinned men.
And thou no longer shalt a widow be,
But with a lion shalt thou live as wife,
A terrible devourer of mankind,
A furious warrior. Then shalt thou become,
365 O hapless one, among all men at once
Invisible, for thou shalt disappear,
Having a shameless soul ; and in its house
Shall the encircling tomb receive thy form
So stately, having once had life within,
370 Cunningly wrought and fit for many chiefs.
And many people will lament for thee
And over thee the king will sorely grieve.
    And then shall an Egyptian servant toil,
Who many years against the Indians bore
375 Her trophies ; she shall serve disgracefully,
And mingle with the river Nile her tears,
For she acquired wealth, and of all good things
•A great store. Nourisher of cities, she
Shall feed a race of sheep-devouring men.
380 Alas, unto how many beasts shalt thou,
O happy Egypt, be a slave and prey !

Line 359. Lacuna in Greek text here.

Line 362. *A lion.*—Reference apparently to Antony; but the writer has embellished this whole portraiture of Cleopatra without much regard for historical accuracy.

Line 368. *Tomb.*—Octavius gave Cleopatra a magnificent burial. The latter part of this passage (lines 368–371) has a corrupt text.

Line 373. *Egyptian servant.*—Egypt herself here conceived as the female slave of oppressing nations.

Line 379. *Sheep-devouring men.*—The Romans, in allusion to the wolf that nourished Romulus and Remus—as if all the Romans were wolves.

(286–304.)

But having given to the peoples laws,
Thou, who didst once exult o'er mighty kings,
Shalt to the peoples be a wretched slave,
385 On account of that people, whom of old,
A pious race, thou didst lead to much woe
Of toils and sorrows, and upon their neck
Didst place a plow, and irrigate the fields
With human tears.   Therefore shall God himself,
390 The king imperishable in the heaven,
Destroy thee utterly, and hurl thee down
Into deep grief ; and thou shalt pay the price
Of what thou didst of old unjustly do,
And know at last that God's wrath came to thee.
395 But I to Python and to Panopeus
Of goodly towers will go ; and then will all
Declare that I am a true prophetess,
And a diviner, but insane in soul.
A messenger. . . . When to the books thou comest
400 Be not afraid, and all things yet to be
And things that were ye shall know from my words.
Then will none longer call a prophetess
Inspired of God an augurer of woe.
But thou, O King, now end my much-loved strain,
405 Driving off frenzy, and the voice divine,
And passion fierce, and give a charming song.

Line 386. *Pious race.*—The Hebrews.

Line 395. *Python . . . Panopeus.*—Shrines of Apollo in Phocis, Greece; Python being put for Delphi, and Panopeus near by.

Lines 396–403.   Comp. book iii, 971–979.

Line 399. *Messenger.*—Lacuna in Greek text after this word.

Line 404. *King.*—God, as in book ii, 412, and xi, 216.

Line 406. *And give a charming song.*—From Hesiod, *Theog.*, 104.   Comp. also close of book xi.

(305–324.)

BOOK X. (XII.)

CONTENTS OF BOOK X. (XII.)

Introduction, 1–22. The first Cæsars, 23–45. The mighty warrior, 46–60. The guileful king, 61–86. The king of wide sway, 87–98. The dreadful and contemptible king, 99–123. The three kings, 124–128. The royal destroyer of pious men, 129–151. The princes famed for filial devotion, 152–159. The peaceful king, 160–181. The venerable king, 182–187. Another warrior king, 188–202. The Celtic warrior, 203–207. The king with the name of a sea, 208–223. The three rulers, 224–237. The wise and pious king, 238–263. The king that sought to rival Hercules, 264–282. Period of Roman dominion, 283–295. The twentieth king, 296–305. The short-lived king, 306–310. The ruler from the East, 311–317. The wily ruler from the West, 318–333. The youthful Cæsar, 334–343. A time of woes, 344–358. Only those who honor God attain happiness, 359–361. The Sibyl's prayer, 362–370.

BOOK X. (XII.)

But bring to me the lamentable time
Of the illustrious Latins, who were first
After the kings of Egypt were cut off,
And had all been borne down into the earth;
5 And also after Pella's citizen,
Under whom all the East had been cast down,
And the rich West; whom Babylon disgraced
And gave a corpse to Philip; not of Jove
Nor Ammon truly boasted to have sprung;
10 And after him, who, from the race and blood
Of great Assaracus, went forth from Troy,
Even he who cleft the violence of fire;
And after many kings, and warlike men,
And after the young children of the beast
15 That feeds on sheep, and centuries six have passed,
And Rome two decades has dictator been,
Then shall arise a king pre-eminent
As from the western sea, and govern Rome,
Exceeding brave and warlike; and his name
20 Begins the letters of the alphabet;
And having bound thee he will hold thee fast
By man-destroying war, thou rich in fruit.

This book is a kind of reproduction of the fifth, and is probably the work of a Christian writer of the third century.

Lines 1-14. Substantially identical with the first fourteen lines of book v. where see notes.

Line 15. *Centuries six.*—Comp. book ix, 340.

Line 17. *King pre-eminent.*—Augustus Cæsar. Comp. book v, 20-26.

Line 22. *Thou rich in fruit.* — Addressed to Egypt. Comp. book ix, 373-394.

(1-17.)

And thou shalt expiate the shameful deeds
To which thou once didst freely give thyself.
25 For this great-souled one will excel in wars.
Him Thrace and Sicily and Memphis fear,—
Memphis, cast to the ground by wickedness
Of leaders, and a woman unsubdued,
Fallen by the spear; and he will institute
30 Laws for the peoples, and subdue all things;
With mighty glory he will long hold sway.
For not a little time will he bear rule,
When yet another scepter-bearing king
Not one hour longer than this one shall rule
35 The Romans, for to him God gave all things,
And showed forth seasons in the divine earth,
Great wonders unto them as signs he showed.
But when a lustrous star, all like the sun,
Appears from heaven in the midst of day,
40 Then shall the hidden Word of the Most High
Come bearing flesh like mortals. But with him
The might of Rome and of the famous Latins
Shall increase. But the mighty king himself
By his own predetermined fate shall die,
45 And to another give the royal power.
    But after this one will a certain man
Famed as a powerful warrior take the lead,
Bearing the purple mantle on his shoulders;
Three hundred numbers he with his first sign.
50 The Medes and arrow-hurling Parthians
He will destroy, and by his mighty strength
Subvert the city of the lofty gates.
And upon Egypt will much evil come,

Line 38. _Star._—The star of Bethlehem. Matt. ii, 2, 9.
Line 40. _Word._—The Logos, as in John i, 1.
Line 49. _Three hundred._—Designating Tiberius, as in book v, 29.
                (18-42.)

And on the Assyrians, and the Colchians,
55 And the Heniochi, and Germans dwelling
By the Rhine's waves beyond the sandy shores.
And he himself will afterwards destroy
The city of the lofty gates beside
Eridanus, that evil things devised;
60 And then will he fall, struck by burning iron.
 And after him another man will rule,
Deep versed in guile, and he will number three
And show it by the initial of his name.
And much gold he will gather, and of wealth
65 There will not be a large sufficiency;
But without sense of shame, collecting more,
Under the earth he will deposit all.
And peace shall come, and Mars shall cease from war.
But he by divination many things
70 Will make known, seeking things of greatest good
For life's support. Yet on him there shall be
A great sign: out of heaven small drops of blood
Shall issue, and the king shall be destroyed.
He will do many lawless things, and place
75 Woes on the necks of Romans, putting trust
In divination. He will also slay
The heads of the assembly. And a plague
Shall seize Campanians, Thrace, and Macedon,
And the Italians; Egypt will alone
80 Feed numerous races. But the king himself
Will craftily destroy the virgin maid,
Deceiving her by means of mysteries.

Line 55. *Heniochi.*—A Sarmatian tribe, near Colchis.

Line 58. *City.*—Cremona seems intended, but the writer has here apparently confused Tiberius with Vespasian, who destroyed this city by fire.

Line 62. *Three.*—The letter Γ, denoting Gaius, or Caius Cæsar, commonly called Caligula, a monster of wickedness.

(43–63.)

But her the citizens in tearful grief
Will bury, but against the king they all
85 Will cherish anger.   Ruin then will come
By a strong hand to blooming powerful Rome.
 Again another of wide sway shall reign,
Whose name the number twenty will denote.
And then shall wars and bitter sorrows come
90 Upon the Sauromatians, and on Thrace,
And the Triballians that hurl the spear,
And all the Romans Mars will fiercely rend.
But while this one rules the Italian land
And the Pannonians, a dread sign shall be:
95 Dark night will come at the mid hour of day
Around them, and a shower of stones from heaven.
Then shall the Italians' mighty prince and judge
By fate divine go into Hades' halls.
 Again another dire and dreadful man
100 Whose name the number fifty shows, shall come.
And many of those in wealth noblest born
Out of all cities he will put to death,
By nature a dire serpent; few his words
Whenever he extends his guiding hands,
105 Works ruin, and brings many things to pass.
Wrestling in contests, driving in the race,
Destroying many lives, and daring still
Ten thousand things.   And he will cleave the mount
Of the two waters and with gore pollute.
110 But also to the Italians he will be
Doubly destructive; making himself God
He will reproach the willing populace.

Line 88. *Twenty.*—The letter K, denoting Claudius (Klaudios). Comp.
book v, 34.
 Line 99. *Dire and dreadful.*—Nero. See on book v, 38–47, and comp.
book iv, 150–157.

(64–86.)

But while he rules there shall be peace profound
And fears among men. By the Ausonian shores
115 The water, rushing from the ocean streams,
Shall come all out of place. Casting about
He will establish contests for the people
Many in number, and, himself presiding,
He will contend with voice and cithara,
120 Along with harp-string uttering a song.
But later, having left the royal power,
He will flee and be miserably destroyed,
Thus making expiation for his deeds.
And after him shall three reign, two of them
125 Obtaining by their names the number seventy,
And after them one, of the letter three.
And one by one shall they all perish, slain
Under the army's hands by mighty Mars.
Thereafter shall a great destroyer come
130 Of pious men, a ruler of strong heart,
A warlike Mars, and seven times ten will show
His number clearly. He will overthrow
Phenicia, and will ruin Lydia.
Also a sword will come upon the land
135 Of Jerusalem, even to the utmost curve
Of the Tiberian sea. Woe, woe to thee,
Phenicia! O how many things will suffer
That sorrow-laden one, with trophies bound!
And every nation shall upon thee tread.
140 Woe on the Assyrians shall come, and babes

Line 125. *Seventy.*—Represented by O, the initial of Otho and Vitellius (Οὐιτέλλιος).

Line 126. *Three.*—Γ, the initial of Galba.

Line 129. *Great destroyer.*—Vespasian. Comp. book v, 49–51. He began the destructive war which ended in the overthrow of Jerusalem.

Line 140. *Assyrians.*—Here denoting, as in book ix, 33, the Hebrews or Jews, who suffered unspeakable woes in the last siege of Jerusalem, and in subsequent exile.   (87–107.)

Shalt thou see serving among hostile men
Along with wivès, and all their sustenauce
And all their wealth shall perish.   For the wrath,
The wrath of God that causes bitter woe,
145 Shall come, because they did not keep his law,
But served all idols with unseemly arts.
And many wars and fights again shall be,
Slaughter of men, famines and pestilence,
And uproar in the cities.   But the king
150 Old and of great soul, and excelling all,
Shall at life's end fall by the army's need.
     Then shall two other princes rule, and love
The memory of their father, the great king,
Glorying in warriors fighting hand to hand.
155 And of these there shall be a noble man,
A ruler, whose name will three hundred show;
Yet he shall also fall by treachery
Even in the army, stretched upon the ground,
Struck in the plain of Rome by two-edged brass.
160   And after him a powerful warlike man,
Of the letter four, shall rule the mighty realm,
Whom all upon the boundless earth shall love,
And then shall war cease over all the world.
But him even from the West unto the East
165 Will all serve willingly, not of constraint,
And cities of themselves will subject be.
For to him will the heavenly Sabaoth,
God the imperishable, who abides
Above the sky, abundant glory bring.

Line 152. *Two . . . princes.*—Titus and Domitian.

Line 156. *Three hundred.*—Represented by T, initial of Titus. Comp.
book v, 53.

Line 157. *By treachery.*—This does not accord with the accredited history
of Titus.

Line 161. *Four.*—Δ, initial of Domitian.

(108–132.)

170 And then will wasting famine much impair
Pannonia, and all the Celtic land,
And they will perish one upon another.
And it shall be with the Assyrians
As though Orontes with creations flowed,
175 And splendor, and whatever better seems.
And these the great king will admire, and love
Some other things far more. But he'll receive
A great wound in the middle of his breast,
Being taken at the end of life in guile
180 By a friend in the sacred royal house,
And he shall fall pierced. After him shall be
A ruler and a venerable man,
Fifty his number, who withal shall slay
Great numbers of the citizens of Rome;
185 But he shall briefly rule; for afterwards,
On account of the king that went before,
Shall he go wounded into Hades' halls.
  Forthwith then shall another king arise,
A warrior, whose rule has the signal mark
190 Three hundred. He shall reign and desolate
The Thracians' varied land, and those that dwell
On the far barbarous borders of the Rhine,

Line 171. *Pannonia.*—Region north of Illyricum on the upper waters of
the Danube. The *Celtic land* was the region now known as France.

Line 173. *Assyrians.*—Comp. line 140, note.

Line 181. *Pierced.*—Domitian was assassinated in his own house by a band
of conspirators.

Line 183. *Fifty.*—Represented by N, and here designating Nerva. He
was a venerable senator of sixty-four years when proclaimed emperor.

Line 187. *Wounded.*—With a keen sense of wrong and disgrace in being
forced to give public approval to certain acts which he was unwilling to
sanction.

Line 190. *Three hundred.*—T, designating Trajan here as in book v, 57–63,
where see notes.

(133–150.)

10*

The Germans, and Iberians that hurl
The arrow.   To the Jews shall also come
195 Another great disaster, and with them
Phenicia shall a shower of murder drink.
And the walls of the Assyrians shall fall
By many warriors, and again shall these
Be by a life-destroying man cut off.
200 And then shall there be threatenings of God's rule,
. Earthquakes and pestilence in every land,
And snow-storms out of season, and fierce lightnings.
And then a king, great in the toil of war,
A Celtic warrior, hastening to the strife
205 Of battle, shameful fate shall not escape,
But he shall die, and foreign dust shall hide
His carcass, having for his name a flower.
And after him another man shall lead,
Of silver helmet; of the sea his name,
210 And the beginning of the alphabet,
And of four syllables, a very Mars.
And priests and temples he will dedicate
In all the cities; traversing the world
With his own foot, and bringing gifts, he will
215 Furnish gold and much amber unto many.
He also will withhold all mysteries
Of the magicians from the sacred temples,
And what is much more excellent for men
Will place . . . [ruling] [thunderbolt] . . .
220 And blessed peace shall be when this king comes,
And he shall also be a rich-voiced bard,

Line 197. *Assyrians.*—Trajan overran Armenia and Mesopotamia, and nearly all the country of the old Assyrians.
Line 208. *Another.*—Hadrian, Greek 'Aδριανός, a word of four syllables. Comp. book v, 63–69, and viii, 63–80.
Line 219. *Will place.*—Lacuna in the original text here leaves it impossible to complete the sentence, or even indicate the thought with any certainty.
(151–173.)

A law observer, and a righteous judge;
But he shall fall destroyed by fate divine.
After him three shall rule, but the third long
225 Shall be in power, three decades holding on.
But known from the first unit yet again
Another king shall rule; and after him
Another ruler, numbering seven times ten ;
Honored shall be their names.   They shall destroy
230 Men marked by many a brand, the mighty Moors,
The Britains, Dacians, and Arabians.
But when of these the youngest is destroyed,
Then shall dire war to Parthia come again ;
And he who wounded them before at last
235 Shall also plunder.   Then the king himself
Shall fall, even by the treachery of a beast,
Baring his hands—a cause itself of death.
And after him another man shall rule
Famed for much wisdom, having for his name
240 The initial number of the first great king
Of the first unit ; good and great is he.
And for the houses of the Latin people
Will this strong one accomplish many things
In memory of his father; and the walls
245 Of Rome will he adorn with gold, and silver,
And ivory ; and with a mighty man

Line 224. *Three.*—The Antonines. See book v, 70, and viii, 81.

Line 226. *First unit.*—A, here denoting Antoninus Pius.

Line 228. *Seven times ten.*—O, Greek initial of Verus (Οὐῆρος).

Line 230. *Moors.*—The Mauri, or Mauritanians, on the north-western coast of Africa.

Lines 232–237. The statements of these lines are inexplicably obscure. Dire war was carried on with the Parthians under command of L. Verus, but the statements of lines 235–237 are not applicable to any of the Antonines, either literally or metaphorically.

Line 241. *First unit.*—Designating Aurelius—that is, Marcus Aurelius.
(174–193.)

Visit the market-places and the temples.
And then by Roman wars will he bring on
Most fearful wounds, and plunder all the land
250 Of the Germans, when there shall appear from heaven
A mighty sign of God; and he will save
For the king's sake and for his piety
The brass-armed, wearied men; for in all things
The God of heaven will hear him when he prays,
255 And out of season send the rain of heaven.
  But when these things are finished which I said,
Then also with the rolling years shall cease
The kingdom of this great and pious king.
And at the end of life will he exhibit
260 Coming into the palace his young child,
And to that ruler with the golden hair
Leaving the royal power, he will expire
By his own fate. Twice ten shall note his name,
Who, having been born king from the royal race
265 Of his own father, shall receive the power.
This man will with superior judgment hold
All things, and the great-hearted Hercules
Will emulate, and be the best in arms
Among the mighty, and have highest fame
270 Both among huntsmen and in horsemanship.
But he will live in peril all alone.
But while he rules there shall appear to him

Line 251. *Mighty sign.*—The marvelous thunder-storm, by aid of which
the emperor and his army gained a great victory over the Quadi, and which
the Romans ascribed to Jupiter Tonans, who heard Aurelius's prayer, but
which the Christians of his army affirmed was in answer to their own
prayers.

Line 260. *Child.*—Commodus, who succeeded him.

Line 263. *Twice ten.*—Represented by K, Greek initial of Commodus,
specially famous for his skill with the bow and other arms, and boasting
himself to be a rival of Hercules.

(193–214.)

A fearful sign; within the plain of Rome
There shall be a great mist, so that a man
275 Will not discern his neighbor.   Then shall wars
And dismal sorrows be when the king himself,
Maddened by love and furious, shall come
Shaming the young race in the nuptial couch,
Shameful with hymeneal songs impure.
280 Then in desertion hidden shall the great man
Destructive, giving himself up to wrath,
Rage in a bath-room, bound by treacherous fate.
    Know, then, that Rome's destructive time is near
Because of zeal for power, and by Mars' hands
285 Shall many perish in Palladian homes.
And then shall Rome be desolate and make
Atonement for all things which she has done.
My heart laments, my heart within me mourns,
For from the time of thy first king, proud Rome,
290 Who gave good law to men upon the earth,
And the Word of the great, immortal God
Came to the earth, until the ending up
Of the nineteenth kingdom, there shall be complete
Two hundred and twice twenty and four years.
295 To these add six months more of other time.
    Then to the widowed race comes the twentieth king,
When in thy houses, smitten by sharp brass
With sword he pours out blood.   His name reveals
The number eighty, and he has old age.

Line 282. *Bath-room.*—Commodus was assassinated by suffocation in a bath-room.

Line 293. *Nineteenth kingdom.*—That is, the nineteenth reign, reckoning from Augustus. Comp. line 296.

Line 294.—This computation is obviously erroneous, for Commodus was assassinated A. D. 192, to which if we add the thirteen years of Augustus before the date of our era we have only two hundred and five years.

Line 299. *Eighty.*—Represented by II, initial of Pertinax, who was sixty-se en years old when made emperor and lived only eighty-seven days thereafter.   (215–239.)

300 And he will shortly make thee desolate
With many warriors, many overthrows,
And murders, homicides, and deadly feuds,
And sufferings for victorious leadership.
And in confusion many a horse and man,
305 Pierced through, shall fall in battles on the plain.
   And then another, with the number ten
As the sign of his name, will come and work
Much woe and grief, and plunder many men,
But short-lived he himself shall be, and fall
310 By mighty Mars, struck by the burning iron.
   Another, of the number fifty, comes,
A warrior, raised up in the East for rule.
As far as Thrace shall come the warlike Mars;
Then will he flee and come unto the land
315 Of the Bithynians, and the Cicilian plain;
But him shall brazen, soul-destroying Mars
Quickly in the Assyrian plains destroy.
   Then shall one become ruler by deceit,
A man of wiles and knowing what is fit,
320 Being raised up from the West, and he shall have
Two hundred as the number of his name,
A sign far above that of royal power.
He will begin war on Assyrian men,

Line 306. *Ten.*—I, here referring to Julianus (Didius Julianus), who after the murder of Pertinax made the highest bid for the empire, but reigned only sixty-six days.

Line 311. *Fifty.*—N, designating Niger, who claimed the empire on the death of Pertinax and was supported by the East, but being repeatedly defeated by the troops of his rival, Severus, he fled for Parthia, but was overtaken and slain.

Line 321. *Two hundred.*—Represented by Σ and designating Septimius Severus.

Line 322. *Sign.*—Alexandre explains this as meaning that the same initial appears in Σεβαστός, *Sebastos*, the Greek equivalent of *Augustus*.

(240–260.)

Assemble all the army, and all things
325 Put under him.   The Romans he will rule
With mighty energy; but in his heart
Is much craft and the baleful wrath of Mars.
A dreadful serpent, terrible in war,
Who will destroy all lofty men on earth,
330 Slaughtering the noble to obtain their wealth,
Despoiling all the land of ruined men,
He will betake him to the Orient.
And with them shall be every artifice.

     *   *   *   *

Then shall a youthful Cæsar with him rule,
335 Having the name of a puissant king
Of Macedon, by the first letter known.
Diverting broils about him, he will fly
The arduous cunning of the coming king
In the bosom of the army, and the one,
340 Who in barbarian usage rules the temple,
Shall suddenly by mighty Mars be slain,
Cut down by burning iron; and even when dead
The people will abuse his lifeless form.
     And then the kings of Persia shall arise

Line 336. *First letter.*—Alexander Severus is denoted, his name reminding
the writer of Alexander the Great of Macedon.

Line 340. *Rules the temple.*—Heliogabalus (or Elagabalus) seems to be
here referred to, who was in early youth trained as a priest in the Temple
of the Sun at Emesa, and who, after he was made emperor, was wont to
wear his pontifical dress and tiara as high-priest of the sun.   But he came
before, not after, Alexander Severus.

Line 344. *Kings of Persia.*—The dynasty of the Sassanidæ, or kings of the
later Persian Empire, founded by Ardechir Babegan, commonly called Artax-
erxes.

The verses which follow are so fragmentary that no certain meaning can
be made out of them.   Lines 353–356 appear to refer to the death of Alexander Severus.

(261–277.)

345 And Roman Mars [will smite] the Roman king.
    And pastoral Phrygia shall with earthquakes groan.
    Woe, woe, Laodicea; woe to thee,
    Sad Hierapolis; for you the first
    The yawning earth received . . .
350 Of Rome,   vast Aus[onia?]
    All things as many . . .
    Shall wail . . . men destroyed
    By the hand of Mars; but when by eastern roads
    He hastens forth to look on Italy,
355 Smitten by burning iron, and all exposed
    He will fall, hated for his mother's sake.

          *   *   *   *

    For horns . . . all things . . . restrains another, . . .
    Burning . . . that all together do not know.
      But not for all are all things; only those
360 Shall unto real felicity attain
    Who honor God and shun idolatry.
    And now, King of the world, of every realm
    The monarch, pure, immortal, for thou hast
    Into my heart set the ambrosial strain,
365 Cease thou the word, for I am not aware
    Of what I say; for all things thou to me
    Dost ever speak. But give me a brief rest,
    And place thou in my heart a charming song.
    For weary has my heart within me grown
370 Of words divine, foretelling royal power.

Line 362. *King of the world.*—Comp. this and the following lines with the conclusion of book ix.

(278–299.)

BOOK XI. (XIII.)

CONTENTS OF BOOK XI. (XIII.)

Introduction, 1–8. A time of wars and woes, 9–15. Persian insurrection, 16–18. The Roman soldier-king, 19–26. The warrior out of Syria and his son, 27–42. Persian war, 43–53. The grain-producing land of Nile, 54–61. Another song announced, 62–66. Wrath on Assyrians, 67–73. Wretched Antioch, 74–79. Cities of Arabia admonished, 80–92. Wars and treachery, 93–101. Roman ruler from Dacia, 102–109. The Syrian robber, 110–125. The Gallic king and dreadful woes, 126–146. Wretched Syria, 147–154. Wretched Antioch, 155–160. Woes on many cities of Asia, 161–177. Murders and wars, 178–195. Allegory of the bull, dragon, stag, lion, and goat, 196–216. Prayer of the Sibyl, 217–218.

BOOK XI. (XIII.)

HE bids me sing again the mighty word,
Even the holy and immortal God
Imperishable, who gives kings their power
And then removes it, and ordains for them
5 The time of life and of destroying death;
Even things the heavenly God enjoins on me
Unwillingly to make known unto kings
Concerning royal power . . .

    *   *   *   *

And Mars of the leaping spear; by him all perish,
10 Youth and age, judging in the market-place.
For many wars, and fights, and homicides,
Famines and pestilences, earthquake-shocks
And mighty thunder-bolts; and many paths
Of the Assyrians through the entire world,
15 And gathering spoil and plundering of temples.
Then of the inventive Persians there shall be
An insurrection, and along with them
Indians, Armenians, and Arabians,
And for these to the Romans there will come
20 A soldier-king, insatiable in war,

Line 1. *Sing again.*—This book is obviously a continuation of the preceding, and perhaps by the same author.   Comp. the style of the opening of books ii and iii.   In the first line and after the words "royal power" in line 8 there are lacunæ in the Greek text.

Line 9. *Mars of the leaping spear.*—Referring probably to Maximinus.

Line 16. *Persians.*—Same as in book x, 344.

Line 20. *Soldier-king.*—Gordian III., who defeated the Persian army under Sapor on the banks of the Chaboras, a branch of the Euphrates, and was soon afterward killed by Philippus (M. Julius Philippus), who succeeded to the empire.

(1–15.)

Marching against the Assyrians, a new Mars,
Who will stretch out to the deep silver stream
Of the Euphrates, having thither sent
A little warlike force . . . [through ignorance]
25 For, by his friend abandoned, he shall fall
Amid the ranks, struck by the burning iron.
   Then will a purple-loving warrior rule,
Appearing out of Syria, fear of Mars,
And by his son, a Cæsar, will persuade
30 The whole world.   Both their names will be obtained
If upon one and twenty there are placed
Five hundred.   But when these shall rule in war,
And enact laws, there shall be, but not long,
Respite from war.   But when unto a flock
35 A wolf makes oath against the white-toothed dogs,
Then will he spoil and hurt the woolly sheep,
And cast them down, in spite of all his oaths.
And then of lawless and perfidious kings
There shall be strife in wars, and terribly
40 Shall the Syrians be destroyed, and Indians,
Armenians, Arabs, Persians, Babylonians,
Through mighty conflict shall destroy each other.
   But when a Roman Mars shall overthrow
The Germans, having in a dreadful war
45 Triumphed upon the ocean, then will be

Line 24. Here the Greek text is somewhat corrupt and uncertain.

Line 28. *Out of Syria.*—The reference is to M. Julius Philippus, who was called the Arabian because of his birth in Bostra, Syria, somewhere to the south of Damascus. Comp. lines 84 and 85.

Line 29. *His son.*—Philippus associated his son, of the same name, with him in the empire.

Lines 31, 32. The Greek letter for five hundred is Φ, initial of Philippus. The "one and twenty" is to be understood as denoting the initials (A=1 and K=20) of Augustus, the title assumed by the father, and Cæsar (Kaisar), the name of his son.

(16–36.)

Among the Persian men of insolence
A war of many years; but victory
Shall not be theirs. For as a fish swims not
Upon the summit of a lofty rock
50 Many ridged, windy, inaccessible,
Nor does a tortoise fly, nor eagle swim
In water, so the Persians in that day
From victory shall be far, while the fond nurse
Of the Italians in the plain of Nile
55 Reposing, and beside the sacred wave,
Shall send the appointed lot to seven-hilled Rome.
These things shall pass, but while the name of Rome
Shall numbers hold of calculable time,
So many years by voluntary act
60 Will the great noble city of the king
Of Macedonia measure out the grain.
    Another toilsome song will I now sing
Unto the Alexandrians, by the strife
Of shameful men destroyed. Those who were strong
65 Aforetime, being then weak, will wish
For peace, because of leaders' wickedness.
    And the wrath of the mighty God shall come
On the Assyrians, and a mountain stream
Shall utterly destroy them, as it comes
70 And injures Cæsar's city of the moon.
The Pyramus will irrigate the city

Line 54. *Nurse of the Italians.*—The land of Egypt as represented in the city of Alexandria, the great source of the grain traffic which supplied the Roman world. Comp. Acts **xxvii**, 6.

Line 57. *Name of Rome.*—Comp. book viii, 187, where the numerical value of the letters of this name is given.

Line 70. *City of the moon.*—Perhaps referring to Seleucia on the Tigris, but the text is doubtful. Comp. line 119.

Line 71. *Pyramus.*—River of Cilicia.

Of Mopsus; then shall the Ægæans fall
Because of battle among mighty men.
   O wretched Antioch, thee heavy war
75 Will not leave; an Assyrian war shall press
Around thee, for within thy palaces
Shall dwell a chief of men, who will fight all
The arrow-hurling Persians, having been
Himself born of the Romans' royal power.
80   Now, cities of Arabia, deck yourselves
With temples and with stadia for the race,
And with broad markets, and with splendid wealth,
With images, gold, silver, ivory;
And of all thou, especially, O Bostra,
85 City of Philip, that thou mayest come
Into great sorrow; for the laughing forms
Of the zodiacal circle, Ram, and Bull,
And Twins, will not assist thee; nor with these
Whatever stars are visible in heaven
90 Determining the hours. O wretched one,
That, having trusted many, afterward
That very man should what is thine pollute!
   Now to war-loving Alexandrians
Will I proceed to sing most dreadful wars.
95 And surely many people will be slain
When cities perish, and opposing states
Wrangle and fight about an odious feud.
And around these will horrid Mars rush on
And stir up war. And then one of great soul

Line 72. *Mopsus.*—More commonly called Mopsuestia, a town situated
on the Pyramus. *Ægæans.*—Inhabitants of the city of Ægæ, near the
mouth of this same river.
   Line 74. *Wretched Antioch.*—Comp. line 155, and book iv, 177.
   Line 84. *Bostra.*—Situated some fifty miles to the south of Damascus.
   Line 87. *Zodiacal circle.*—These allusions refer to a notable devotion to
astrology on the part of the people of this region.

100 Along with his own mighty son shall fall
By means of the treachery of the older king.
And after him another great-souled man
And skilled in war, shall rule strong verdant Rome,
Proceeding from the Dacians, of the number
105 Three hundred, also of the letter four.
Many will he destroy ; and then all brothers
And friends will the king slay, even kings being killed.
Then also on the former king's account
Will thefts and murders suddenly occur.
110   Then when a very crafty man shall come,
A robber, out of Syria appearing,
Ignoble Roman, also craftily
A race of Cappadocians will approach,
And fall in siege, insatiable of war.
115 Then, Tyana and Mazaca, shall be
Thy conquest ; thou shalt be in servitude
And bear a heavy yoke upon thy neck.
And Syria shall mourn for men destroyed;
Nor will the moon her holy city save,
120 When he first out of Syria, sore beset, ·
Shall flee the Romans through Euphrates' streams,
No longer like the Romans, but the fierce

Line 100. *Mighty son.*—The son referred to in line 29.

Line 104. *From the Dacians.*—Pannonia and Dacia joined each other, and the two names were easily interchangeable with a poet.

Line 105. *Three hundred . . . four*—T, the numeral for 300, is the initial of Trajan, Δ (=4) here represents Decius.

Line 110. *Crafty man.*—Probable reference to Cyriades, one of the so-called "thirty tyrants," or pretenders, that arose in various parts of the empire about this time. Alexandre adds to this line the conjectural reading *of twenty*, which, having K for its letter, would also denote Cyriades [Kuriades].

Line 115. *Tyana and Mazaca.*—Chief cities of Cappadocia.

Line 119. *Her holy city.*—Seleucia on the Tigris, noted for the worship of the moon. Comp. line 70.

Dart-hurling Persians, then the Italian lord
Broken will fall, struck by the burning iron,
125 Having left his world ; his children perish too.
But when a Gallic king shall govern Rome,
Then also to the Romans there shall come
Unstable nations,—to the walls of Rome
Mars the destroyer with his bastard son.
130 Then also shall come famines, pestilence,
And wasting thunder-bolts, and dreadful wars,
And tumults of the cities suddenly,
And the Syrians shall be terribly destroyed,
For on them shall come wrath of the Most High.
135 And straightway there shall be a rising up
Of the inventive Persians, and conjoined
With Persians shall the Syrians overthrow
The Romans; but, controlled by the decree
Of power divine, they shall not conquer laws.
140 Alas ! how many will flee from the East
With their goods unto men of other tongues !
Alas ! the dark blood of how many men
The land shall drink !   For this shall be the time
In which the living will with their own mouths
145 Call the dead happy.   Beautiful to die,
They will exclaim, and it will flee from them.
Now over thee, O wretched Syria,
I weep in sorrow, for to thee shall come
A dreadful blow from arrow-hurling men,
150 Which thou didst hope would never come to thee.

Line 123. *Italian lord.*—That is, Decius, who was slain by a shower of
darts while fighting with the Goths.

Line 126. *Gallic king.*—Gallus Trebonianus, who was proclaimed emperor
by the legions on the death of Decius.

Line 129. *Bastard son.*—Reference to Volusianus, son of Gallus.

Line 145. Comp. books ii, 367, and viii, 440.

(100–121.)

Also the fugitive of Rome shall come,
Lifting on high his spear, and, passing through
Euphrates with his many myriads,
He will burn thee, and all things ill-dispose.
155   O wretched Antioch, thee they no more
Will call a city, when beneath the spears
Thou shalt fall down by thine own lack of sense;
And having spoiled and stripped thee of all things,
They leave thee coverless, without a house,
160 And whoso sees thee will at once lament.
And thou, O Hierapolis, shalt be
A triumph; thou, Berœa, too; weep ye
At Chalcis for the children newly slain.
Alas, alas, how many shall abide
165 By high Mount Cassius, by Amanus, too;
As many also as the Lycus laves,
And Marsuas and silvery Pyramus.
For even to Asia's borders they will take
The spoil, strip cities, and all idols take away,
170 And cast down temples to the nursing earth.
And then to Gallia and Pannonia,
To Mysians and Bithynians there shall be
A mighty sorrow, when the soldier comes.
O Lycians, Lycians, there will come a wolf
175 To lick thy blood, whenever Sannians come

Line 151. *Fugitive.*—Comp. book iv, 175.

Lines 155–157. Comp. book iv, 177–179.

Lines 161–163. *Hierapolis ... Berœa ... Chalcis.*—Cities of Syria, eastward from Antioch.

Line 165. *Cassius.*—Rising to the south of Antioch. *Amanus.*—A mountain range north of Antioch and overlooking the valley of the Pyramus.

Line 166. *Lycus.*—River of Pontus.

Line 167. *Marsuas.*—Or *Marsyas*, river of Syria, a branch of the Orontes.

Lines 171–177. The mention of these widely-separated provinces depicts the broad range of the desolating wars of this period.

(122–140.)

11

With city-wasting Mars, and Carpians
Draw near to fight with the Ausonians.
   And then by his own shameless recklessness
A bastard son will put the king to death,
180 And he himself for his impiety
Will straightway perish.   After him again
Will yet another rule, whose name presents
The first of letters ; quickly shall he fall
By mighty Mars, struck by the burning iron.
185   And yet again the world shall be confused,
Men perishing by pestilence and war.
And the Persians shall again force on the toil
Of warfare, maddened by the Ausonians.
And then there shall a flight of Romans be.
190 But then shall come a priest, the last of all
Sent by the sun, from Syria appearing,
And he will all things by deceit effect.
And then shall be a city of the sun,
And around it [the Persians] will endure
195 The fearful menaces of the Phenicians.
   But when two leaders, warlike men, shall rule
The mighty Romans, one of whom shall have
The number seventy, one the number three,
Then the proud bull that digs the earth with hoofs,

Line 179. *Bastard son.*—The same as in line 129.

Line 183. *First of letters.*—Evidently denoting Æmilianus, who was himself in turn cut off before he had reigned four months.

Line 187. *Persians again.*—Under Sapor, who captured Valerian, put the Romans to flight, and spread destruction over Syria and Cappadocia.

Line 190. *Priest.*—Odenatus.

Line 193. *City of the sun.*—Here referring to Palmyra.

Line 198. *Seventy . . . three.*—The first is represented by O, initial of the Greek form of the name Valerian [Οὐαλῆριανος], and the second by Γ, initial of Gallienus.

Line 199. *Bull.*—Here representing Valerian, who dealt out many ills to the Persians, but was himself destroyed.

(140–157.)

200 And raises up the dust with double horns,
    Shall do the dark-skinned reptile many ills,
    Which draws a trailing furrow with his scales,
    And he himself shall perish. After him
    Shall come another, beautiful-horned stag,
205 Hungry upon the mountains, craving strong
    To feed upon the venom-shedding beasts.
    Then shall a fierce and dreadful lion come,
    Sent from the sun, and breathing plenteous flame.
    And then with much and shameless recklessness
210 Will he destroy the rapid, well-horned stag,
    And the huge beast so venomous and dread
    That sends forth many a cry, and the he-goat,
    Bow-legged, and renown will follow him.
    And he himself, obtaining all by lot,
215 Uninjured and insatiable, shall rule
    The Romans, and the Persians shall be weak.
    But thou, O Prince, King of the world, God, end
    The song of my words, and give charming song.

Line 201. *Dark-skinned reptile.*—Sapor, King of the Persians.

Line 204. *Stag.*—Macrianus, the Roman general.

Line 207. *Lion.*—Odenatus.

Line 211. *Huge beast.*—The Persians.

Line 212. *He-goat.*—Reference doubtful. Alexandre suggests Balista, one of the so-called "thirty tyrants," who made pretension to the throne in the reign of Gallienus.

Line 214. *He himself.*—Odenatus.

Lines 217-218. Comp. conclusion of books ix and x.

BOOK XII. (XIV.)

CONTENTS OF BOOK XII. (XIV.)

Warning against the lust of power, 1–13. The bull-destroyer, 14–20. The man known by the number one, 21–24. Two rulers of the number forty, 25–31. Young ruler of the number seventy, 32–51. Ruler of the number forty, 52–60. Ruler known by the letter A, 61–68. Three kings of haughty soul, of the numbers one, thirty, and three hundred, 69–87. King known by the number three, 88–92. The old king of the number four, 93–114. The venerable king of the number five, 115–128. Two kings of the numbers three hundred and three, 129–140. The king of many schemes, 141–152. King of the number three hundred, 153–165. King like a wild beast, of the number thirty, 166–181. Ruler of the number four, 182–196. Ruler out of Asia, of the number fifty, 197–207. Ruler out of Egypt, 208–214. The man of potent signs, 215–224. The peaceful king of the number five, 225–235. Many tyrants, 236–244. The holy king known by the letter A, 245–251. Burning and restoration of Rome, 252–261. Woe for various Greeks, 262–267. The fratricide, 268–272. The fierce king of the number eighty and the terrors of his time, 273–296. Many obtain royal power, 297–300. Three kings and their destruction, 301–316. Many spearmen, 317–321. God's judgment on the shameless, 322–328. Plots and suffering followed by rest, 329–337. Last race of Latin kings, 338–342. Egypt and her prudent king, 343–358. The Alexandrians, 359–378. The Sicilians, 379–385. The lion and lioness, 386–389. Much massacre, 390–396. The dragon and the ram, 397–402. Second war on Egypt, 403–422. The Messianic era, 423–440.

BOOK XII. (XIV.)

MEN, why in vain, as though ye were immortals,
And being in power but for a little time,
Do ye imagine such exalted things,
All of you wishing over men to reign?
5 Not understanding that the lust of power
God himself hates, and most the insatiate kings,
Malevolent, ungodly, and on such
Brings darkness; for instead of noble deeds
And righteous thoughts, ye all choose purple robes.
10 These, loving wars and miseries and murders,
Short-lived will be made by the immortal God,
Who dwells in heaven, and will exterminate,
And upon one another ruin them.
    But when, fair-haired and terrible, shall come
15 The bull-destroyer, trusting in his might,
He also will slay all, and tear the shepherds,

This book is the most obscure and inexplicable of the entire collection. Its date and authorship are quite uncertain. After the opening lines against the lust of power (1–13) there appears to be an allusion to the closing part of the preceding book; but the writer goes on to designate a long succession of emperors and conquerors, giving the initial letter of most of the names as in previous books, and otherwise describing them, yet so inconsistently with what we know of history as to leave it impossible to identify with any certainty the individuals and events intended. Ewald has attempted to identify most of these names with known characters of Roman and Byzantine history (*Abhandlung*, pp. 99–111), but the results of his study have commanded no following. In the following notes we insert for the benefit of the reader his more plausible conjectures, but with no conviction that they represent the persons intended by the author.

Line 15. *Bull-destroyer.*—That is, the lion mentioned in book xi, 207, symbolizing Odenatus.

Line 16. *Shepherds.*—Chiefs of the various tribes and nations whom Odenatus subdued.

(1–14.)

And they will have no strength, except the dogs,
With swift foot eagerly pursuing on,
Encounter in the strife, and then the dog
20 Will chase the lion that destroyed the shepherds.
   Then shall there be a man, four-syllabled,
Trusting in might, made clearly known by one;
But quickly him will brazen Mars destroy
By battles of insatiable men.
25   Then shall two other princely men bear rule,
. Both of the number forty ; and with these
Great peace shall be throughout the world, and right
And justice to all people ; but even these
Will men with gleaming helmet, wanting gold,
30 And for the sake of silver, basely slay,
Having taken them in their hands. And then shall reign
A terrible young warrior, ruler known
By the number seventy, hot with deadly wrath,
Who basely to the army shall betray
35 The Roman people, slain by wickedness
Through wrath of kings, and shall hurl to the earth
Even every city of the illustrious Latins.
Rome is no longer to be seen or heard,
Such as of late the traveler's eye beheld,
40 For all those things shall in the ashes lie,
And of her works not any shall be spared.
For wrathful he will come, and out of heaven
Send lightnings from the sky, and thunderbolts,

Line 19. *The dog.*—Mæonius, the assassin of Odenatus. Comp. book viii, 199.

Line 21. *Four-syllabled.*—Aureolus.

Line 26. *Both . . . forty.*—Macrianus, father and son of same name. But from this point onward the identification of the persons intended is purely conjectural and uncertain.

Line 33. *Seventy.*—Represented by O, and possibly denoting the Achaian pretender, Valens.

Upon mankind—even God, the immortal One;
45 And some he will destroy by burning blasts,
And others with his chilling thunder-bolts.
And then shall children of Rome, mighty Rome,
And the Latins slay the shameless ruler dire;
Nor on him, dead, shall the dust lightly lie,
50 For he shall be a sport for dogs, and birds,
And wolves, for he destroyed a warlike tribe.
     After him, numbering forty, there shall rule
Another, famous Parthian-destroyer,
German-destroyer, slayer of fierce beasts
55 That kill men, who upon the ocean's streams
And the Euphrates press unceasing on.
And then again shall Rome be as before.
But when there comes a great wolf in thy plains,
A ruler from the West, then he shall die
60 By mighty Mars, pierced through with the sharp brass.
     Then o'er the valiant Romans there shall rule
Another great-souled warrior, brought to light
Out of Assyria, and his name begins
The letters ; in subjection he himself
65 Will bring all things by wars, and he at once
Over the armies will exhibit power
And laws establish. But him brazen Mars
Will soon destroy, in treacherous armies fallen.
     After him three of haughty soul shall reign,
70 One having the first number, one three tens,
And the other king three hundred will partake.

Line 53. *Parthian-destroyer.*—Macrinus (M—40).

Line 58. *Wolf.*—Reference, perhaps, to Quintilius, the brother of Claudius. *Lines* 61–68. Aurelian.

Line 69. *Three.*—Their names beginning with A, L (Λ—30), and T (—300), the reference might be to Achilleus, whom the people of Palmyra invested with the purple, and Lollian and Tetricus, who, however, belonged to the western provinces.

(37–60.)

11*

Cruel, they gold and silver in much fire
Will melt, statues for temples made with hands,
And to the armies they, being armed, will give
75 Money for victory, and costly things
Will they distribute, numerous and good,
Devising shameful things, so they shall harm
The arrow-hurling Parthians of the deep
And swift Euphrates, and the hostile Medes,
80 And fair-haired warriors the Massagetæ,
And the strong Persians, quiver-bearing men.
  But when the king by his own fate shall fail,
Leaving the royal scepter to his sons
More valiant, urging them to what is right,
85 Then they, unmindful of their father's prayers,
And girding on the implements of war,
Will rush in conflict for the royal power.
  And then a king, known from [the number] three,
Shall rule alone, and, smitten by the spear,
90 Shall quickly see his fate. And after him
Shall many perish at each other's hands,
Strong mortals, wrestling for the royal power.
  And one of mighty soul shall then bear rule
Over the mighty Romans, an old king,
95 Of the number four, and all things well dispose.
And then shall war unto Phenicia come
And conflict, when the nation shall approach
Of arrow-shooting Persians ; and how many
Shall fall down under men of barbarous speech!
100 Sidon, and Tripolis, and Berytus

Lines 82–87. These lines fittingly describe Septimius Severus and his sons, Geta and Caracalla, but seem out of place in this connection.

Line 88. *Three.*—The reading is doubtful, and the reference altogether uncertain.

Line 95. *Four.*—Represented by Δ, initial of Diocletian.

(61–83.)

The loudly boasting, shall each other see
Covered with blood and bodies of the dead.
Wretched Laodicea, round thyself
Thou shalt a great and unsuccessful war
105 Stir up through the impiety of men.
O hapless Tyrians, ye shall gather in
An evil harvest, when in the day-time
The sun that lighteth mortals shall retire,
And his disk not appear, and drops of blood,
110 Thick and abundant, shall come down from heaven
Upon the earth. And then the king shall die,
Betrayed by his companions. After him
Shall many shameless leaders still promote
The wicked strife, and one another kill.
115 And then shall be a venerable king
Sagacious, with a name that numbers five,
Confiding in great armies ; him will men
Love for his royal power, and of a name
Illustrious, he shall do illustrious deeds.
120 While this king reigns there shall be a great sign:
'Twixt Taurus and Amanus, clad with snow,
From the Cilician land shall be destroyed
A certain city, new and beautiful
And mighty, by a powerful-flowing stream.
125 And in Propontis and in Phrygia
There shall be many earthquakes ; and the king
Of great renown shall under his own fate
By wasting, deadly sickness end his life.
And after him shall rule two princely kings,
130 One's name three hundred, and the other three.

Lines 107–111. Comp. book ii, 21 ; iii, 948–958 ; x, 72, 73.
Line 116. *Five.*—Represented by E, initial of Eugenius.
Line 130. *Three hundred.*—Represented by T, and, according to Ewald's conjecture, here designating Theodosius by his Latin initial. *Three.*—Γ, initial of Gratian.

So also he will utterly destroy
Many upon the seven-hilled city Rome,
That he the mighty kingdom may obtain.
And then unto the Senate there shall be
135 A deep misfortune ; it shall not escape
The angry king, against it holding wrath.
And furious rains and snow-storms shall there be,
And hail shall ruin fruits upon the earth,
And men shall fall in battles, overcome
140 By mighty Mars in the Italian wars.
   And then another king, of many schemes,
Shall bear rule, all the army summoning,
And for the sake of war distributing
Treasures to those with brazen breastplate clad.
145 The corn-abounding Nile beyond the shores
Of Libya shall for two years irrigate
The plain of Egypt and the fertile land.
But famine will on all things seize, and war,
Robberies, murders, slaughter of mankind.
150 And many cities shall by warlike men
Be overthrown ; and at the army's hands
Himself, betrayed, shall fall by burning iron.
   After him one whose number is three hundred
Shall rule the Romans and the mighty men,
155 And he will stretch a deadly javelin forth
Against the Armenians, and the Parthians,
The Assyrians, and the Persians, bold in fight.
And then a structure there shall be at Rome,
Magnificently built of gold and amber,
160 Silver and ivory and beauty rare.
   And in it many people shall abide

Line 153. *Three hundred.*—If the T of line 130 could represent Theodosius, this would most naturally refer to Theodosius the Younger, whom
Gratian invested with the purple.

From all the East, and from the prosperous West;
And for it other laws the king will make.
Him afterward upon a boundless isle
165 Shall wasting death and mighty fate receive.
    Another man, of ten times three, shall reign,
Like a wild beast, with mane, and terrible,
And from the Greeks shall he his lineage trace.
And then in fertile Phthia shall the city
170 Of the Molossi fall, and also famed
Larissa, situate on Peneus' banks.
And then in horse-abounding Scythia
Shall there be insurrection, and dire war
Beside the waters of Mæotis' lake,
175 At the outpourings of the utmost draught
Of Phasis' watery fountain on the meads
Of asphodel. And many then will fall
By powerful warriors. Ah, by fiery brass
How many Mars will seize! And then the king
180 Will utterly destroy the Scythian race,
And die in his own lot, releasing life.
    Then shall another rule, made evident
By the number four, a fearful man, whom all
The Armenians, even as many as shall drink
185 The thick ice of Araxes' flowing stream,
And the brave Persians shall much fear in war.
Between the Colchians and Pelasgi strong
Shall there be fearful wars and homicides,
And Phrygia's land and cities of the land
190 Propontis, making bare their two-edged swords,
Shall smite each other in base wickedness.

Line 166. *Ten times three*—Δ, initial of Leo, who was acknowledged emperor of the East in A. D. 457.

Line 183. *Four*—Δ, representing, as Ewald suggests, Dreskyllas, another form of the name Threskyllas.

Then a great sign with the revolving years
Will God from heaven display to mortal men,
A falcon, omen of pernicious war.
195 The king will not escape the army's hands,
But die at their hands, cut by burning iron.
   After him, numbering fifty, there shall reign
Another, out of Asia, terrible,
A fierce antagonist, and he will place
200 War even on the famous walls of Rome,
And on the Colchians, and the Henochians,
And the milk-drinking Agathyrsians,
The Euxine Sea and Thracia's sandy bay.
The king will not escape the army's hands,
205 Whom, even dead, they will abuse his corpse.
And then, the king destroyed, illustrious Rome
Shall be a desert, and much people perish.
   And then again one terrible and dread
From mighty Egypt will bear rule, and slay
210 The great-souled Parthians, and the Medes, and Germans,
And Agathyrsians of the Bosporus,
Britons, Hibernians, and Iberians
That bear the quiver, crooked Massagetæ,
And Persians thinking themselves more than men.
215   And then a famous man upon all Greece
Will turn his eye, and act the enemy
To Scythia and windy Caucasus.
And while he rules a potent sign shall be:
Crowns altogether like the beaming stars
220 From heaven will shine forth in the south and north.
Then he will leave unto his son, whose name

Line 194. *Falcon.*—Greek φάλκη (a bat?).
Line 197. *Fifty*—N, initial of Nepos, emperor in A. D. 474.
Lines 208–214. The reference is unknown, and the allusions of the rest of
the book defy even the ingenuity of Ewald to make even plausible.

(158–182.)

Begins the alphabet, the royal power,
And forthwith by his fate into the house
Of Hades will the noble king depart.
225   And when his son rules in the land of Rome,
Known from one, there shall be on all the earth
Great peace much longed for, and the Latin people
Will love the king even for his father's worth.
Him, urgent to go to the East and West,
230 The Romans will hold firmly fast at home
Against his will, and in command of Rome,
Because among all there is friendly soul
Felt for the royal and illustrious prince.
But ruinous death will snatch him out of life,
235 Short-lived, given over to his destiny.
   Other strong warriors afterward again
Shall smite each other, forwarding base strife,
Not exercising royal power of kings,
But that of tyrants. And in all the world
240 Will they accomplish many evil things,
But chiefly to the Romans, till the time
Of the third Dionysus, until Mars
With gleaming helmet shall from Egypt come,
Whom they Prince Dionysus then will call.
245   But when a murderous lion and lioness
The famous purple royal robe shall rend,
They will upon the inmost vitals seize,
The kingdom being hard pressed ; and then a holy king,
Whose name has the first letter, will exchange
250 Hostile chiefs for the sake of victory,
And leave them as a prey for dogs and birds.
Woe, woe to thee, thou city burned with fire,
O powerful Rome ! How many things for thee
To suffer when all these things come to pass!
255 But afterward the great and famous king
(183–210.)

With gold and amber, silver and ivory,
Will altogether raise thee up again,
And in the world thou shalt be first in goods,
And temples, markets, riches, stadia ;
260 And thou again shalt be a light for all,
Even as thou hast been in the former time.
    Woe, wretched Cecrops, and ye Argive Greeks,
Laconians, too, and those around Peneus,
And by Molossos' stream thick grown with reeds,
265 Tricca, Dodona, Ithome cut on high,
Pierus' neck, and great Olympus' peak,
Ossa, Larissa, and high-gate Calydon.
    But when for mortals God works a great sign
And day becomes dark twilight round the world,
270 Even then to thee, O king, the end shall come,
Nor wilt thou find it possible to flee
A brother's piercing bow against thee thrown.
    And then a life-destroying one shall reign,
Unspeakable, fierce, of the royal line.
275 Who shall have Egypt's race, much heavier armed
And stronger than his brother ; he obtains
The number eighty as initial mark.
Then all the world will in its bosom feel
The grievous wrath of the immortal God
280 For penalty.   And there shall come on men
Famines, and plagues, and wars, and homicides,
And ceaseless darkness also on the earth,
Mother of peoples, and disordered times,
And wrath severe from heaven, and earthquake shocks,
285 And flaming thunder-bolts, and stones, and storms,
And squalid drops.   A quaking also moves
The lofty summits of the Phrygian land,
The bases of the Scythian mountains shake ;
The city trembled, trembled all the earth,
               (211-237.)

290 Along with those of the Hellenic land.
And many cities, God being very wroth,
Shall fall prone under flaming thunder-bolts
And lamentations ; and to flee the wrath
And make escape is not even possible.
295 Then at the army's hand the king shall fall,
Struck down, as no one, under his own men.
 After him of the Latins many men
Will be raised up, and on their shoulders place
The purple mantle, longing to obtain
300 By lot the royal power. And then three kings
Shall be upon the famous walls of Rome,
Two having the first number, but the one
The name of victory as no other bears.
Concerned for men, they will have love for Rome
305 And all the world, and there shall be for them
No relaxation. For not to the world
Has God been gracious, nor will he to men
Be kind, since they have many evils done.
Therefore made he for kings a shameful soul,
310 Much worse than that of panthers and of wolves.
For them will men, in brazen helmets clad,
Seizing unsparingly with their own hands,
And for their scepters utterly destroy,
Even kings, like helpless women cleft for naught.
315 Woe, wretched lofty men of glorious Rome,
Trusting in false oaths, ye shall be destroyed.
 And many spearmen then upon the world,
Men rushing forward, will the offspring seize
From blood of first-born men. . . .
320 Twice may not demon such a lot first lead ;
And all men he will with their works destroy.
 But God again those having shameless soul
Will bring into the judgment yet to come,

Line 319. Lacuna in Greek text.
(238–267.)

As many as are marked ; these, sent away
325 Into that condemnation of wickedness,
Are fenced in, striking one upon another.
And many stars, and brilliant comet, [sign]
Of much war and of battle-strife to come.
　But when one gathers many oracles
330 Concerning islands, planning with strange guests
War and fierce strife and harm to sacred things,
And in the Roman houses gathers wheat
And barley, pressing for abundance on,
For twelve months long, the city in those days
335 Shall suffer hardship.　But straightway again
It shall be prosperous not a little while ;
And rest will come when ruling is destroyed.
　And then the last race of the Latin kings
Shall come, the kingdom will again grow up,
340 And children and the children's race shall be
Unshaken, for it shall be known to them
When God himself shall be the ruling king.
　There is a land, fond nourisher of men,
Situate in an open plain ; the Nile
345 Around it borders, wafting blessings on
All Libya and Ethiopia.
And short-lived Syrians, some here and some there,
Shall plunder all the substance of that land.
And it shall have a great and prudent king ;
350 Sending one of the children as a light,
And meditating dreadful things for such
As are exceeding dreadful unto all,
He will of all high-minded Italy
A mighty helper bring.　And when he comes
355 Unto Assyria's dark-colored sea,
He will spoil the Phenicians in their homes,

Lines 327, 328. Comp. book viii, 237–240.
(268–293.)

Unloosing foul war and dire battle-din.
Of the two rulers one shall rule the earth.
Now will I of the Alexandrians sing
360 The painful end.   Barbarians shall dwell
In sacred Egypt, unharmed, quiet land,
Whenever envy shall from some place come.
Winter will become summer ; then will all
The oracles to their fulfillment come.
365 But when three youths in the Olympia
Shall conquer, and to them, while they take heed,
Thou speak the oracle invoked of God
To cleanse them first by blood of tender beasts,
Thrice then may the Highest move his awful neck.
370 Whenever he the long and mournful spear
Shall stretch out upon all, much barbarous blood
Will flow amid the dust, when by strange guests
The city has been plundered utterly.
Happy is he who died, and happy he
375 Who has no child.   For under slavish yoke
Shall he be placed that formerly was free,
And famous once for plans himself revolved.
Such is the various slavery of kings.
And then of the Sicilians there shall come
380 A host ill-fated, carrying dire alarm,
When a barbarian nation shall approach.
When they grow fruit they will divide the land.
To them will God, the lofty thunderer,
Evil for evil give ; continually
385 Guest plundering guest of gold will go away.
But when all see the fearful lion's blood,
And when unto the body there shall come

Lines 363, 364. Comp. book viii, 266.
  Lines 386–400. Here there seems to be a return to the allegory of book
xi, 199–213.

The murderous lioness, then he will rend
Away from him the scepter from his head.

390　As when in Egypt at the friendly feast
The people all eat, and complete great works,
One finds another, and there is among them
Much shouting, also thus alarm shall be
Among men, while the conflict rages round,

395　And many perish, and they massacre
Each other in impetuous battle fray.
And then one covered with dark scales shall come.
Two others shall come hostile to each other;
With them a third, a great ram from Cyrene

400　Of whom I spoke before, who flees in battle
Along the streams of Nile.　But yet not thus
Do all complete the unsuccessful way.
　　And then the lengths of the great rolling years
Shall be all tranquil.　Yet a second war

405　Shall then again on Egypt be imposed;
And they shall boast, but have no victory.
O wretched craftsmen of a noble city!
And in wars there shall not be booty long.
And then the neighboring men of a large land

410　Shall flee in fear, and lead their fearful sires.
And then, obtaining a great victory,
Shall they upon the city light again;
They will destroy courageous Jewish men,
Slaughtering by war far as the hoary sea,

415　Both shepherds for their fatherland and sires.
But to the dead there shall succeed a race
Of trophy-bearing men.　Alas! how many men
Around the waves shall swim!　For multitudes
Will lie exposed upon the sandy shores;

420　Heads covered with the golden hair shall fall
Under the swift Egyptians; then indeed
　　　　　　(318–346.)

Shall follow the Arabians' mortal blood.

But when wolves pledge themselves by oaths to dogs

Upon a sea-girt isle, then shall there be

425 A rising up of towers, and men will dwell

In the city that has suffered many things.

No more will treacherous gold and silver be,

Nor earthly wealth, nor toilsome servitude,

But one fast friendship and one mode of life

430 Will be with the glad people, and all things

Will common be, and equal light of life.

And wickedness from earth in the vast sea

Shall sink away.   And then the harvest-time

Of mortals is near.   Strong necessity

435 Is laid upon these things to be fulfilled.

Nor then will any other traveler say,

Recalling, that men's perishable race

Shall ever cease.   And then o'er all the earth

A holy nation will the scepter hold

440 Unto all ages with their mighty sires.

Line 426. *City that suffered.*—Jerusalem.

Lines 427–440. Messianic picture of the coming golden age.

(347–361.)

INDEX.

THE NUMBERS DESIGNATE PAGES.

Acheron, 46, 67, 153.
Achilles, 92.
Acrostic, 185.
Adam, four-lettered, 72.
Ægæans, 238.
Æneas, 208.
Agathyrsians, 254.
Aggon, 96.
Alexandria, 87, 132, 211, 212.
Alexandrians, 237, 238, 259.
Alps, 168.
Amalek, 187.
Amanus, 241, 251.
Ammon, 127, 210, 219.
Antandrus, 90.
Antigone, 87.
Antioch, 87, 121, 238, 241.
Apis, 164.
Apollo, 118.
Arabia, 238.
Arabians, 97, 209, 227, 235, 236, 261.
Ararat, 44.
Araxes, 253.
Argives (see Greeks), 256.
Armenia, 119.
Armenians, 235, 236, 252, 253.
Asia, 79, 87, 88, 89, 91, 92, 93, 100, 113, 116, 117, 121, 133, 134, 143, 151, 152, 178, 181, 210, 211, 254.
Assaracus, 127, 208, 219.
Assyria, 211, 249, 253.
Assyrian, 202, 205.
Assyrian-Babylon, 78, 175.
Assyrians, 60, 75, 81, 83, 85, 115, 145, 204, 208, 209, 221, 223, 225, 226, 230, 235, 236, 237, 238, 252.
Astypalia, 87.
Athenagoras, citation of Sibyl, 76.
Augustine, citation of Sibyl, 185.
Ausonia, 128, 223, 232.
Ausonians, 242.

Babylon, 76, 85, 89, 118, 127, 128, 135, 136, 150, 211, 219.
Babylonians, 134, 236.

Bactria, 118.
Baptism, allusion to, 48.
Barca, 187.
Basil, citation of Sibyl, 25.
Basilis, 87.
Beliar, 60, 74.
Bercea, 241.
Berytas, 166, 250.
Bethlehem, star of, 197.
Bithynia, 209.
Bithynians, 134, 230, 241.
Bosporus, 254.
Bostra, 238.
Britons, 138, 227, 254.
Byzantium, 92.

Cæsars (see Emperors), 213.
Calydon, 256.
Camarina, 106.
Campania, 94, 221.
Cappadocians, 97, 239.
Carchedon (see Carthage), 118.
Caria, 79, 81, 94, 117, 121.
Carians, 143.
Carpians, 242.
Carthage, 95.
Cassius, 241.
Caucasus, 254.
Cebren, 87.
Cecrops, 256.
Celtic land, 168, 225.
Celtic mountaineer, 129.
Celtic warrior, 226.
Chalcedon, 92.
Chalcis, 241.
Chaldeans, 150.
Chios, 91.
Cilicia, 211, 230.
Cilician, 251.
Clement of Alex., citation of Sibyl, 24, 25, 26, 101, 113, 114.
Cleopatra, 213.
Clitos, 87.
Cœle-Syria, 166.
Colchians, 221, 253, 254.

Colophon, 87, 166.
Comet, sign of evil, 86, 183, 258.
Constellations, 238.
Constellations, conflict of, 139, 155.
Corcyra, 144.
Corinth, 95, 119, 139, 166.
Corsica, 94.
Creation, 33, 196.
Crete, 96, 151, 177.
Cross, the, 160, 187.
Croton, 117.
Cumæ, 144.
Cyagra, 87.
Cyprus, 93, 120, 121, 151, 163.
Cyrene, 138, 260.
Cyzicus, 92, 118.

Dacians, 227, 239.
Dardans, 96.
David, 164, 187.
Delphi, oracle of, 8.
Delos, 88, 163, 182.
Deluge, 42.
Demeter, 77.
Dia, 77.
Diana, temple of, 143.
Dione, 77.
Dionysius Halicarnasseus, account of Sibyl, 10.
Dionysus, 255.
Dodona, 77, 256.
Dorylæum, 99.

Egypt, 73, 78, 80. 81, 85, 87, 100, 101, 116, 127, 131, 132, 133, 137, 146, 151, 152, 153, 154, 164, 175, 202, 203, 204, 207, 212, 221, 252, 254, 255, 256, 259, 260.
Egypt, kings of, 181, 182, 212, 215, 219, 220.
Egyptians, 142.
Emperors, Roman, designated by initial letters, 127–130, 175–178, 219–232, 239, 242, 248–257.
Elysian fields, 67.
Ephesus, 87, 93, 143, 144.
Erebus, 38, 103.
Eridanus, 135, 144. 221.
Ethiopia, 78, 81, 86, 258.
Ethiopians, 97, 138, 139, 154, 164, 204, 209.
Etna, 117.
Euphrates, 116, 119, 120, 133, 150, 208, 236, 239, 241, 249, 250.
Europe, 87, 88, 89, 91, 93, 113, 210, 212.
Eurotas, 78.
Eusebius, citation of Sibyl, 185.
Euxine, 254.

Fates, the three, 139.
Firmianus (see Lactantius), use of the Sibylline verses, 22.
Floyer, trans. of Sibylline Oracles, 16.

Gabriel, 62, 196.
Gaia, 76, 77.
Galatians, 95, 96, 146.
Gallia, 241.
Gallic king, 240.
Gauls, 138.
Gaza, 87.
Gehenna, 37, 65, 123, 168.
Germans, 221, 226, 228, 236, 249, 254.
Glaucus consults Pythian oracle, 8.
Gog, 85, 96.
Greece, 118, 135, 209, 210, 254.
Greeks (see Hellas and Hellenes), 97, 98, 99, 102, 142, 180, 207, 253.
Gregory Nazianzen, citation of Sibyl, 25.

Hades, 36, 46, 49, 61, 89, 93, 95, 137, 179, 182, 184, 186, 207, 222, 225, 255.
Hades, Christ in, 190.
Hæmus, 94.
Hebrews, 49, 81, 82, 181, 203.
Hector, 92.
Hellas (see Greece), 105, 116, 117, 207, 257.
Hellenes, 79, 80.
Hellespont, 116, 145.
Henochi, 221, 254.
Hermes, 146.
Heraclitus quoted, 7.
Hercules, 132, 228.
Hierapolis, 87, 144, 232, 241.
Hibernians, 254.
Holy race, 99, 100, 141.
Homer, referred to, 91, 209.
Honorius, orders destruction of Sibylline Books, 15.

Iassus, 87.
Iberians, 184, 226, 254.
Ilion (Ilius), 91, 92, 166, 207.
India, 204, 211.
Indians, 138, 139, 235.
Ionians, 204.
Iselastic contest, 54, 59.
Isis, 130, 153.
Isthmus, cleft, 129, 140, 182.
Italians, 118, 221, 222, 236.
Italy, 94, 119, 120, 135, 136, 146, 151, 175, 179, 206, 232, 258.
Ithome, 256.

Japetus, 76.
Jerusalem (see Solyma), 223.
Jesus Christ, 47–49, 167, 188, 189, 190.
Jesus Christ, acrostic of, 185.
Jews, 212, 228, 260.
Jews, land of (see Judea), 120.
Joppa, 141.
Josephus, citation of Sibyl, 75.
Jove (Jupiter), 182, 184, 185, 177, 208, 210, 219.
Judea, 142, 145.
Judgment, the, 62, 63, 75, 103, 115, 123, 184, 185.
Juno, 77, 185.
Justin Martyr, citation of Sibyl, 25, 105, 114.

Kronos, 76, 77, 78, 80, 177, 210.

Laconians, 256.
Lactantius, account of the Sibyls, 11.
Lactantius, citation of Sibyl, 24, 25, 26, 27, 29, 85, 49, 87, 98, 101, 107, 108, 114, 115, 141, 147, 150, 159, 160, 169, 175, 177, 184, 186, 187, 188, 189, 190, 191, 193, 194.
Laodicea, 94, 118, 148, 164, 232, 251.
Lapithæ, 185.
Larissa, 253, 256.
Latin kings, 180, 181.
Latins, 127, 219, 220, 227, 255, 257, 258.
Letters, initial, 128–130, 202, 205, 208, 211, 212, 213, 236, 239, 242, 248–258.
Letters in mystic name, 89.
Letters in name of Adam, 72.
Letters in name of Jesus, 47.
Lesbos, 134, 144.
Libya, 81, 86, 138, 204, 215, 252, 258.
Locrian race, 92.
Lycia, 92, 97, 134.
Lycians, 241.
Lycurgus, 144.
Lycus, 94, 164, 241.
Lydia, 79, 93, 97, 223.
Lydians, 143, 146, 152, 209.

Macedonia, 78, 79, 80, 89, 100, 117, 118, 145, 147, 152, 175, 210, 221, 237.
Macedonians, 169.
Mæander, 121, 145.
Mænades, 130.
Mæotis, 86, 253.
Magnesia, 87.
Magog, 85, 96.
Mars, 165, 181, 210, 211, 214, 221, 222, 223, 229, 230, 231, 232, 235, 236, 238, 242, 249, 252, 253, 255.
12

Marson, 96.
Marsyas (Marsuas), 44, 241.
Mary, the Virgin, 196, 197.
Massagetæ, 134, 250, 254.
Maurians (Moors), 97, 227.
Muzaca, 239.
Medes, 115, 116, 128, 135, 151, 175, 209, 220, 250, 254.
Media, 78, 204.
Memphis, 128, 131, 137, 202, 203, 212, 220.
Meropeia, 87.
Messiah, 141, 149, 182.
Michael, 62.
Miletus, 145.
Millennial glory, 104, 105, 107, 150, 170, 261.
Molossi, 253.
Molossus, 256.
Mopsus, 238.
Moses, a type, 187.
Mygdonia, 168.
Mykene, 87.
Myra, 119.
Myrina, 87.
Mysia, 79, 95, 97.
Mysians, 241.

Nemea, 180.
Neptune (see Poseidon), 90, 136.
Nereus, 43.
Nice, 87.
Nile, 116, 131, 153, 164, 209, 213, 215, 237, 252, 258, 260.
Noah, preaching of, 40, 41.

Olympia, 259.
Olympus, 169, 256.
Orontes, 225
Ossa, 256.

Palladium, 176.
Pamphylia, 79, 81, 97.
Pamphylians, 146, 204.
Pandonia, 87.
Pannonia, 225, 241.
Pannonians, 222.
Panopeus, 216.
Pantheia, 87.
Paphos, 120, 151.
Paradise, 34.
Parthia, 227.
Parthians, 150, 208, 220, 249, 250, 252, 254.
Patara, 92, 119.
Pausanias, account of the Sibyls, 8.
Pelasgi, 253.

Peleus, 92.
Pella, 127, 211, 219.
Peneius, 78.
Peneus, 135, 253, 256.
Pentapolis, 138.
Pergamos, 134.
Persis, 78, 79, 80, 84, 93, 135, 141, 231.
Persians, 116, 117, 128, 133, 134, 150,
     165, 175, 182, 203, 204, 209, 235,
     236, 237, 238, 240, 242, 243, 250,
     252, 253, 254.
Phasis, 253.
Phenicia, 79, 95, 134, 151, 166, 223,
     226, 250.
Phenicians. 242, 258.
Phenix, 181.
Philip, 127, 219, 238.
Phocylides, his admonitory poem, 55-
     59.
Phœbus, 145.
Phrygia, 41, 44, 77, 79, 80, 90, 97, 116,
     134, 163, 207, 232, 251, 253, 256.
Phthia, 253.
Pierus, 256.
Pisideans, 146.
Pitane, 134.
Pluto, 77.
Poseidon. 77.
Priam, 92.
Propontis, 92, 251, 253.
Pyramus, 118, 237, 241.
Python, 216.

Raphael, 62.
Ravenna, 189.
Resurrection, 49, 62, 122, 184.
Rhea, 77, 78, 90, 134, 177.
Rhine, 221, 225.
Rhodes, 93, 118, 163, 182.
Rhyndacus, 92.
Romans, 148, 235, 242, 243, 248, 249,
     250.
Rome, 73, 78, 79, 87, 88, 120, 121, 135,
     140, 151, 152, 169, 176, 178, 179,
     180, 181, 182, 219, 220, 222, 225,
     227, 229, 237, 239, 240, 252, 254,
     255, 257.

Salamis, 120, 151.
Samos, 88, 93, 117, 182.
Sannians, 241.
Sardinia, 168.
Sardis, 143.
Sauromatians, 222.
Schürer on Sibylline Oracles, 18.
Scythia, 253, 254, 256.
Serapis, 153.

Sibyl, general account of, 7.
Sibyl, names of, 8, 21.
Sibyl, Cumæan, 7.
Sibyl, Jewish, 13.
Sibyl, her account of herself, 45, 67,
     109, 110, 130, 171, 216, 232, 235.
Sibyl, impersonating God, 192.
Sibylline books, destroyed by fire, 12.
Sibylline books, character of those now
     extant, 12, 13.
Sibylline books quoted by Fathers,
     14.
Sibylline books, editions of in Greek,
     16.
Sibylline books, literature of, 17.
Sicilians, 209, 259.
Sicily, 117, 128, 163, 220.
Sicyon, 95.
Sidon, 93, 250.
Sidonians, 139.
Sinai, 83.
Sinope, 87.
Smyrna, 87, 88, 134, 144.
Solomon, 79.
Solyma (Jerusalem), 119, 120.
Son of God, 159.
Sozomen, citation of Sibyl, 160.
Sparta, 91.
Styx (Stygian), 78, 123.
Susa, 118.
Sybaris, 118.
Syene, 188.
Syria, 120, 134, 139, 169, 236, 239, 240,
     242.
Syrians, 180, 258.

Tanagra, 87.
Tanais, 86.
Tarquinius Priscus, his treatment of
     Sibyl, 10, 21.
Tartarus, 33, 37, 38, 65, 123, 137, 192.
Taurians, 134.
Taurus, 251.
Temple (of Solomon), 50, 81, 86, 119,
     135.
Temple in Egypt, 154.
Tenedos, 95.
Tentyris, 188.
Tertullian, citation of Sibyl, 76.
Tethys, 72.
Thebans, 169, 203.
Thebes, 117, 137, 182.
Theodoret, citation of Sibyl, 25.
Theophilus, citation of Sibyl, 24-29,
     75.
Thermodon, 144.
Thessaly, 135, 166.

Thmois, 132.
Thrace, 94, 96, 128, 145, 209, 210, 220,
    221, 222, 225, 230, 254.
Thracians, 152.
Tiber, 136.
Tiberian Sea, 223.
Tigris, 116, 204, 208.
Tishbite, coming of, 61.
Titan, 76, 77, 78.
Titans, 46, 62, 78, 80.
Tower of Babel, 76, 175, 201.
Trallis, 93, 143.
Triballi, 154, 222.
Tricca, 256.
Tripolis, 145, 250.
Trojan car, 181.
Troy, 80, 127, 207, 208, 219.
Tyana, 239.

Tyre, 117, 151, 166.
Tyrians, 251.

Ur, 81.
Uranus, 76
Uriel, 62.

Varro, account of the Sibyls, 9.
Venus, 77.
Vesta, 77.
Vulcan, 53.

Woman, rule of, 74, 184.
Word of God, 197, 220, 229.

Xois, 132.

Zion, daughter of, addressed, 191.

THE END.

Milton Keynes UK
Ingram Content Group UK Ltd.
UKHW022007181223
434628UK00005B/292

9 781016 148054